NISHAPUR REVISITED

NISHAPUR REVISITED
Stratigraphy and Ceramics of the Qohandez

Rocco Rante
&
Annabelle Collinet

with contributions by

Rajabali Labbaf Khaniki, Iranian Centre of Archaeological Research (ICAR)
A. Bouquillon, Y. Coquinot, C. Doublet, Y. Gallet, A. Genevey, E. Porto and A. Zink
Centre de Recherche et de Restauration des Musées de France (C2RMF)

OXBOW BOOKS
Oxford and Oakville

Published by
Oxbow Books, Oxford, UK

© Oxbow Books and the authors, 2013

ISBN 978-1-84217-494-4

A CIP record for this book is available from the British Library

This book is available direct from:

Oxbow Books, Oxford, UK
(Phone: 01865-241249; Fax: 01865-794449)

and

The David Brown Book Company
PO Box 511, Oakville, CT 06779, USA
(Phone: 860-945-9329; Fax: 860-945-9468)

or from our website

www.oxbowbooks.com

Library of Congress Cataloging-in-Publication Data

Rante, Rocco.
Nishapur revisited : stratigraphy and ceramics of the Qohandez / Rocco Rante, Annabelle Collinet ; with
contributions by Rajabali Labbaf Khaniki and the C2RMF.
    pages cm
  Includes bibliographical references.
  ISBN 978-1-84217-494-4
  1. Nishapur (Iran)--Antiquities. 2. Excavations (Archaeology)--Iran--Nishapur. 3. Pottery, Iranian--Iran--Nishapur.
4. Geology, Stratigraphic--Iran--Nishapur. I. Collinet, Annabelle. II. Labaf Khaniki, Rajab'ali, 1948 or 1949- III. Centre
de recherche et de restauration des musées de France. IV. Title.
  DS325.N57R36 2013
  935'.792--dc23
                           2012040604

Cover image: Nishapur, north-eastern part of the Qohandez (© Rante 2005)

Printed in Great Britain by
Short Run Press
Exeter

Contents

Foreword

This book presents the results of the most recent archaeological study in Nishapur, the ancient city of Khorasan. It is focused on the stratigraphy and the pottery of the Qohandez (citadel). The archaeological material in this volume has been gathered by the Irano-French mission in charge of excavating the citadel between 2005 and 2007. The joint mission was organized by the ICAR (Iranian Centre of Archaeological Research), MAEE (Ministère des Affaires étrangères et européennes), CNRS (Centre National de la Recherche Scientifique) and the musée du Louvre.

The ceramics analysis was undertaken by the Département des Arts de l'Islam of the musée du Louvre following agreement in 2008 of a joint framework between that Department and the C2RMF (Centre de Recherche et de Restauration des Musées de France). As part of that agreement, a final season of work in Nishapur was organised by the joint team in 2009. This mainly aimed to gather data and take radiation measurements needed for thermoluminescence and archaeomagnetism analyses.

Rocco Rante, archaeologist at the Département des Arts de l'Islam of the musée du Louvre, has been active in Nishapur since 2005 and became the field director of the French team in 2006. He continues to head the French mission under the authority of the MAEE and the Louvre.

Annabelle Collinet, scientific advisor at the Département des Arts de l'Islam of the musée du Louvre, has been in charge of the study of Nishapur ceramic material since 2006. She has was also a member of the Nishapur mission in 2006 and 2007.

The results of the stratigraphic and ceramic analyses presented in this volume constitute an important contribution to the knowledge of the archaeology of Nishapur and towards the resolution of decades of debate. Beyond this major issue, the book also represents a useful tool for future comparative studies on the urbanism and material culture of the Greater Khorasan and beyond.

Chahryar Adle
President of the International Scientific Committee for the publication
of the *History of the Civilizations of Central Asia* (UNESCO)
Research Director Emeritus, CNRS (Paris)

Acknowledgements

This book is the result of collaborative work by an Irano-French team comprising the ICAR, the CNRS and the musée du Louvre who carried out excavations at Nishapur between 2005 and 2007. First, we would like to thank the Iranian authorities, the ICAR and the ICHHTO as well as the Miras-e Faranghi of Mashhad. Without their permissions for excavation and authorisation of the subsequent analyses this work would not have been realised. In this respect, we particularly thank Rajabali Labbaf Khaniki and Meysam Labbaf, respectively the director and assistant director of the Iranian team. They and the Miras-e Faranghi of Mashhad made it possible to transport the pottery assemblage to France for analysis. We also thank Abulfazl Mokaramifar, who granted permission for us to continue our work here in Paris. Many thanks also go to the French Institute in Tehran (IFRI) for logistical support.

We sincerely thank, Henri Loyrette, President-Director of the musée du Louvre, as well as the Director of the Département des Arts de l'Islam, Sophie Makariou, and particularly our colleagues Delphine Miroudot and Carine Juvin, who were with us on the field.

Finally, many thanks to our colleagues of the C2RMF team, who are included in this book.

List of Illustrations

List of tables

Introduction

The aim of this study is to revisit the history and material culture of Nishapur, from its foundation to the Mongol conquest, through its archaeology and the study of its pottery. It also aims to integrate the city into the regional context of Khorasan. This research, focused on the Qohandez (or citadel), has generated important results, adding specific detail to some historical and cultural elements and completing others. In terms of resolving the problems of understanding Khorasan, this study can represent only the current state of research in this region, but it nevertheless provides precise and detailed data for use as a comparison model for other sites and future studies.

To achieve these aims, some questions have been posed and problems addressed. First we question the long accepted relationship between the toponym of Nishapur[1] and its history. In other words, when was the city founded? Is Nishapur a Sasanian city? Was it founded by the Sasanian king Shapur I or II, as the toponym sets out and written sources mention? These questions are also posed in the light of former studies published by Bulliet (1976), whose conclusions concerning the foundation of the city diverged from those of Charles Wilkinson, director of the American Archaeological Mission in Nishapur (1935–1940, 1947).

The second problem was to define the chronology of occupation and the sequence of the ceramic culture of the city, essentially during late antiquity and medieval times, in order to refine the data concerning the ceramic ware types used and produced in Nishapur.

The third question concerns the real extent of the archaeological area of Nishapur. The existing plans of the site made by Wilkinson (Fig. 5) and later by Bulliet (1976, pl. I) were sketches and did not accurately record the topography of the area. It has, therefore, been necessary to carry out a detailed study of the topography of the site, including all archaeological mounds and previously excavated zones. This is still incomplete.

To answer these various questions a new excavation was opened on the site. In 2004 the ICAR (Iranian Centre of Archaeological Research), directed by Masud Azarnoush, invited a French team (headed by Monique Kervran[2]) to excavate Nishapur in collaboration with an Iranian team (headed by Rajabali Labbaf Khaniki[3]). The latter was already active in Shadyakh, another site in the area of Nishapur. The Irano-French Mission[4] began in 2004 under the aegis of the MAEE[5]-CNRS. The French team was composed of CNRS and musée du Louvre members.

As previously mentioned, the first purpose of the Irano-French archaeological mission was to study the most ancient places of this area to find elements concerning the foundation of the city. The 'historical topography' conducted by Bulliet in 1976 brought to light interesting elements pointing to the eastern area as being the oldest. Here, the Qohandez ('ancient fortress' or citadel) and the Shahrestan ('inner city') constituted an interesting nucleus, even though

---

[1] Honigmann and Bosworth 1993.
[2] Former archaeologist, CNRS, Orient et Méditerranée (UMR 8167).
[3] Former archaeologist of Miras-e Faranghi Mashhad.
[4] The members of the Nishapur Mission (2004–2007) were: V. Bernard, M. Hoveyda, D. Rosati and L. Vallières (architects and topographs); J. Cuny, M.-E. Etemadi, Y. Karev, M. Labbaf, A. Mohammadi, A. Pezier, R. Rante and P. Wormser (archaeologists); A. Collinet, Z. Delarami, C. Juvin, J. Kamalizad, S. Khozaymeh, D. Miroudot, A. Mousazadeh, A. Péli and H. Sharifan (ceramologists); Cl. Cosandey and E. Fouache (geomorphologist and hydrologist).
[5] Ministère des Affaires Étrangères et Européennes.

already examined by the American team in the 1930s. The Irano-French Mission exclusively focused its excavation activity on the Qohandez, considered to be the oldest part of the site. In 2007 a very accurate survey was also carried out in the Shahrestan and the mosque situated to its south. Some of the shards collected here have been analyzed and used as comparative material to complete the study of the Qohandez pottery.

Although the quantity of material discovered was significant and the stratigraphical cross-sections detailed, unfortunately no dating elements were found during any of the excavation seasons. Only a Pahlavi inscribed pottery fragment and a seal in the surface levels were brought to light. This left the questions concerning Nishapur's foundation and occupation sequence unanswered.

In 2009 the DAI (Département des Arts de l'Islam) of the Louvre, in collaboration with the C2RMF,[6] began a project to study and analyse the Nishapur material, headed by the authors. This project, concerning absolute dating on the one hand and study of the ceramic material on the other, involved various kinds of analyses. The dating analyses were performed by Thermoluminescence, Archaeomagnetism and Radiocarbon. The first two of these were performed on ceramic fragments officially imported from Nishapur to Paris; the last was performed on a supposed wood sample taken on the site.

To ensure the better performance of the Thermoluminescence programme, a mission of dosimetry measurements was organised in 2009 in Nishapur, headed by Rocco Rante with the expertise of Antoine Zink and Elisa Porto for measurements. The data acquired were employed to refine the Thermoluminescence ages of the ceramic fragments analyzed. To attain a much more precise result, the C2RMF and Louvre teams elaborated a system of cross data between the TL dates and the Archaeomagnetism Intensity. The results have been cross-matched with the stratigraphy.

The second thrust of the laboratory analyses concerns the study of the ceramics. Chemical and petrographic[7] analyses have been performed. The aim of these studies was to define the fabrics and glaze compositions, as well as their production types and places. These analyses, together with stratigraphic study of the material, brought to light a ceramic sequence from Nishapur's foundation to the Mongol invasion.

This sequence of ceramic typology has been compared with other ones inside the Khorasanian region, as well as its geographical *limes*. Even if incomplete, due to the absence of more precise elements obtained from other major cities, this research is a first step in the definition of the cultural limits of Khorasan to the east and to the west in different periods. The geographical area studied in this precise context corresponds to the Sasanian and medieval Khorasanian borders. The limits have been drawn in correlation with the Sasanian administrative provinces, known by numismatic and seal study, and the Arab written sources. In the inscription of Paikuli, Herzfeld identified the Eastern territories of the Sasanian Empire, even if no specific mention was made of the toponym 'Khorasan' (Humbach 1978).

In his division of Sasanian provinces, Ammianus Marcellinus (*Rest Gestae* XIV, VIII, 1)[8] does not mention Khorasan. Might this suggest that the Khorasanian toponym did not exist before the second half of the 4th century?

During the 8th century, the *T'ang Shu* written source mentions 'Tegin, King of Khorasan', recognising this territory also as a political and not only a geographical entity (Harmatta and Litvinsky 1996, 376).

Nevertheless, the first clear occurrences of the 'Khorasan' toponym were noticed in the Arab written sources. At the end of the ninth century, Yaqubi (Marquart 1901, 47) includes in the Khorasanian territory not only the main capitals of Merv, Nishapur, Balkh and Herat, but also

---

[6] Centre de Recherche et de Restauration des Musées de France.
[7] Carried out by Anne Bouquillon, Yvan Coquinot and Christel Doublet, C2RMF.
[8] Ammianus Marcellinus.

Gurgan and Bukhara. He also affirms, in his *Kitab al-Buldan* (Wiet 1937, 101), that the centre of Khorasan corresponds to Balkh. He gives the borders of this province: Ferghana, Rayy, Sistan, Kerman, Kashmir, Khorazm and Multan.

At the end of the 10th century, around 100 years later than Yaqubi, Ibn Hawqal (Kramers and Wiet 1964, 413) locates Khorasan into Sistan and India to the east, the desert of Ghuzz and the Gurgan region to the west, Transoxiana to the north and the Fars desert and Qumis to the south. According to this last description, Khorasan seems to be smaller than previously. This perimeter persists, as shown by later medieval written sources.[9]

---

[9] See Juzjani's Tabaqat-i Nasiri (Raverty 1995 (1st ed. 1881), 49–50, 248, 252, 914–916, 930–931). See also al-Yaqut (Barbier de Meynard 1861, 197–198).

Chapter 1

Historical and Geographical Background

1. Geographical setting of Nishapur

Nishapur is located in the Khorasan region, in the eastern part of Iran (Fig. 1). This part corresponds to the northern boundaries of the Iranian Plateau, beyond which the landscape corresponds to the Central Asian steppe land. The territory of the archaeological site is situated in a fertile zone (see Nasir al-Din Shah Qajar 1889, 171). It is limited on the northeast by the foothill of the Binalud range (Fig. 2), culminating at 2000 m up to the plain, and on the southwest by the brackish and marshy course of the Shurah Rud (also Shurirud) above the site (Barthold 1984, 95). Some southern areas of the plain are, in fact, unsuitable for agricultural exploitation.

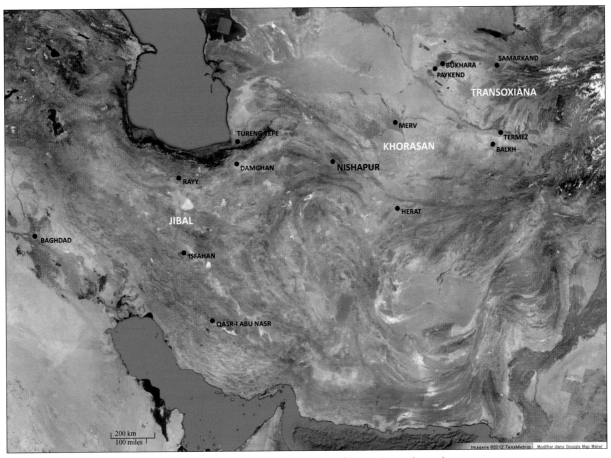

Figure 1: Geographical map of Iran (© Google Earth 2012).

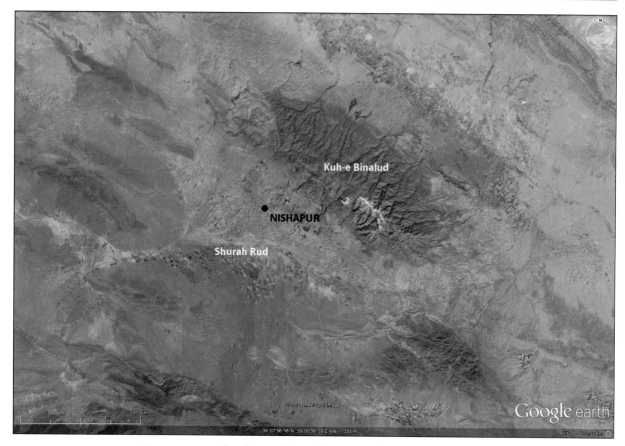

Figure 2: Geographical map of the Nishapur area (© Google Earth 2012).

From the mountain in the north, rain and snow fall to irrigate the farmland below. Thus, the Nishapur area is irrigated upstream by surface precipitation and downstream by a system of draining galleries known as *qanats*. The orientation of the urban plan is determined by the course of water flows descending from the Binalud Range.[1]

The archaeological area is today located around 2 km from the southeastern part of the modern city (Fig. 3). Between them, the Mausoleum of Omar Khayyam is set inside a magnificent and well-maintained garden. Fortunately, the archaeological zone has been, more or less, spared from modern urbanization. The reasons for this shift in urban location are probably due to various historical and natural events, such as several invasions and earthquakes (see *the historical setting of Nishapur*). However, the sole railway branch to the east, principally to Mashhad, constructed in the middle of the last century, crosses the site from northwest to southeast, cutting the archaeological landscape between the oldest part (Qohandez and Shahrestan) and the probable Great Mosque of the ancient city.

Nishapur was an important crossroads linked to Central Asia and China by way of Merv, Paykend, Bukhara and Samarkand; to Afghanistan and India by Herat; to the Persian Gulf by Yazd and Isfahan; and finally to the west by Damghan, Rayy and Hamadan. It was one of the main cities on the Silk Road (Rtveladze 2009, 226). The last excavation has shown that, during late antiquity and the medieval epoch, the city had the dual characteristic of a residential as well as a production place. These characteristics are specific to different periods of the city. Nishapur could be considered as an important residential city as well as a 'storehouse' along this segment of the Silk Road. The city was, like the other cities of the Silk Road, strongly protected by ramparts. Its position between the plain and the mountain, situated in a natural

---

[1] For more information about the geomorphology and hydrology of the Nishapur area, see Fouache *et al.* 2011.

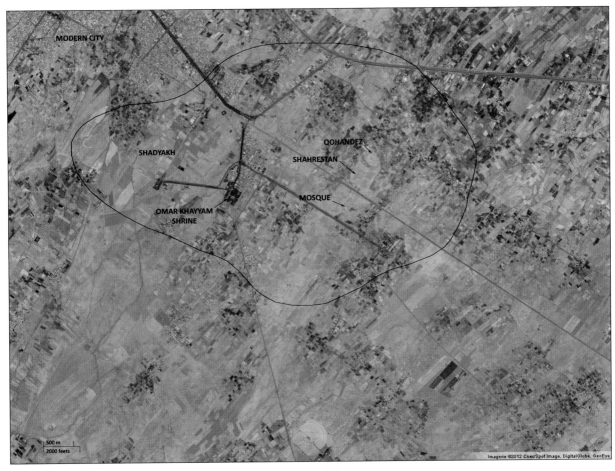

Figure 3: Nishapur, satellite view of the archaeological area (© Google Earth 2012).

Figure 4: Nishapur, Qohandez, present state of the site ruins (© Collinet 2006).

corridor on the main route of the caravan road, easily exposed it to strong attacks and invasions.

Following a centuries-long period of abandonment, the medieval site was turned into a quarry and exploited by brick makers (d'Allemagne 1911, 129) (Fig. 4). Their first actions were to take the baked bricks of the late occupation on the top of the site and reuse them to build the surrounding villages. Later, the mud brick buildings at a lower level were destroyed in order to fertilize fields that covered the site and the surrounding plain (*ibid.*, 117–118). The occasional discovery of antique objects, many of them very valuable, promoted illegal excavations.

2. Former excavations and studies

The American and Iranian excavations in Nishapur

The Metropolitan Museum's excavations

The Metropolitan Museum's excavations, headed by Walter Hauser, Joseph M. Upton and Charles K. Wilkinson, took place between the years 1935 and 1940. Halted by World War II, the work ended with a final mission in 1947. The leading aim of the excavations was clearly the discovery of objects and architectural decorations for the Museum (Hauser 1937; Wilkinson 1937) and the drawing up of their chronology. The architectural ornaments and the artefacts discovered were divided – under the authority of the Iranian Ministry of Education and Fine Arts and following the Iranian antiquities law of 1930 – between the MET in New York and the Tehran Museum (Hauser 1937, 27; Wilkinson 1961, 103).

In the parts of the archaeological area of Nishapur which were not urbanized, the excavations were nevertheless limited by fields and public paths. The excavations were mainly focused on the area situated between the site of Shadyakh and the citadel or Qohandez (Fig. 5).

After several test digs and the uncovering of restricted parts of other mounds, the American excavations were principally concentrated on two mounds: 'Tepe Madraseh' and 'Tepe Sabz Pushan'. These two areas produced most of the Nishapur objects owned by the two museums.

The final publications of the excavations and of the finds were written by Wilkinson (after the death of Hauser and changes in Upton's activities) and by other scholars who published the most important finds. They were released by the Metropolitan long after the interim reports published in the *Bulletin* of the Museum. The ceramics were first published by Wilkinson (1973). In his final report of the excavations proper, eventually released after his death (Wilkinson 1986), he essentially concentrates on the architectural decorations (stucco panels and wall paintings) discovered. Finally, the metal objects were studied by J. W. Allan (1982) and the glass wares by J. Kröger (1995).

The question of the Sasanian city

The American team did not identify any vestige of the Sasanian Period during the survey and the excavations of the site (Hauser *et al.* 1938, 4; Hauser and Wilkinson 1942, 119). In Wilkinson's opinion, 'the Sasanian city was used at least a whole century after its capture by the Arabs. The city was then rebuilt several miles away in the same plain as is customary in Persia'. This was the city excavated by the Museum (Wilkinson 1950, 61).

He considered that the mound on which the citadel stands ('Tepe Alp Arslan' or Shahr-i Kuhna) 'was erected in the ninth century and formed the platform on which the citadel was built' (Wilkinson 1950, 62), and that the Sasanian city was not in this area (1986, 39). Wilkinson was, on that subject, contradicted by Bulliet (1976) and Melville (1980, 103), and the recent excavations and the TL dates of some ceramic shards show that they were correct.

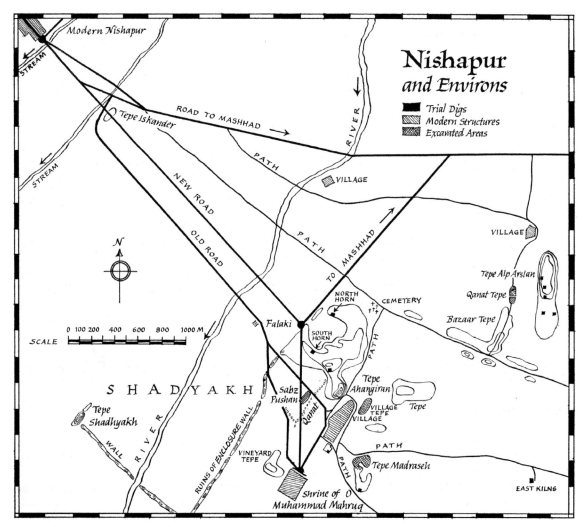

Figure 5: Nishapur and Environs, Excavation Map, The Iranian Expedition at Nishapur, The Metropolitan Museum of Art (The Metropolitan Museum of Art Image © The Metropolitan Museum of Art, Drawing by Joseph P. Ascherel).

The Islamic Period

The American excavations revealed structures and objects dated by the excavators from *circa* the late 8th to the 12th centuries, but they did not provide any stratigraphy. A refined chronological sequence of the finds thus cannot be established. In addition, the objects discovered were not considered as stratigraphical assemblages. We do not know which types of ceramics, glass wares, metals and so on were contemporary with one another (Allan 1982, 13; Kröger 1995, 23). Thanks to the patient study of the glass wares and of their respective findspots, when known, Wilkinson's opinion of the contemporary occupation of 'Tepe Madraseh', 'Sabz Pushan', 'Qanat Tepe' and 'Village Tepe' (Kröger 1995, 30), mostly *circa* the 10th century AD, was nonetheless confirmed.

Other mounds were explored at the beginning of the American researches. The citadel, locally called 'Tepe Alp Arslan' after the name of the Seljuk Sultan, was the object of seven test digs opened in order to identify the ruins. During these excavations, 13 coins, of which nine date from the 8th or early 9th century, were discovered (Wilkinson 1937, 19; Upton 1937, 37). Other test soundings were opened on different spots of the identified archaeological area: five near the tomb of Omar Khayyam and the mound 'Tepe Ahangiran'; one trial dig in 'Vineyard Tepe' and in 'Village Tepe' (Wilkinson 1937, 17, 19–20), in which the 'lower level' was dug in 1937 (Hauser *et al.* 1938, 3).

The 'Vineyard Tepe' was more thoroughly excavated, but over a small area. The structures uncovered were probably part of an important house or palace adorned with stucco panels and wall paintings. The mansion discovered was contemporary with those in 'Tepe Madraseh', as suggested by coin finds, dating to the second half of the 8th–first half of the 10th century. It may have been abandoned earlier than 'Tepe Madraseh', as no fritware was discovered in 'Vineyard Tepe' (Wilkinson 1986, 188–189).

However, the main excavations were, at the same time, concentrated first in the locally named 'Tepe Sabz Pushan' (or the 'green-covered mound'), where stucco panels and wall paintings were discovered (Upton 1936, 179–180; Hauser 1937). During the second season in 1936, six test digs were opened in the mound, in which several rooms were cleared (Wilkinson 1937, 8). The first construction of the building partially uncovered was dated (mainly with the oldest coins found) to the second half of the 8th century. Its repair was dated to around the late 9th century, and the stucco ornaments were attributed to the late 10th century. There were no traces of any Seljuk occupation in the structures (Hauser 1937, 32–35). Of the 38 coins coming from the *tepeh*, 31 are of the 8th or the early 9th century, and three are of the late 10th century. Wilkinson thus thought that there was a gap in the occupation of the site (Upton 1937, 37–38; Hauser *et al.* 1938, 6). The uncovering of the structures was extended in 1937 to find other ceramic wares and architectural decorations for the MET (Hauser *et al.* 1938, 3). Very many coins were again discovered: 12 are dated 731–760; 118 to 760–800; 24 to 800–820; 102 to 731–820 AD; and more than 15 Samanid coins were also found. In addition, the several Sasanian coins discovered in the excavations (one of which may be Parthian) were considered to be residual, for no other 'pre-Islamic objects' were found (*ibid.*, 5–6). The area excavated was identified as a residential quarter of the city, which was already derelict at the arrival of the Seljuks in 1037 (*ibid.*, 8) and abandoned by the 12th century (Wilkinson 1986, 221).

Coins of the Khwarezm Shah 'Ala' al-Din Muhammad ibn Tekish (596–617 H/1200–1220) were, in addition, found in the nearby area between the citadel and Shadyakh, to the northeast of 'Tepe Sabz Pushan' (Upton 1937, 38).

The most extensive excavation of the American team, in 'Tepe Madraseh', began during the 1937 season with a test dig (Hauser *et al.* 1938, 22) and was extended in 1938 (Hauser and Wilkinson 1942). The structures uncovered were interpreted as a 'part of a palace or a series of government or public buildings' and a mosque, lavishly adorned with brick designs, stucco panels and wall paintings. Most of the objects discovered during the American excavations come from this site. The occupation periods were dated between the early 9th and the 12th century. According to the excavators, the complex, which was partly cleared, was probably already ruined at the arrival of the Seljuks in 1037 (Hauser and Wilkinson 1942, 92–97). Three levels of structures were defined. In the lowest, a coin in the name of Harun al-Rashid was found on a floor. The 'middle level' is associated with most of the stucco panels discovered. Five dinars found in a well were associated with this phase: the latest are in the name of al-Mustakfi and dated 944 (?) (Wilkinson 1986, 57). The other numerous coins found in the structures were 42 from the second half of the 8th century; 23 from the 8th–9th centuries; 15 from the 9th century; 26 from the 10th century; and a few coins from the 11th–late 12th centuries and the Mongol Period (*Ibid.*, 54). The brick inscription and the fragments of inscribed glazed tiles which were associated with the highest level of the structures (*ibid.*, 110–116) nevertheless suggest an occupation during the 11th–12th centuries.

The Iranian excavations in Shadyakh, 1995–2002
Shadyakh is said to have been occupied firstly during the Tahirid Period in the early 9th century, and during the Samanid Period it may have become an integral part of the city of Nishapur. From 556 H/1161 AD onwards the population of Nishapur moved there (Melville 1980, 105–106,

Figure 6: Nishapur, Shadyakh, view of the Iranian excavation (© Collinet 2006).

table II). The site was partly excavated by an Iranian team under the direction of Dr Labbaf Khaniki. The research was focused on the small enclosure which occupies the southern part of the site (Fig. 6): a large residence was discovered, which may have been the administrative centre and the mansion of the ruler. The rich stucco panels uncovered, as the quality of the numerous metalwares and fritwares also discovered in that site, corroborate this hypothesis.

The kilns and ceramics of Nishapur

Discoveries of ceramic kilns

The ceramic kilns discovered between 1935 and 1940 were partially described and mapped on the topography established by the American team (Figs 5; 7).

According to Wilkinson, none of the kilns discovered was from the 9th or 10th century: the kilns for the 'buffware' and the 'imitation of opaque white wares' were not found (Wilkinson 1961, 107). But the 'discovery of a waster and another spoiled base in the area of some kilns' of painted on slip and under glaze type may be from the 10th–11th centuries (*ibid.*, 113).

Some later kilns were identified to the north of 'Tepe Sabz Pushan' and further (no. 3) (Wilkinson 1937, 19). They were used for the manufacture of coarse unglazed wares and perhaps moulds and moulded wares. Five kilns situated southwest of the citadel were later examined. They were 'used in making the fine, gritty, fritlike blue and white wares usually decorated with transparencies of a rather crude type and assignable here to the eleventh century' (Hauser *et al.* 1938, 3, 22). Other ceramic kilns were found at the southeast of 'Tepe Madraseh' (Hauser and Wilkinson 1942, fig. 27). They were one of the main focuses of the final mission, in 1947.

Figure 7: East Kilns, Inlcudes the largest kiln (right) with three rings of baton holes in wall, Nishapur, from the Iranian Expedition at Nishapur, The Metropolitan Museum of Art (Photograph by the Iranian Expedition at Nishapur, The Metropolitan Museum of Art Image © The Metropolitan Museum of Art).

Without specifying their location, he writes that three of the kilns discovered were completely cleared: they contained coins from the 11th century and, in his opinion, they could thus not have been in use before the 12th century. In the vicinity of the kilns were 'broken pottery, stilts and other supports, fragments of wasters, ash, lumps of quartz, evidence of one kind or another of the manufacture of frit for glaze, and fragments of moulds' (Wilkinson 1959, 235–236).

The site of 'Qanat Tepe', interpreted as the 'home of potters and glassmakers' was, according to Wilkinson, occupied from the early 9th to the late 11th or early 12th century. While three of the coins found were Sasanian, most are dated between the 8th and 10th centuries. Eight are Ghaznavid, and three coins are from the Seljuk to the Mongol Periods (Wilkinson 1986, 261). The ceramic kilns (more than three) found there (unexcavated) and later than the occupation periods may have produced 'white and fritlike (wares) decorated with streaks of blue or given a turquoise glaze'; 'T'ang type glazed pottery', that is to say splash wares; and sphero-conical vessels (Hauser and Wilkinson 1942, 84, 89; Wilkinson 1986, 263). The two glass slabs discovered in 'Qanat tepe' may be linked with the production of glazed pottery, but glass may also have been made near the pottery kilns (Kröger 1995, 20).

In 1965 several other ceramic kilns of baked bricks were discovered (Kambakhsh Fard and Mahani 1965). Some were uncovered and partially destroyed during works at the north of the village of Khormak, situated in the archaeological area. They are situated to the west of the area studied by the American team and in the northeastern part of Shadyakh. Two of the kilns were excavated. The larger one, of circular plan (D. 2.30 m), has an underground fire room (H. 0.70 m) surmounted by a domed circular chamber with a firing platform. A smaller kiln (D. 1.85 m), situated nearby, presented the same characteristics. Next to the kilns were circular rubbish wells (*ibid.*, 17–21). The larger kiln contained glazed earthen wares and smaller unglazed ones. In another part of the archaeological zone, between the villages of Filkhaneh and Lak-Lak Ashian, kilns were uncovered after repeated salvage diggings. Two of these kilns were excavated. They were of the same plan as the two kilns describe above, but one was larger (H. 3.45 m; firing platform D. 2.70 m). They were used for the manufacture of underglaze painted wares.

From the ceramic types (*sgraffiato* and underglaze painted wares; moulds for fritwares) associated with the kilns and their area, they may have been in use *c.* 10th–12th centuries.

C. K. Wilkinson and the ceramics of Nishapur

Wilkinson considered that the ceramic wares discovered were local products, apart from two major types of imports: Chinese celadons and stonewares of the T'ang Period (618–906 AD) on the one hand, and polychrome and monochrome lustre wares from Iraq (9th–10th centuries) on the other hand (Hauser *et al.* 1938, 14).

A first chronological sequence was proposed for the ceramics long before the final publication of 1973 (*ibid.*, 14–21), in which the main ceramic types studied were presented. They are mainly 'Samanid wares', which are the best 'Nishapur wares' known since Wilkinson's book. The 'Samanid phase' was in fact the best recognized after the excavations opened by the American team. The main glazed ceramic types associated with that phase were further defined by Wilkinson. The unglazed types were much less studied, but some of the finest unglazed wares – basically the fine pitchers – were published. On the contrary, the most common material has not been. A few types of unglazed wares (jugs and drinking jugs) were published in an article dealing with the water supply of the city (Wilkinson 1943).

The view given on Nishapur ceramics by C. K. Wilkinson was incomplete: he does not discuss the material of the early Islamic Period, and does not really study the ceramics of the 11th–12th centuries, at least the well-identified fritwares. Basically, he seemed to consider that in that part of Iran, far away from great ceramic centres as Rayy or Kashan, the main wares made or in use were mostly earthen glazed wares. The focus on the clayey glazed wares, most of them considered 'Samanid', leaves the account on unglazed wares and on fritwares almost absent from his book. Very fine quality moulded wares, their moulds and wheel-turned fritwares were nonetheless discovered during the American excavations, but Wilkinson quite neglected this material.

Being, up to now, one of the most important publications on Eastern Iran ceramic wares, the picture presented by Wilkinson on the ceramic of Nishapur wares widely persists.

3. Historical setting: between textual sources and new results

The main historical sources concerning the city of Nishapur have been almost completely edited and studied (for a complete bibliography see Bulliet 1972; 1976: 67–89). The main historical reference is the *Ta'rikh-i Naisabur* of Abu 'Abd Allah Muhammad al-Hakim al-Naisaburi, who died in 405 H/1014 AD.[2] However, the history of the city concerns several other manuscripts, which have been well-mentioned in Richard Frye's *Ta'rikh-i Nisapur* (1965, xxxii, 405–420). Our intention here is to provide some historical acknowledgement, not to perform another analysis of Nishapur's history from the sources. Our aim is, therefore, to develop a framework to establish our context as well as to specify some details from our results which remain vague in the sources (Table 1).

Legend attributes the foundation of the Qohandez of Nishapur to the king Turan Afrasiab (al-Hakim: f57a–f58a). Other authors, instead, mention different founders of the city. In his *Choose History*, for example, Mustawfi (see Barbier de Meynard 1861, 578, n. 1) told us that Tahomers was the founder of Nishapur, from whose ruins Ardashir Babagan rebuilt another city called Nih. The Persian toponym 'Nishapur' comes from the Old Persian *Niv-Shahpuhr* ('the good of Shahpuhr'; Marquart 1901, 74; Le Strange 1966, 383).[3] Its province, Abarshar (Marquart 1901, 74–75), is attested in the Sasanian sigillography (Gyselen 1989, 42; 2002, 126, 190). The name of the city is mentioned as the location of a Nestorian diocese in 430 AD (Marquart 1901,

---

[2]   We are using the al-Hakim persian text (Nishapuri, *Tarikh-i Nishapur*, ed. B. Karimi, Téhéran 1960).

[3]   See also see EI² s.v. 'Nishapour'.

75; see also Vine 1937, 57). Arab historiography perpetuated the names of both Nishapur and Abarshar, the second toponym used in the minting of Umayyad and early Abbasid dirhams (Le Strange 1930, 383). Ibn Hawqal, for example, tells us that the city of Nishapur is known under the name of Abrashahr (Ibn Hawqal, 431; Kramers and Wiet 1964, 417). The survival of the name New-Shahpuhr/Nishapur until the present day should already be a sign of the long-term life of the site before and after the Arab conquest of 651 AD. Nevertheless, the period of its foundation, as well as the name of its founder, is still in question, even if the present work may help to find a possible answer. The historical sources disagree on a probable Shapur I (241–272 AD) or Shapur II (309–379 AD) foundation.[4] The former is mentioned by many of them, as shown by Marquart (1901, 75): 'the capital of Nev-Shahpuhr was built by Shahpuhr, the son of Artashir ...'. Hamza al-Isfahani (1848, 48) attributes the foundation of Nishapur to Shapur I, while Tabari and the local chronicler al-Hakim al-Naisaburi, among others, attribute it to Shapur II. The administrative and architectural reorganizations undertaken by the latter, according to the sources, could be an answer to this diatribe (Gyselen 1989, 43). However, the analyses carried out for the present work show another possible way. As we will demonstrate in the following chapters, the results of a work on the Thermoluminescence and Archaeomagnetism analyses on the ceramic material from excavation, as well as the cross-referencing with the stratigraphical sequence, have shown that the first architectural activity on the Qohandez of Nishapur belongs to the period corresponding with Shapur II's rule and later (4th–5th centuries). At that epoch, Nishapur should have been more a fortified eastern outpost on the Silk Road than a purely residential place. It is in the Islamic Period, under the Tahirid dynasty (9th century) that the city becomes an important capital of Khorasan (Barthold 1984, 96), as well as an important place of manufacture. The Persian geographer Hamd Allah Mustawfi (14th century) recounted that the perimeter of the town was 15,000 paces long and, at the time of the Khusroes I, the city plan resembled a chessboard (Le Strange 1919, 147; Barbier De Meynard 1861, 578, n. 1).

Nishapur was taken by the Arab armies at around 651 AD (Ya'qubi: 85; Barbier de Meynard 1861, 579; Jackson 1911, 251). Al-Baladhuri (Hitti 1976, 161) tells of the conquest of the city by Ibn 'Amir after having besieged its population for several months. Al-Hakim al-Naisaburi relates the Arab conquest with further details, leaving most important topographic and historiographic data, as the construction of three mosques in the Qohandez, Shahanbar (the southern part of the Shahrestan) and Ma'qil Street (al-Hakim, f66b, f61b, f21b). Concerning this last part of the city, Bulliet provides us with an argument as to its location. In fact, he locates this zone in the Baghak ('little garden") quarter, where Ma'qil Street was, which was connected with one of the four gates of the 'inner city" (Shahrestan), called Ma'qil Gate. He recognized this gate as the eastern gate of the Shahrestan. Therefore, the Baghak quarter was at the eastern part of the ancient city (Bulliet 1976: 81). Concerning the Qohandez, the construction of the mosque inside it is mentioned by al-Hakim as located at one of the two gates of the citadel (al-Hakim, f59a, 67b; Bulliet 1976, 72). Written sources are more or less silent about the period after the conquest of the Qohandez. However, the discovery of three coins struck by Abu Muslim 'Abd al-Rahman (748 AD), during the American excavations, could be a proof of this (see Wilkinson 1986, 40).

'Abd Allah ibn Tahir became governor of Khorasan in 829–30 AD (see the governor succession account of Ya'qubi, 307–308; Wiet 1937, 136–138). Ya'qubi (278; Wiet 1937, 85) recounted that 'Abd Allah ibn Tahir settled his residence in Nishapur. Ibn Hawqal related, moreover, that the governmental residence was displaced from Merv and Balkh to Nishapur during this epoch (Ibn Hawqal, 434; Kramers and Wiet 1964, 420). He built a splendid building there and erected a minaret (Ya'qubi, 278; Wiet 1937, 85). According to Yaqut's chronicle (Barbier de Meynard 1861, 340), Shadyakh was a garden close to the town belonging to 'Abd Allah ibn Tahir. 'Abd Allah b. Tahir chose this garden as a military camp for his troops. He had a residence built in

---

[4] For a summary on the sources disagreeing see A. V. W. Jackson (1911, 249–51).

Shadyakh[5] and ordered to his soldiers to build their houses around his own. This place soon enlarged into a vast quarter adjacent to the town.

The Sistani dynasty of the Saffarids (see Barthold 1981, 215–220), under the command of Ya'qub ibn Layth, transferred its capital to Nishapur after the overthrow of the Tahirid dynasty in 873 AD (Barthold 1984, 96). Even if for a few years the Saffarid dynasty ordered important works, it was under the government of 'Amr ibn Layth (r. 879–900 AD), brother of Ya'qub ibn Layth, that a *dar al-imara* was constructed in the town, tentatively located by Bulliet northeast from the present tomb of Omar Khayyam (Bulliet 1976, pl. 1). According to Ibn Hawqal, 'Amr ibn Layth built the Great Mosque of Nishapur (Le Strange 1930, 384; see also the relation of Hafiz Abru (1420 AD), quoted by Schefer 1881, 279–280). Maqdisi gives some more precise details about this building, confirming that it was situated below the walled city (Maqdisi, 316). During this short period of rule, however, the Saffarid government was instable. The city was, in fact, conquered again by Muhammad ibn Tahir in 882 AD, who was in 885 AD again declared viceroy of Khorasan (Barthold 1981, 219). Finally, in less than 30 years, Nishapur was besieged several times by Saffarids and Tahirids.

As for the Samanid Period, thanks to the abundance of sources, there are more details about its history and topographic development. In that epoch the capital of the Emirate was transferred to Bukhara, but we know that Nishapur remained the seat of the government of Khorasan (Barthold 1981, 229). Thus, the countries down the Oxus were administrated by the governor of Nishapur. The governor was not only the chief of the administration and the army (wali), but also the khatib (preacher), since often this latter was Persian or Turkish by birth and hardly a master of the Arabic language used for the sermon (Barthold 1981, 233). Concerning Samanid Nishapur, however, we do not have copious information from the historical sources. Data about construction activity in the Qohandez is rare. The results of the Irano-French archaeological excavation, however, showed that the layers on the top of the tepe presented occupation levels as well as the architectural structure of this epoch. We do not know the extension of these levels as the excavation concentrated only on some zones of the tepe. However, it is not impossible that the entire citadel had been reoccupied during this period by quarters.

Nishapur remained the capital of Khorasan under the Ghaznawid and Seljuk Periods (Barthold 1984, 98). In 1038 AD Toghrïl Beg made Nishapur his capital. He named his nephew and successor Alp Arslan (1063–1072 AD) (Jackson 1911, 254, n. 2; see Mustawfi, tr. Gantin 1903, 199). Until the 1950s the Qohandez and the Shahrestan were identified as Tepe Alp Arslan. Today they are called Tepeh Torbabad, after the small adjacent village. In 1145 AD the city was destroyed by an earthquake (Melville 1980, 105).[6] This was not the only destructive event; two other major earthquakes successively destroyed the city in 1270 and 1389 AD (*ibid.*, table 1). In 1153 AD the Ghuzz incursions and sacking of the city caused a significant emigration of its leading families (*ibid.*, 105, 117). Some information about history of Nishapur during the Seljuk and Ghurid Periods are given by al-Juzjani, who describes the Seljuk rule over the city and the conquest by the Ghurids in 596 H and later by the Mongols in 617 H (Raverty 1881, 180–182, 380, 393, 1028, 1226). The devastation of the Mongol invasion (1221 AD) was one more action concerning the decline of the Qohandez, as well as of the old city. However, this does not necessarily mean an abandonment of the site. The Iranian excavation showed clear layers of occupation at Shadyakh dated to the Il-Khanid Period by coins.[7] Moreover, some ceramic fragments found in a well on top of the monumental door of the Qohandez, datable to the pre-Mongol epoch, showed that the citadel was still occupied – probably sporadically – during this period.

---

[5] Ya'qubi's account also mentions 'a wonderful building, Shadyakh' (278; Wiet 1937, 85). Nevertheless, in this case, Shadyakh is called the building proper and not the area occupied.

[6] For an exhaustive account of the earthquakes in Nishapur, see Melville 1980.

[7] Kind information of Dr. Labbaf Khaniki, Iranian Director of the Archaeological Mission at Shadyakh.

Table 1: Chronology, Urbanization and Pottery evolution synthesis.

	DATE	URBANIZATION PHASE	POTTERY MAJOR CHARACTERISTICS
PERIOD I	450 BC–150 BC	No architectural phase	Storage material
PERIOD II	late 4th–late 8th centuries	Foundation of Nishapur and Islamic Conquest (651 AD)	Storage and cooking utilitarian material. Less fine material. Appearance of monochrome glazed wares
PERIOD IIIA	2nd half of 8th–early 11th centuries	Lost of the main military character of the city and development of the rich habitats on the Qohandez	Storage and cooking utilitarian material. Growth of fine material and monochrome and polychrome glazed wares. First appearance of fritware
PERIOD IIIB	11th century–1165 AD	Development of the rich habitats and progressive depopulation of the Qohandez. Introduction of baked brick construction material	Storage and cooking utilitarian material. Large representation of fine unglazed and glazed material. Preponderance of fritware glazed monochrome wares

Chapter II

The Excavation and the Absolute Chronology

with contributions by A. Zink[1], E. Porto[2], A. Genevey[3] and Y. Gallet[4]

1. Introduction to the Irano-French excavation

The Qohandez of Nishapur covers a surface area of *c.* 3.5 ha and sits at an altitude of 1191.60 m above sea level (Figs 8–9). Today, the site presents an extremely damaged and jumbled mass, rendering archaeological analysis arduous (Fig. 10). In fact, the landscape of the citadel is composed of shapeless masses of mud brick, resulting from the active exploitation of this material for agricultural purposes as well as by treasure-hunters. In this confused and 'lunar' landscape, almost two areas of the Qohandez are most suitable for excavation: one corresponds with the northeastern zone, where the historical sources mentioned the 'old fortress'; the second with the central zone. The two parts are at different altitudes. The central part is lower, at around 1197 m, and the second is at 1201 m. The discontinuity of the two areas, and their different altitudes, obviously rendered study of the citadel complex and it could not be examined in its entirety. The advantage, however, is that it provided one zone in which it was possible to reach the lower layers quickly, and a second where it was possible to explore the last occupations of the site.

Within this framework, the choice of the French mission was to concentrate excavation on the northeastern part of the Qohandez. The eastern part is occupied by an open space (Fig. 8–9) whose nature remained unknown. The first large mud brick structure appearing in this part of the citadel rises 6 m from the present ground, at an altitude of 1203 m. The first examinations of this structure revealed its function as the doorway of the citadel. Further, more detailed analyses showed that this doorway was constructed above a platform built of three levels of mud bricks. However, this platform was only observable in the area close to the doorway. The same platform was not traceable inside the Qohandez although, in some places, one can find an arrangement of mud brick as well as that platform.

[1] C2RMF, 14 Quai François Mitterrand, 75001 Paris.
[2] C2RMF, 14 Quai François Mitterrand, 75001 Paris.
[3] C2RMF, UMR CNRS 171, 14 Quai François Mitterrand, 75001 Paris (at present Université Pierre et Marie Curie, Sorbonne Universités, UMR CNRS 8220 LAMS.
[4] Paleomagnetism Team, Institut de Physique du Globe de Paris, Sorbonne Paris Cité, UMR CNRS 7154, 1 rue Jussieu, 72238 Paris Cedex 05.

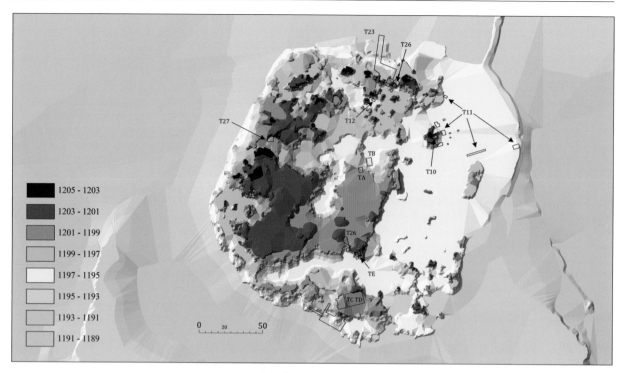

Figure 8: Nishapur, Qohandez, 3D plan and tests (© Rosati 2010).

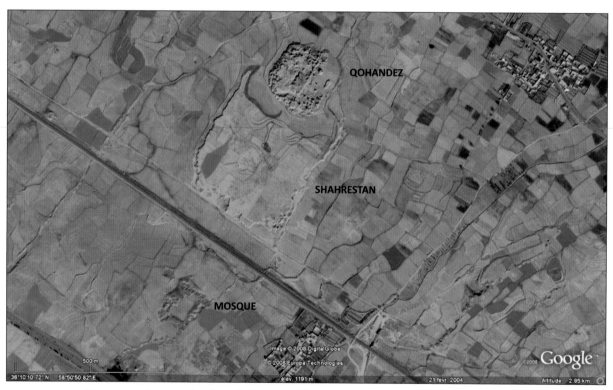

Figure 9: Nishapur, Qohandez, Shahrestan and mosque, satellite view (© Google Earth 2008).

Figure 10: Nishapur, view of the north-eastern part of the Qohandez (© Rante 2005).

Figure 11: Nishapur, Qohandez, view of the Iranian team excavation (© Rante 2005).

This structure leads inside the Qohandez, where a large depression is surrounded by the same shapeless masses of mud bricks. This depression is at an altitude of around 1196 m, almost the same as that of the platform of the citadel at the eastern edge of the mound. The south and southwestern parts of this zone were occupied by the upper part of the Qohandez. The eastern and northeastern parts were, instead, occupied by a series of mud brick structures, independent from one another. The topography of this last area nevertheless showed an organized sequence of structures, leading to the interpretation of a single architectural structure, square in shape and certainly fortified.

The excavated areas

Our first archaeological tests began (Fig. 8), between the doorway and this depression, and inside the fortified building. At the same time, our Iranian colleagues investigated the southern part of the Qohandez (Fig. 11), where they brought to light a large part of the original southern rampart and some 11th–12th century

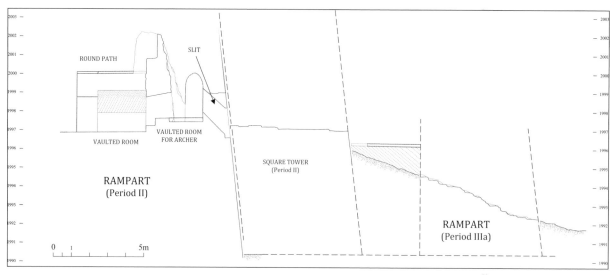

Figure 12: Nishapur, Qohandez, Northern Rampart, cross-section N–S (© Rosati 2010).

occupation constructed above it. In 2007, Test-pit T27 was opened at the western extremity, the only one in this part of the Qohandez, providing us with important stratigraphical data.

In 2005 two stratigraphical test-pits were opened in the area of the depression. This zone was later interpreted as being outside the fortified northern building. Test-pit TB was opened on a slope, between the altitude of 1197 m and 1195.50 m, to reach the first occupations of the site and the virgin soil more quickly. Test-pit TA, some metres to the west of the former, at altitude 1201 m, was opened to study the sequence of the last occupations of the site. Three test-pits (TC, TD, TE) were opened at the southern part of the Qohandez by our Iranian colleagues. TC and TD were situated above the southern rampart, TE more centrally, on the slope, at altitude *c.* 1201 m. This test-pit has been very promising because of the discovery of some Sasanian administrative material[5]. In 2006 Test-pit T10 was opened on the top of the doorway (at 1203 m). The aim of this test-pit was to obtain the entire stratigraphy of the site, to study the evolution of the doorway and the development of the different occupations. After identifying the jambs of the door, the beginning of the arch was observed, visible only for 40 cm. T10 was opened at the top of the structure, between the two jambs. Test-pit T12 was opened the same year inside the fortified building as a stratigraphical comparison with TB and as a control of the general stratigraphy. Other test-pits, not stratigraphical (T15, T17 and T18), were opened inside the fortified building with the aim of identifying correspondences between the different structures. The results of this work were not satisfactory. In fact, the extreme approximation of the proposed conjunctions of the walls suggested in order to construct a more or less logical sequence of spaces and rooms results in too unlikely a possible architectural reality. At present, it is impossible to recognize the ambient arrangement in this area.

In 2007 a different approach was adopted. First, a stratigraphical test-pit, T27, was opened at the extreme western part of the Qohandez. This test-pit gave us some details concerning the occupation sequence, showing some interesting differences with the northeastern area. Test-pit T26 was opened close to the previous TE to help interpret this interesting zone of the Qohandez. Test-pit T26 gave us some new stratigraphical details to confirm the probable administrative nature of this southern part of the citadel. T23 was opened at the northern part of the Qohandez with the aim of examining the rampart. It permitted us to reach the lowest layers of the northern rampart, at an altitude of 1190.40 m (Fig. 12), which is *c.* 1.30 m lower

---

[5]   One Sasanian seal and one Sasanian clay bulla were found in this area.

Figure 13: Nishapur, Dosimetry Mission for Thermoluminescence (TL) analyses (© Porto and Rante 2009).

Figure 14: Nishapur, Qohandez, mission TL, the gamma inspection with the gamma-meter instrument (© Porto and Rante 2009).

than the virgin soil attained in TB and T12. Therefore, the northern rampart was dressed, excavating a foundation trench more than 1.30 m through the virgin soil, testifying to the birth of the citadel of Nishapur. According to our recent researches, the rampart, and thus the birth of the citadel, is datable to early Period II, corresponding to the 4th–5th centuries, according to the TL and Archaeomagnetism[6] data (see below).

Finally, some surveys were carried out between the monumental door of the Qohandez and the slope of the mound to verify the nature of the northeastern open space of the Qohandez which is, unfortunately, still unknown.

2. Dating problems

As previously stressed, the impossibility of establishing an absolute chronology is due to the absence of dating material. The only two objects permitting one to suggest a Sasanian occupation, a seal and a *bulla*[7], fall outside the stratigraphical context. No other dating elements were found during several archaeological seasons. Moreover, the pottery assemblages were too poor to constitute concrete proof of the dating of the supposed pre-Islamic material. Nevertheless, the constitution of these assemblages has been the first and necessary step for the following analyses.

To circumvent the problem of the dating of the Qohandez occupations, in 2008 a large analysis program was begun in collaboration with the C2RMF. Among the various problems tackled in this Archaeometric study, the relationship between stratigraphy and absolute dating was one of the priorities. The thermoluminescence (TL) process was the first analysis to be carried out. In this framework, one campaign of dosimetry in the field was organized in April 2009, with

---

[6]   The synthesis of TL and Archaeomagnetism gives a more precise chronology, slightly earlier than the 5th century.
[7]   See Fouache *et al.* 2011, 100.

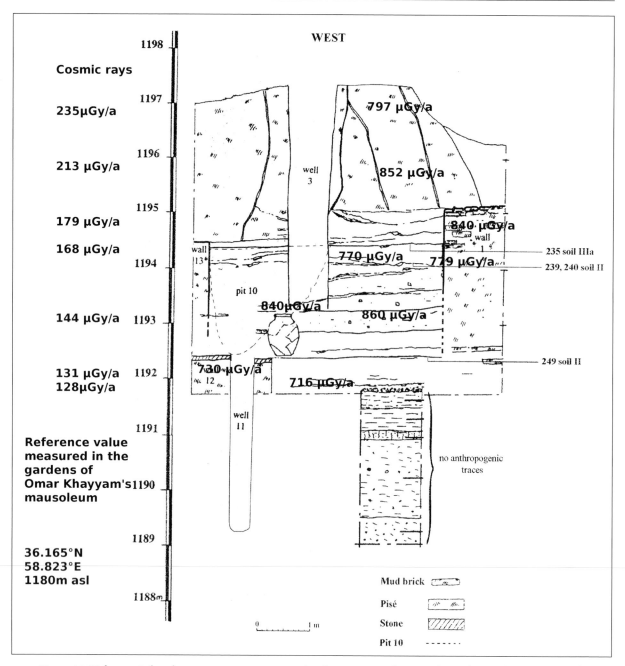

Figure 15: Nishapur, Qohandez, some measurements realized on Test B and Test 10 (© Zink 2010 from Rante 2005).

the expertise of Antoine Zink and Elisa Porto (Fig. 13). The results of the thermoluminescence were later cross-matched with Archaeomagnetic analysis.[8]

The thermoluminescence field measurement mission had two major objectives: detecting the ground composition of the different layers and phases of the Qohandez and collecting the pottery fragments belonging to these layers and phases. The ground analyses were carried out with a gamma-meter (Fig. 14). This instrument points out all the ground composition at the depth of 30 cm (Fig. 15). This permits one to interlace the data with the radiation analyses of the pottery fragments, to define their age through the gamma rays.

The measurements were made inside test-pits TB and T10, the two most representative stratigraphical test-pits of the Qohandez. The former shows the first occupations of the site, while the latter shows the entire sequence from the upper layers to the platform of the

---

[8]   No C14 dating was performed because no organic samples have been collected.

monumental door. In both cases several layers were analyzed from the relative chronology illustrated by the archaeological sequence of excavation. Finally, other measurements were made concerning the atmosphere and the cosmic background. Then, some pottery fragments, linked to the recorded layers, were chosen in both test-pits. The results of the analyses showed a completely new stratigraphical and occupational background.

3. Thermoluminescence analysis (TL)

The luminescence methods are based on the faculty of minerals to accumulate energy from ambient radioactivity. The previously accumulated energy is released by heating, thus producing a luminescence signal. The amount of light emitted is proportional to the absorbed energy. In the laboratory, the amount of light produced by heating the sample is compared with that obtained after the irradiation of the sample at a calibrated radioactive source. We deduced a dose equivalent to that received by the object since its last heating. To estimate the age, one must also estimate the dose received annually by the artefact. The annual dose consists of the sum of four components. For the alpha and beta radiation with low penetration power, the knowledge of their contribution within the sample is sufficient. In contrast, gamma and cosmic rays come from a far-ranging path; their contribution is from the environment surrounding the artefact, and not from the artefact itself. The age is obtained by dividing the equivalent dose by the annual dose.[9]

Sample preparation

The potshards listed in Table 7, for which no particular precautions were taken during the travel to France, were previously identified as being suitable for this analysis.

The potshards were sampled using a 1.8 mm diameter Tungsten carbide drill under dim red light. Some 100 mg of powder was collected for luminescence measurements. After etching with HCl 10% and washing with water, ethanol and acetone, the 4–13 μm fractions were selected by sedimentation into 8 cm heights of acetone and deposited on 9.8 mm diameter stainless discs. All these operations, apart from the HCl etching, were automated (Zink *et al.* 2002). Finally, 16 discs were prepared for thermoluminescence measurements and four for OSL.

Measurement apparatus

The luminescence measurements were performed with a Risoe TL/OSL DA-15 equipped with an EMI 9235QA PMT and incorporated 90Sr/90Y source (6.71 Gy/min on 1 January 2009). For optical stimulation, we used an infrared laser diode (830±10 nm; 50% of 450 mW/cm² full power – IR-OSL) or 21 pairs of blue diodes (470±30 nm; 50% of 19 mW/cm² full power – BL-OSL) and the optical luminescence was detected through a 7.5 mm thick U-340 filter. The thermo-luminescence was detected through a combination of 7–59 × HA-3 Filters.

The irradiations were produced using a Daybreak 801 multi sample irradiator including beta 90Sr/90Y source (3.25 Gy/min; 1/1/2009) and alpha 238Pu source (7.39 μm–2/min; 1/1/2009). Alpha counting was carried out with three Daybreak 582/583 alpha counters using a 12 mm diameter cell. X-ray analysis was carried out by energy dispersion spectrometry (EDS) using a Philips scanning electronic microscope. The external gamma and cosmic ray contribution to the annual dose was measured with a spectrometry using a 2 × 2 in NaI(Tl) probe (NanoSpec, Target Gmbh).

---

[9]   More details can be found in Aitken (1985).

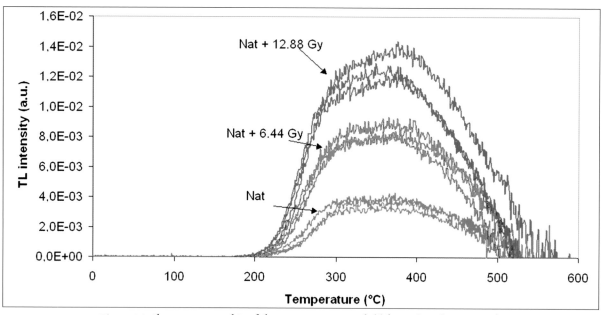

Figure 16: Glow curves graphic of the measurement on field (© Zink and Porto 2010).

Luminescence tests

A test was conducted by thermoluminescence using the regenerative additive method (TL SARA). The doses estimated by this method range from 3.1 to 22.3 Gy. A first test using a single aliquot regeneration OSL (SAR-OSL) protocol was unsuccessful. Concerning the N06 Tr12 158b sample, no luminescence was detected under optical stimulation for our samples.

Palaeodose

The luminescence measurements were made by additive TL (Zink and Porto, 2005), with a storage of 3–4 weeks in the dark at 50°C and a preheating of 220°C during 1 second. The anomalous fading was investigated using SAR-fading protocol on 1.5 decade (Auclair *et al.* 2003; Zink 2008). Figure 16 shows standard glow curves. The results are presented in Table 2.

Annual dose

The annual dose rate is the sum of contributions from inside the sample (alpha and beta radiations) and contributions from the surroundings (gamma and cosmic rays). The internal contribution (alpha and beta radiation) of the annual dose was determined by alpha counting for uranium and thorium contents and by X-ray analysis using scanning electron microscope and PIXE for the potassium content. We observed a variation between potassium contents measured by SEM and those obtained by PIXE. We are not aware if it is an experimental bias between both methods, or simple dispersion due to the lack of homogeneity of the samples. Concerning the calculations, the average of both methods was used (Table 2). The internal radionuclide content was relatively homogeneous and close to the contents of surrounding sediments.

The external gamma contribution was based on measurements of gamma spectrometry (threshold technique on the entire spectrum between 500 keV and 2780 keV) made in trench TB, listed in Table 4. The TB was selected as having a complete stratigraphical profile. The homogeneity of the sediment throughout the citadel surmised that the gamma dose rate is homogeneous throughout the site. In fact, we observed no significant variation in our measures on all levels of the TB with dispersion of values lower than 6% (Table 8). Hence, we took a mean value for the entire site of 0.801±0.045 mGy/a.

The contribution of cosmic radiation (energy range between 3 and 10 MeV) was monitored in the plain (the gardens of Omar Khayyam's mausoleum), 1 km away from the archaeological site (36.165°N, 58.823°E, 1180 m above sea level). The result was compared with that obtained on the site of Marsal (France, 48.78°N, 6.60°E, 200m asl).

D (Nishapur) = 1.113 D (Marsal)
It was consistent with that obtained from the tables of Prescott and Stephan (1982):

D (28.50°; 1180 m asl) = 1.132 D (50.32°; 200 m asl).
We deduced the cosmic dose rate at the surface:

D (Nishapur) = 245 mGy/ka (±5%)
This value is insensitive to variations in altitude on the site [±15 m = ±0.3%]. On other hand, it varies with depth into the soil (Prescott and Hutton 1988).

Numerical simulation

The Bayesian approach (Buck *et al.* 1995) sought to define the probability distribution of ages based on data and parameters listed in Table 9 with their associated distributions. To maintain a reasonable calculation time, we did not start from the real measured data (equivalent dose and supralinearity based on alpha and beta radiation, and alpha counting). The calculation thus does not take into account the uncertainties due to calibration (uncertainty Ur4 in Table 5). They will be added to the final result.

The likelihood function establishes a connection between the data and the age θ, according to the following system of equations:

Db = (bu * U+ bh * Th + bk * K2O) / (1 + WFh * WF/100)   beta annual dose
Da = (au * U+ ah * Th) / (1 + WFu * WF100)   alpha annual dose
DA = a* Da + Db+ Dg + Dcos   total annual dose
fadcorr = (1-g/100*log((θ*1000*365,25*24*60)/(exp(1)*t0)))   correction factor for fading
De = DA * θ * fadcorr   age equation

We have implemented all the data and the above equations as a function written in R language (R 2.9.1, R Development Core Team, 2009) running WinBUGS software (WinBUGS14) via R2WinBUGS package (R2WinBUGS 2.1–14). The simulation was done using three chains of 50,000 iterations (taking every 5th simulation after discarding the first 25,000 iterations).

Results

Table 2 shows the individual ages of the shards (Figs 17–18), which are plotted on Figure 19. Three groups are clearly visible. Most of our data belongs to only one group with a probability of 95%. We order the three groups:

3000 years > group 1 > group 2 > group 3> present day

We use the 'greater than' symbol '>' to denote that a group is earlier than another. The ages of the three groups were between the present day and 3000 years ago, with group 1 older than group 2, which is older than group 3, the belonging to different groups being based on Figure 20.

Using the above observation, we made a new Bayesian treatment to define the limits of each group:

Lower boundary (group 3) = 940 (120) years
Upper boundary (group 3) = 1170 (95) years

Figure 17: Shards from the Qohandez dated by TL (© Collinet 2010).

Lower boundary (group 2) = 1360 (85) years
Upper boundary (group 2) = 1510 (95) years
Lower boundary (group 1) = 1810 (175) years
Upper boundary (group 1) = 2280 (255) years
(The number in parentheses is the numerical value of the combined standard uncertainty)
We inferred that the age of a potshard belonging to:[10]

The first group has a probability of 95% of being within the coverage interval [350 BC–530 AD];
The second group has a probability of 95% of being within the coverage interval [405–785 AD];
The third group has a probability of 95% of being within the coverage interval [775–1235 AD].

From the allotting of the potshards to the different groups, we performed a seriation of our stratigraphical units (Table 6). The result is compared to distributions of archaeological units at different periods made by archaeologists (last column of Table 6).

The same stratigraphical unit may have potshards belonging to different groups. This result is not surprising if one accepts that potshards can be found in higher layers following a reworking

---

10 This dating exclusively concerns the TL analyses, without the Archaeomagnetism support.

110-E4 (n°18)

110-4 E5 (no.21)

110-E3 (no.11)

110-E6 (no.26)

116-E1 (no.3)

200-E1 (no.33)

203-E1 (no.32)

5   cm

Figure 18: Shards from the Qohandez dated by TL (© Collinet 2010).

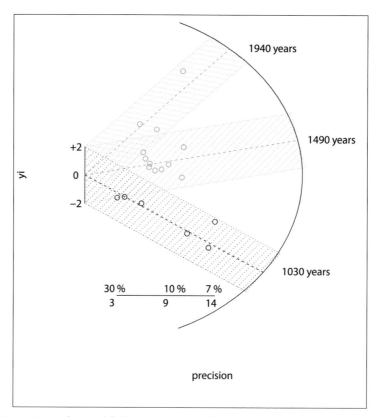

Figure 19: Graphic model showing the individual ages (© Zink and Porto 2010).

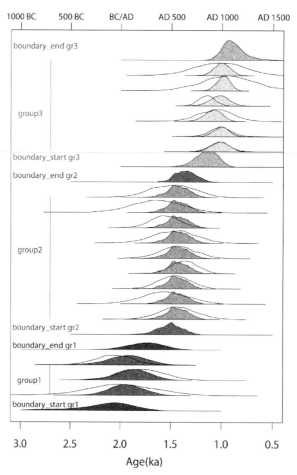

Figure 20: Graphic showing the probability distribution of luminescence ages. For each age, two distributions have been plotted: one in outline which is the result of extended Bayesian treatment using vague prior uniform distribution between present days and 3000 years; and a solid one based on the model assuming three ordered groups: 3000 years > group 1 > group 2 > group 3> present day '>' meaning 'older than'). Other plotted distributions correspond to estimated date of begin and end of the different groups (© Zink and Porto 2010).

Table 2: Thermoluminescence Analysis (© Zink and Porto 2010).

Field campaign	Trench	Sample	Q (Gy)	I (Gy)	De (Gy)	DA (mGy/a)	Fading rate (%/decade)	Age (years)	Uncertainty (%)
N 06	T 10	418–1	**2.2±0.2**	**+1.8±0.3**	4.0±0.4	4.1	**0.0±0.8**	1025	± 11
N 06	T 10	418 box	**3.1±0.4**	**+2.7±0.6**	5,8±0.7	4.2	**0.0±0.5**	1380	± 13
N 06	T 10	418–16	**3.0±0.2**	**+2.1±0.2**	5.1±0.4	5.2	**0.0±0.2**	1020	± 10
N 06	T 10	420	**2.8±0.5**	**+3.0±0.7**	5,8±0.9	4.0	**0.8±0.1**	1540	± 13
N 06	T 12	148	**3.7±0.3**	**+2.4±0.4**	6.1±0.6	4.2	**0.0±0.8**	1555	± 11
N 06	T 12	158	**3,9±0.6**	**+3.1±1.0**	6,9±1.2	3.4	**0.0±0.4**	2070	± 18
N 06	T 12	158 box	**3,9±0.1**	**+2.0±0.2**	5,9±0.2	4.2	**0.0±0.2**	1470	± 8
N 07	T 26	110 E1	**4.2±0.4**	**+2.5±0.6**	6,7±0.7	5.0	**0.0±0.2**	1365	± 11
N 07	T 26	110 E3	**2.5±0.4**	**+2.0±0.5**	4.5±0.6	4.5	**0.7±0.1**	1020	± 14
N 07	T 26	110 E4	**5.3±0.4**	**+2.7±0.7**	8.0±0.9	4.6	**0.0±0.9**	1810	± 13
N 07	T 26	110-4 E5	**3.5±0.1**	**+1.3±0.2**	4,8±0.2	4.8	**2.4±0.1**	1125	± 8
N 07	T 26	110 E6	**4.4±0.5**	**+2.4±0.7**	6,8±0.9	4.9	**0.0±0.3**	1455	± 17
N 07	T 26	UF 113	**5.3±0.2**	**+2.3±0.4**	7.6±0.4	5.2	**0.0±0.5**	1540	± 8
N 07	T 26	116 E1	**6.6±0.7**	**+1.4±1.0**	8.0±1.2	5.0	**0.0±0.4**	1585	± 16
N 07	T 26	200 E1	**2.5±0.7**	**+1.7±1.0**	4.2±1.2	4.5	**0.0±0.2**	935	± 29
N 07	T 26	203 E1	**6.4±0.4**	**+2.1±0.5**	8.5±0.6	4.3	**0.5±0.1**	2095	± 8
N 07	T 27	515–603	**3.6±0.6**	**+0.5±0.8**	4.0±1.0	3.9	**0.0±0.8**	1085	± 25
N 07	T 27	516	**3.4±0.4**	**+2.6±0.6**	6.0±0.7	4.0	**0.0±0.4**	1600	± 14

Notes: In bold – measured parameters

Q – Equivalent dose to the archaeological dose received by the sample since its last heating uncorrected from the supralinearity – unit Gray – Gy; I – Supralinearity correction- unit Gray-Gy; De – Equivalent dose to the archaeological dose received by the sample since its last heating De = Q + I – unit Gray – Gy; DA – Annual dose or dose rate – dose received by the sample during one year – it is composed of contributions in alpha, beta, gamma and cosmic as described in Table 3 – Unit milligray per year – mGy/a (equivalent to Gray per kilo-annum (thousand years) – Gy/ka); Fading rate – correction factor due to anomalous fading – unit percent per decade -%/decade; Age – ages calculated from measurements of dose equivalent, effective alpha, fading rate, the average values of alpha counting, content of potassium oxide and external dose and estimation of humidity. Bayesian approach with non-informative prior (uniform distribution between 0 and 4000 years). The simulation was done using three chains of 50,000 iterations (taking every 5th simulation after discarding the first 25,000 iterations) – years; Uncertainty – based on the combined standard uncertainties as described in Table 4.

Table 3: Uranium, thorium and potassium oxide contents (© Zink and Porto 2010).

Field campaign	Trench	Sample	Cα (cp/ks)	Cα corr (cp/ks)	U (ppm)	Th (ppm)	K2O (%)
N 06	T 10	418-1	**0.82 ± 0.03**	0.81 ± 0.08	2.8 ± 0.3	8.8 ± 0.9	2.98± 0.20
N 06	T 10	418 boite	**0.86 ± 0.03**	0.85 ± 0.08	2.9 ± 0.3	9.2 ± 0.9	2.70 ± 0.06
N 06	T 10	418-16	**0.91 ± 0.03**	0.90 ± 0.08	3.1 ± 0.2	9.8 ± 1.0	4.17± 0.02
N 06	T 10	420	**0.70 ± 0.02**	0.70 ± 0.07	2.4 ± 0.2	7.5 ± 0.7	2.83± 0.23
N 06	T 12	148	**1.09 ± 0.03**	1.08 ± 0.08	3.7 ± 0.4	11.7 ± 1.2	2.40± 0.10
N 06	T 12	158	**0.59 ± 0.02**	0.58 ± 0.08	2.0 ± 0.2	6.3 ± 0.6	2.56± 0.08
N 06	T 12	158 boite	**0.69 ± 0.02**	0.68 ± 0.07	2.3 ± 0.2	7.4 ± 0.7	3.70 ± 0.44
N 07	T 26	110 E1	**0.81 ± 0.02**	0.80 ± 0.08	2.7 ± 0.3	8.7 ± 0.9	3.49± 0.12
N 07	T 26	110 E3	**0.77 ± 0.02**	0.76 ± 0.08	2.6 ± 0.3	8.3 ± 0.8	3.26± 0.01
N 07	T 26	110 E4	**0.84 ± 0.02**	0.83 ± 0.08	2.8 ± 0.3	9.0 ± 0.9	2.52± 0.13
N 07	T 26	110-4 E5	**0.86 ± 0.03**	0.85 ± 0.08	2.9 ± 0.3	9.2 ± 0.9	3.50± 0.11
N 07	T 26	110 E6	**0.91 ± 0.03**	0.90 ± 0.08	3.1 ± 0.3	9.8 ± 0.9	3.30± 0.60
N 07	T 26	UF 113	**0.86 ± 0.02**	0.85 ± 0.08	2.9 ± 0.3	9.2 ± 0.9	3.86 ± 0.41
N 07	T 26	116 E1	**0.83 ± 0.02**	0.82 ± 0.08	2.8 ± 0.3	8.9 ± 0.9	3.39 ± 0.06
N 07	T 26	200 E1	**0.66 ± 0.02**	0.65 ± 0.08	2.2 ± 0.2	7.1 ± 0.7	3.58 ± 0.05
N 07	T 26	203 E1	**0.63 ± 0.02**	0.64 ± 0.08	2.1 ± 0.2	6.8 ± 0.7	3.23 ± 0.06
N 07	T 27	585	**0.55 ± 0.01**	0.54 ± 0.05	1.9 ± 0.2	5.9 ± 0.6	2.75± 0.12
N 07	T 27	610	**0.50 ± 0.02**	0.50± 0.05	1.7 ± 0.2	5.4 ± 0.5	2.94 ± 0.37

Notes: In bold - measured parameters

Cα – counting alpha – alpha radiation measurement using zinc sulphide screen 12.4 mm diameter – unit kilo-counts per second – cp/ks; Cα corr – alpha counting after correction of over-counting: corr Cα = Cα xs with over-counting factor s = 1.01 ± 0.04 – unit counts per kilo-seconds – cp/ks; U - uranium content – U = Cα corr/0.292348 (Aitken, 1985) unit parts per million – ppm; Th – thorium content – Th = 3.167 × U (Aitken, 1985) – unit parts per million – ppm; K2O – potassium oxide content – unit percent -%

Table 4: Annual dose rate (© Zink and Porto 2010).

Field campaign	Trench	Sample	U (ppm)	Th (ppm)	K2O (%)	Alpha Effectiveness	D'α (mGy/a)	Dβ (mGy/a)	Dext (mGy/a)
N 06	T 10	418-1	2.8 ± 0.3	8.8 ± 0.9	2.98±0.20	**0.069 ±0.001**	0.7	2.4	0.97 ± 0.07
N 06	T 10	418 wood	2.9 ± 0.3	9.2 ± 0.9	2.70 ±0.06	**0.088 ±0.001**	1.0	2.3	0.97 ± 0.07
N 06	T 10	418-16	3.1 ± 0.2	9.8 ± 1.0	4.17±0.02	**0.085± 0.001**	1.0	3.2	0.97 ± 0.07
N 06	T 10	420	2.4 ± 0.2	7.5 ± 0.7	2.83±0.23	**0.089 ±0.001**	0.8	2.2	0.95 ± 0.07
N 06	T 12	148	3.7 ± 0.4	11.7 ± 1.2	2.40±0.10	**0.071 ±0.001**	1.0	2.3	0.88 ± 0.07
N 06	T 12	158	2.0 ± 0.2	6.3 ± 0.6	2.56±0.08	**0.068 ±0.001**	0.5	2.0	0.88 ± 0.07
N 06	T 12	158 wood	2.3 ± 0.2	7.4 ± 0.7	3.70± 0.44	**0.061 ±0.001**	0.5	2.8	0.88 ± 0.07
N 07	T 26	110 E1	2.7 ± 0.3	8.7 ± 0.9	3.49± 0.12	**0.117 ±0.002**	1.2	2.7	1.00 ± 0.07
N 07	T 26	110 E3	2.6 ± 0.3	8.3 ± 0.8	3.26± 0.01	**0.095 ±0.002**	0.9	2.6	1.00 ± 0.07
N 07	T 26	110 E4	2.8 ± 0.3	9.0 ± 0.9	2.52± 0.13	**0.129 ±0.001**	1.4	2.2	1.00 ± 0.07
N 07	T 26	110-4 E5	2.9 ± 0.3	9.2 ± 0.9	3.50± 0.11	**0.092 ±0.001**	1.0	2.8	1.00 ± 0.07
N 07	T 26	110 E6	3.1 ± 0.3	9.8 ± 0.9	3.30± 0.60	**0.103 ±0.001**	1.2	2.7	1.00 ± 0.07
N 07	T 26	UF 113	2.9 ± 0.3	9.2 ± 0.9	3.86 ±0.41	**0.108 ±0.001**	1.2	3.0	0.99 ± 0.07
N 07	T 26	116 E1	2.8 ± 0.3	8.9 ± 0.9	3.39 ±0.06	**0.130 ±0.001**	1.4	2.7	0.96 ± 0.07
N 07	T 26	200 E1	2.2 ± 0.2	7.1 ± 0.7	3.58 ±0.05	**0.095± 0.001**	0.8	2.7	1.03 ± 0.07
N 07	T 26	203 E1	2.1 ± 0.2	6.8 ± 0.7	3.23 ±0.06	**0.102 ±0.001**	0.8	2.4	0.99 ± 0.07
N 07	T 27	585	1.9 ± 0.2	5.9 ± 0.6	2.75± 0.12	**0.126 ±0.003**	0.9	2.1	0.92 ± 0.07
N 07	T 27	610	1.7 ± 0.2	5.4 ± 0.5	2.94 ±0.37	**0.136 ±0.003**	0.9	2.2	0.91 ± 0.07

Notes: In bold – measured parameters; U, Th, K2O average values derived from Table 2; Effectiveness alpha – correction factor reflecting alpha dose rate in equivalent beta (or gamma) dose rate – It is the a-value as defined in Aitken (1985) – dimensionless unit 1; D'α – contribution of alpha particles to the annual dose: $D'\alpha = a \times (2.31 \times U + 0.611 \times Th) / (1 + 1.5 \times WF)$ (Adamiec G. and Aitken, 1998) – unit milligray per year – mGy/a; Dβ – contribution of beta radiation to the annual dose rate: $D\beta = (0.146 \times U + 0.0273 \times Th + 0,649 \times K2O) / (1 + 1.25 \times WF)$ (Adamiec and Aitken M. J., 1998) – unit milligray per year – mGy/a; WF – Wetness 5 ± 3 %; Dext – contribution of the environment (cosmic and gamma) to the annual dose rate – Gamma dose rate is estimated from measurements made in the trench B (Zink and Porto, 2009, cf. table 7) and the contribution of cosmic rays is based on tables provided by Prescott and Hutton, 1988.

Table 5: Summary of standard uncertainty components (© Zink and Porto 2010).

Source of uncertainty	Type	U(xi)	Ci	Uri(y)
Luminescence measurements Ur1	A			8.6 %
Archaeological dose UrQ (TL)	A	7.5 %	0.4	3.0 %
Supralinearity UrI (TL)	A	20 %	0.4	8.0 %
Alpha Effectiveness Ury (TL)	A	2.0 %	0.2	0.4 %
Annual dose measurements Ur2	A			4.2 %
Alpha counting Uαobs	A	3.0 %	0.3	0.9 %
X-rays analysis UK	A	10.0 %	0.4	4.0 %
External gamma dose rate	A	5.4 %	0.15	0.8 %
External cosmic dose rate	A	5.0 %	0.05	0.25 %
Calibrations Ur4	A/B			4.3 %
Beta source	B	5 %	0.8	4.0 %
Alpha Source	B	5 %	0.2	1.0 %
Alpha over-counting	A	4 %	0.3	1.2 %
Parameters Ur5	B			2.7 %
Parameters linked to alpha	B	5 %	0.2	1.0 %
Parameters linked to beta	B	5 %	0.5	2.5 %
Uranium/thorium ratio Ur6	B	5 %	0.1	0.5 %
Wetness Ur7	B	15 %	0.1	1.5 %
Dosimetry Ur9	B			5.0 %
Gammameter calibration	B	25 %	0.2	5.0 %
Fading Ur10 (TL)	A			5.0 %
Combined standard uncertainty Urc				13.0 %

Notes: The values presented here are based on the average values of the various samples: Type: A – uncertainty evaluated by statistical analysis; B – uncertainty evaluated by means other than statistical analysis; U(xi) estimated uncertainty of the input xi; Ci sensitivity coefficient $Ci = y / xi$; Uri(y) contribution due to the input xi in the total uncertainty $Uri(y) = Ci\, U(xi)$; The calculation of uncertainties Ur1 to Ur9 is based the appendix B of Aitken (1985). The fading, Ur10 is estimated by comparing the standard deviations of Monte-Carlo simulation with and without fading (Zink, 2008); The combined standard uncertainty Urc is the square root of the quadratic sum of standard uncertainties: $Urc^2 = \Sigma\, Uri^2 = (i)\ 1, 2, 4, 5, 6, 7, 9, 10$.

Table 6: Seriation matrix. For each stratigraphical unit we reported the number of potsherds belonging to the various groups (see Figure 2). In the case where a potsherd may belong to two groups, we counted 2/3 for the most likely group and 1/3 for the other. The matrix was diagonalized. The last column gives the Period for each unit as provided by the archaeologists (© Zink and Porto 2010).

	Group 3	Group 2	Group 1	Period
N06 T10 418	2	1	0	IIIa
N07 T26 110	2	3+1/3	2/3	IIIa
N07 T27 515–603	2/3	1/3	0	III
N07 T26 200	2/3	1/3	0	III (reemploy of a more ancient wall)
N06 T10 420	0	1	0	II (ancient sherd in a IIIa layer)
N07 T26 113	0	1	0	II
N06 T12 148	0	1	0	II
N07 T26 116	0	2/3	1/3	II
N07 T27 516	0	2/3	1/3	II
N06 T12 158	0	1+1/3	2/3	II
N07 T26 203	0	0	1	I

Table 7: List of samples from Nishapur (© Zink and Porto 2010).

Field campaign	Trench	Unit	Sample	No C2RMF	No TL
N 06	T 10	418	1	C2RMF68418	530
N 06	T 10	418	Box	C2RMF68417	525
N 06	T 10	418	16	C2RMF68419	542
N 06	T 10	420		C2RMF68420	543
N 06	T 12	148	1	C2RMF68422	531
N 06	T 12	158	Box	C2RMF68423	526
N 06	T 12	158		C2RMF68421	532
N 07	T 26	110	E1	C2RMF68665	534
N 07	T 26	110	E3	C2RMF68662	535
N 07	T 26	110	E4	C2RMF68661	536
N 07	T 26	110-4	E5	C2RMF68663	537
N 07	T 26	110	E6	C2RMF68664	538
N 07	T 26	UF 113		C2RMF68424	527
N 07	T 26	116	E1	C2RMF68660	539
N 07	T 26	200	E1	C2RMF68659	540
N 07	T 26	203	E1	C2RMF68658	541
N 07	T 27	585		C2RMF68426	544
N 07	T 27	610		C2RMF68425	528

Table 8: Locations of external dose rate measurements, TB (© Zink and Porto 2010).

No	Location	Stratigraphical Unit	Gamma dose rate (mGy/ka)
NI 1	Period III (adobe wall), vertically		797 (± 6.2%)
NI 2	Period III, horizontal to approximately 2.50 m above ground level		852 (± 3.9%)
NI 3	Period III, vertically		840 (± 5.4%)
NI 4	Period II, vertically	SU 220	775 (± 2.1%)
NI 5	Period II, vertically	SU 242, 243, 244. Mainly SU 242 and 243	770 (± 5.3%)
NI 6	Early Period II, horizontally	SU 246	860 (± 6.9%)
NI 7	Period I, horizontally, possibly first occupations and virgin soil	SU 248	746 (± 4.0 %)
NI 8	Period I, horizontally	SU 248	840 (± 4.3%)
NI 9	Period I, vertically	SU 248	733 (± 6.2%)
Average			801 ± 45

Table 9: Variables used in Bayesian treatment (© Zink and Porto 2010).

VARIABLE	DISTRIBUTION	REFERENCE
Equivalent dose	De ~ N(μDe, σDe)	cf. table 1
Alpha efficiency	a ~ N(μa, σa)	cf. table 3
Fading rate	g ~ N(μg, σg)	cf. table 1
Radionuclide contents	X ~ N(μX, σX) (X= [U], [Th], [K2O];	cf. table 2
Storage between irradiation and measurements	t0 ~ N(μt0, σt0)	The duration was estimated for each potsherd from about 3 to 4 weeks, with an accuracy of eight hours
Cosmic dose rate	Dcos ~ N(μDcos, σDcos)	Prescott and Hutton (1988); Zink and Porto (2009)
Gamma dose rate	Dg ~ N(μDg, σDg)	Zink and Porto (2009)
Wetness	WF ~ N(μWF, σWF)	cf. note to table 3
Wetness parameters	WFx ~ N(μWFx, σWFx) (x=u, h,k)	Aitken (1985)
Conversion factors	xy ~ N(μxy, σxy) (x=a, b ; y= u,h,k)	Adamiec G., Aitken M. J. (1998)

Note: Each of these data is represented by its mean μ and standard deviation σ and its probability distribution function follows a normal distribution (notation N (μ, σ)).

of the sediments. Except for the stratigraphical unit N06 T10 420, the Islamic stratigraphical units contain fragments of group 3. On the other hand, the pre-Islamic units do not. Thus group 3 is characteristic of the Islamic period. The transition period is more difficult to analyze and seems to be shared between groups 2 and 3. However, the two levels associated with this period each contain a single potshard. The stratigraphical unit 158 N06 T12 contains a mixture of group 1 and group 2. Hence, group 1 would be older than that unit.

In terms of the TL, group 2 appears to be relatively homogeneous. It is difficult to attribute it to one period rather than another. Our sample is relatively small per stratigraphical unit and per period. It is possible that this group represents only a single period. It would be a sampling or a taphonomic bias. But it is also possible that this group corresponds to several periods, close enough in time to be indiscernible.

4. Insights from archaeomagnetic analysis

The archaeomagnetic study was conducted by Agnès Genevey (CNRS-UPMC)[11] and Yves Gallet (OPGP-CNRS)[12] (text below © Genevey and Gallet). The aim of the study was to use archaeomagnetic analysis to bring chronological constraints to the site of the Qohandez at Nisapur. Most baked clay fragments analysed were also studied using the thermoluminescence technique (© Zink and Porto), allowing the results obtained from both methods to be contrasted within the archaeological context.

The archaeomagnetic analysis

Archaeomagnetism is a dating method which relies on the knowledge of the secular variation of the Earth's magnetic field (e.g. Gallet *et al.* 2009 and references therein). These variations

---

[11] C2RMF, UMR CNRS 171, 14, Quai François Mitterrand, 75001 Paris (at present Université Pierre et Marie Curie, Sorbonne Universités, UMR CNRS 8220 LAMS)

[12] Equipe de Paléomagnétisme, Institut de Physique du Globe de Paris, Sorbonne Paris Cité, UMR CNRS 7154 (1, rue Jussieu, 75238 Paris cedex 05, France).

can be recovered from the magnetic properties of well-dated baked clay archaeological materials, such as fragments of kiln, oven, tile, brick or ceramic. These objects have indeed acquired a thermoremanent magnetization (TRM) during their cooling consecutive to the final heating (typically higher than 600°C), whose direction and intensity are respectively parallel and proportional to that of the ambient geomagnetic field (e.g. Dunlop and Özdemir 1997). Structures found *in situ*, such as kilns which have not moved since their final heating–cooling, can provide information on both the direction and intensity of the ancient magnetic field. In contrast, for displaced artefacts, such as ceramics for which one cannot retrieve their original position during their manufacturing (and thus during the acquisition of their TRM), the directional information is lost but it is still possible to determine the ancient geomagnetic field intensity.

Thanks to its rich historical past and to the numerous archaeological excavations conducted each year, the Middle East region has been the target of several archaeomagnetic studies (e.g. Burakov and Nachasova 1978; Burakov *et al.* 1982; Hussain 1983; 1987; Aitken *et al.* 1984; Nachasova *et al.* 1986; Burlatskaya and Chernykh 1989; Burlatskaya and Chelidze 1990; Nachasova and Burakov 1994; 1997; Odah *et al.* 1995; Odah 1999; Genevey *et al.* 2003; Gallet *et al.* 2006; 2008; Gallet and Al-Maqdissi 2010). These studies were mainly focused on the determination of the ancient geomagnetic field intensity and allow one to describe the main characteristic of the regional geomagnetic field intensity variations covering the past eight millennia. Although this curve is still in progress, it can be used to obtain some chronological constraints for undated or poorly dated archaeological artefacts discovered in the Middle East. With this objective, we analyzed several baked clay fragments that were found during the archaeological excavations conducted on the site of the Qohandez at Nishapur. Most of those fragments were also analyzed with a Thermoluminescence (TL) technique (see above), which should allow us to contrast the dating constraints provided by these two very different methods. The main objective of this study was to determine whether the analyzed fragments could reveal the presence of a first Sasanian occupation period that would correspond to the foundation of the city of Nishapur.

Sample collection and magnetic properties

The collection of baked clay fragments that was analyzed for archaeointensity determination is composed of 19 fragments previously measured for TL dating (17 from pottery and two from bricks), plus five potshards from Unit 110 of Trench 26 (Table 10). Each fragment was labelled with an archaeomagnetic reference number, the corresponding TL identification number and a C2RMF number as indicated in Table 10.

Archaeointensity experiments require heating the samples to high temperatures of up to ~550°C. This thermal treatment may induce an alteration of the magnetic mineralogy and, as a consequence, a failure in the intensity determination. For this reason, we first tested the stability of the magnetic mineralogy of the different fragments upon heating. This was made possible by carrying out low-field susceptibility measurements on a few grams (~2 g) of powder collected from each fragment. Each series of measurements, performed using a KLY3/CS3 susceptibility bridge, involved undergoing a heating-cooling cycle between room temperature and 550°C.

We observe for most fragments a satisfactory reversibility of the thermomagnetic susceptibility curves (Fig. 21, a–k), which underlines the good stability of their magnetic mineralogy and their potential for intensity analysis. Alteration was detected in only six fragments, which were therefore discarded from further magnetic experiments (Fig. 21, l–m). The remaining fragments were next subjected to Isothermal Remanent Magnetization (IRM)

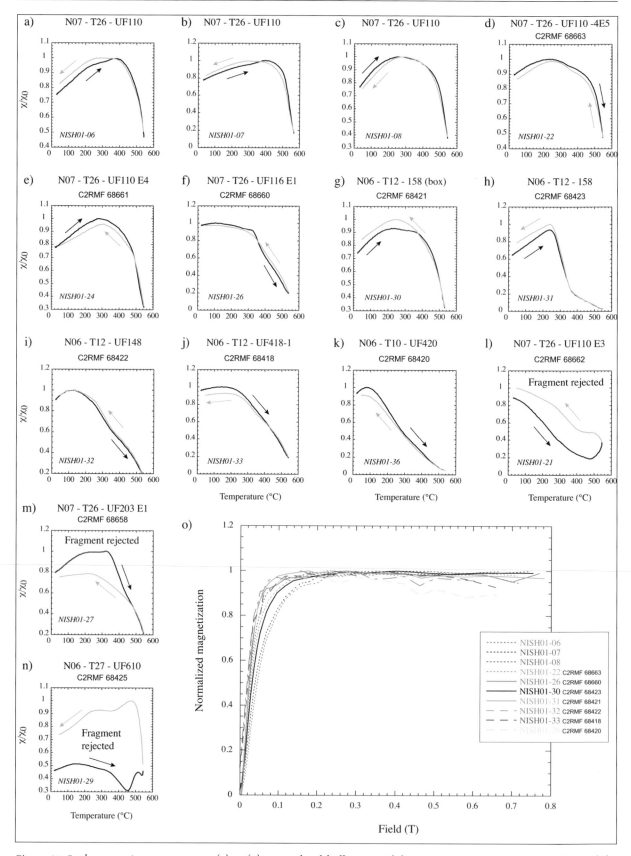

Figure 21: Rock magnetic measurements (a) to (n): Normalized bulk susceptibility versus temperature curves obtained for different fragments with (a) to (k) fragments showing a favorable behavior for archeointensity determinations and (l) to (n) three examples of rejected fragments because of magnetic alteration during heating. (o) Normalized IRM acquisition curves obtained for ten fragments for which we successfully performed intensity measurements (© Genevey and Gallet 2010).

up to a maximum field of 0.8 T (Fig. 21, o). For all these fragments, the magnetization reaches saturation in a field strength of between 0.3 and 0.5 T, indicating a magnetic mineralogy dominated by a mineral of the titanomagnetite family. The different shapes of the thermomagnetic curves further indicate that the titanium contents may vary according to the fragments. It is worth mentioning that we did not find evidence of high-coercivity (>1 T) minerals, such as hematite, in our collection. Altogether, the magnetic properties observed for the Iranian fragments appear relatively common for archaeological baked clay artefacts and, in particular, they are very reminiscent of those previously reported from Syrian pottery and baked brick fragments (Genevey *et al.* 2003; Gallet and Al-Maqdissi 2010).

Intensity experiments

The intensity experiments were performed using a Triaxe, a specially designed laboratory magnetometer, which allows continuous magnetization measurements at high temperatures (Le Goff and Gallet 2004; Gallet and Le Goff 2006). The methodological protocol designed for the Triaxe magnetometer, hereafter referred as to the Triaxe protocol, is derived from the classical Thellier and Thellier (1959) method. The latter relies on the proportionality between the thermoremanent magnetization (TRM) and the geomagnetic field intensity that induced that magnetization, and on the laws of additivity, reciprocity and independence, which apply to the TRM acquisition (Thellier and Thellier 1959). Essentially, the experimental protocol implies the replacement of the original thermoremanent magnetization, called the natural remanent magnetization (NRM), acquired by the objects during their manufacturing by a new TRM acquired in the laboratory in controlled field conditions.

The Triaxe protocol allows one to study the magnetization of a small cylindrical sample, 1cm in diameter and height. The cycle of measurements comprises a succession of five steps: the sample is first heated in a zero magnetic field from room temperature to a high temperature T_2, so that its NRM is almost completely demagnetized (step #1); still in a zero field, the sample is then cooled down to a low temperature T_1, usually 150°C (step #2), and heated up again to T_2 (step #3); the sample is next cooled down from T_2 to T_1 in a magnetic field whose intensity is set to be close to that expected at the supposed date of the fragment and whose direction is adjusted to be close to that having induced the NRM (step #4); the newly acquired TRM is demagnetized by again heating the sample in a zero field up to T_2 (step #5) before the sample is finally cooled down to room temperature.

At each running temperature T_i, every ~5°C, between T_1 to T_2, we compute the ratio between the NRM and TRM fractions demagnetized between T_1 and T_i, both fractions being corrected from the thermal variations of the remaining NRM above T_2. An estimate at T_i of the ancient field intensity is then obtained after multiplication of this ratio by the laboratory field intensity (parameter $R'(T_i)$). For each sample, we thus derive a 'characteristic' magnetic intensity value from the averaging of all $R'(T_i)$ data computed between T_1 and T_2. It is worth pointing out that when a second magnetization is isolated during the NRM demagnetization, say between the room temperature and a temperature T'_1 with $T'_1 > T_1$, the averaging of the $R'(T_i)$ data is then performed between T'_1 and T_2.

We highlight the fact that the Triaxe protocol takes into account both the TRM anisotropy and cooling rate effects, which may significantly bias the intensity determinations. These two effects are linked to the manufacturing process of the analyzed objects (stretching of the clay paste for the TRM anisotropy and cooling conditions for the cooling rate effect) and to the fact that the cooling conditions in which the laboratory TRM is acquired may not reproduce those having prevailed for the NRM acquisition. Because the laboratory field is set so that the acquired TRM direction is very close (within a very few degrees) to the NRM direction, the Triaxe protocol makes unnecessary any TRM anisotropy correction. For the cooling rate effect, it was experimentally shown that, although the cooling time used for the laboratory TRM acquisition is much faster that the original one (½ hour versus several hours or tens of hours), the intensity values computed from the R'(Ti) data are almost independent from this effect. This was further demonstrated by the agreement, generally within ±5%, between several datasets obtained using both classical intensity methods (involving correction of the cooling rate effect) and the Triaxe protocol (Genevey *et al.* 2009; Hartmann *et al.* 2010).

Archaeointensity results

Among the 18 fragments showing a stable magnetic mineralogy upon heating (as deduced from the thermomagnetic susceptibility curves), three fragments were found too weakly magnetized to be measured with the Triaxe magnetometer. The intensity experiments were therefore performed on a final collection of 15 fragments (11 of which had been previously measured with luminescence technique).

It is important to indicate that our analyses are currently performed on groups of fragments of the same date. Intensity means are then computed from the average of the results obtained from the different fragments, with quality criteria requiring the dispersion of the data around the mean to be less than 10%. Such an approach was however not possible in this study where only individual fragments were made available for our archaeointensity analysis. To partly circumvent this issue, we analyzed several specimens per fragment.

Between two and six specimens were thus measured per fragment and we used the strict selection criteria defined by Gallet and Le Goff (2006) and Genevey *et al.* (2009) to only retain the most reliable intensity results. Four fragments were rejected on the basis of these strict selection criteria. The results obtained from the 11 remaining fragments are reported in Figure 22, where each panel displays the R'(Ti) data obtained from the different specimens analyzed for one fragment. We recall briefly that the R'(Ti) data are first averaged at the specimen level, before the mean values are themselves averaged to derive a mean intensity value at the fragment level. Regarding Figure 22, one can first note a limited scatter at low temperatures on some R'(Ti) curves, which only reflects the fact that the demagnetized fractions of NRM and TRM are very small for these first demagnetization steps (between T1 and Ti). It is important to note that these initial R'(Ti) data do not significantly affect the intensity determination performed over a much wider temperature interval. The case is different for the specimens analyzed for fragments NISH01-32 and NISH01-33, for which the scatter in R'(Ti) data concerns the entire temperature range. These fluctuations are linked to the weak magnetization characterizing the specimens, which however provide very consistent R'(Ti) curves. As a general matter, a very good consistency is observed between the specimens analyzed for each fragment (Figure 22). This allows one to compute for all fragments precise mean intensity values, in each case defined with a standard deviation of less than 3% of the corresponding mean (Table 10).

Discussion

The mean intensity value determined for each fragment reflects the intensity of the Earth's magnetic field prevailing at the time of the manufacture of the corresponding pottery assumed made close to Nishapur. Dating constraints on these artefacts can then be derived by comparing data with a reference geomagnetic intensity variation curve constructed for this area.

Archaeomagnetic data from Iran are very sparse with only a few recent results obtained by Gallet *et al.* (2006) on dated brick fragments from the Elamite sites of Haft Tepe, Chogha Zanbil and from Susa for the more recent Achaemenid Period. A large number of dated intensity

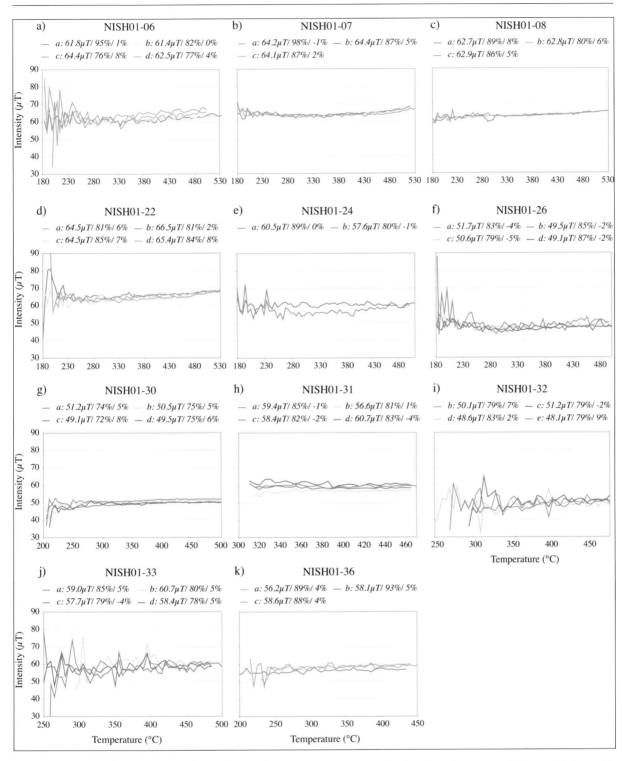

Figure 22: Intensity determinations obtained using the Triaxe magnetometer for the eleven fragments which provided suitable intensity results. Two to four specimens were analyzed per fragment providing each individual R'(Ti) curve in the different panels. For all specimens, the intensity value obtained is reported above each relevant panel together with two percentages indicating for the first one, the percentage of the magnetization fraction involved in intensity computation and for the second, the percentage of the slope of the R'(Ti) data after their fitting with a linear trend (see Gallet and Le Goff 2006 for further details) (© Genevey and Gallet 2010).

Table 10: Archaeointensity results obtained from baked clay fragments collected in the citadel of Nishapur. 'Archaeomag#', 'C2RMF#' and 'TL#' columns indicate respectively the archaeomagnetic reference number and the C2RMF and Thermoluminescence numbers (when relevant) associated to each baked clay fragment analyzed. 'Field campaign', 'Trench', 'UF' and '#' columns display the archeological information on the fragments. 'n specimen' column indicates the number of successfully analyzed specimens per fragment or the reason for which the fragment was not analyzed in intensity: either 'Rejected (χ(T))' for fragments rejected because of an unstable magnetic mineralogy upon heating or 'too weakly magnetized' for fragments whose magnetization was too low to be measured using the Triaxe magnetometer. 'Fmean±σF ($_{MT}$)' column reports the mean intensity value obtained per fragment with its standard deviation in micro Tesla or the 'Rejected (Triaxe)' label for fragments, which were rejected due to a non ideal behavior observed during the intensity experiments (© Genevey and Gallet 2010).

ARCHAEOMAG#	FIELD CAMPAIGN	TRENCH	UF	#	C2RMF#	TL#	AGE TL	dAGE TL	PHASE	n SPECIMEN	FMEAN±σF (mT)
NISH01-06	N 07	T 26	UF 110							4	62.5±1.3
NISH01-07	N 07	T 26	UF 110							3	64.2±0.2
NISH01-08	N 07	T 26	UF 110							3	62.8±0.1
NISH01-09	N 07	T 26	UF 110							Too weakly magnetized	X
NISH01-16	N 07	T 26	UF 110							2	Rejected (Triaxe)
NISH01-19	N 07	T 26	UF 110	E6	C2RMF68664	538	590 AD	215	IIb	6	Rejected (Triaxe)
NISH01-20	N 07	T 26	UF 110	E1	C2RMF68665	534	610 AD	155	IIb	2	Rejected (Triaxe)
NISH01-21	N 07	T 26	UF 110	E3	C2RMF68662	535	950 AD	150	IIIa	Rejected (χ(T))	X
NISH01-22	N 07	T 26	UF 110	-4 E5	C2RMF68663	537	880 AD	100	IIIa	4	65.2±1.0
NISH01-23	N 06	T 26	UF 110							Rejected (χ(T))	X
NISH01-24	N 07	T 26	UF 110	E4	C2RMF68661	536	210 AD	235	I	2	59.1±1.5
NISH01-25	N 07	T 26	UF 200	E1	C2RMF68659	540	1030 AD	255	III	Rejected (χ(T))	X
NISH01-26	N 07	T 26	UF 116	E1	C2RMF68660	539	380 AD	245	IIa	4	50.2±1.2
NISH01-27	N 07	T 26	UF 203	E1	C2RMF68658	541	60 BC	205	I	Rejected (χ(T))	X
NISH01-28	N 07	T 26	UF 113		C2RMF68424	527	500 AD	150	IIb	5	Rejected (Triaxe)
NISH01-29	N 07	T 26	UF 610		C2RMF68425	528	463 AD	233	II	Rejected (χ(T))	X
NISH01-30	N 06	T 27	UF 158	Box	C2RMF68421	532	543 AD	148	IIa	4	50.1±0.9
NISH01-31	N 06	T 12	UF 158		C2RMF68423	526	50 BC	350	I	4	58.8±1.7
NISH01-32	N 06	T 12	UF 148		C2RMF68422	531	568 AD	223	IIa	4	49.5±1.4
NISH01-33	N 06	T 10	UF 418	-1	C2RMF68418	530	1000AD	110	IIIa	4	59.0±1.3
NISH01-34	N 06	T 10	UF 418	Box	C2RMF68417	525	610 AD	180	IIb	Too weakly magnetized	X
NISH01-35	N 06	T 10	UF 418	-16	C2RMF68419	542	990 AD	90	IIIa	Too weakly magnetized	X
NISH01-36	N 06	T 10	UF 420		C2RMF68420	543	460 AD	250	IIIa	3	57.6±1.3
NISH01-37	N 07	T 27	UF 585		C2RMF68426	544	935 AD	245	IIIa	Rejected (χ(T))	X

results were however obtained in nearby countries, such in Turkmenistan, Uzbekistan, Georgia, Azerbaijan and Syria (e.g. Burakov and Nachasova 1978; Burakov *et al.* 1982; Nachasova *et al.* 1986; Burlatskaya and Chernykh 1989; Burlatskaya and Chelidze 1990; Nachasova and Burakov 1994; 1997; Genevey *et al.* 2003; Gallet *et al.* 2006). Those data can be used to construct a regional reference curve. Indeed, for a region of limited geographical extension and for the time scales of interest here, the variations of the Earth's magnetic field are nearly identical. Data obtained from different sites of such an area can then be reduced to a single reference site with a formula for latitude correction using the hypothesis of an axial dipole field.

For selecting data for our reference curve, we used the ArcheoInt compilation, which includes all intensity data obtained for the past 10,000 years (Genevey *et al.* 2008; http://archeoint.free. fr). The data are from the geographical area displayed on Figure 23. They were filtered by age to keep only the results dated between 800 BC and 1500 AD. We further selected the results that meet a set of reasonable quality criteria as defined in Genevey *et al.* (2008) which are based on the dispersion of the data about their mean intensity value as well as the number of samples analyzed per site. The dots in Figure 23 indicate the sites where the retained data were obtained, with often several results associated to a same location.

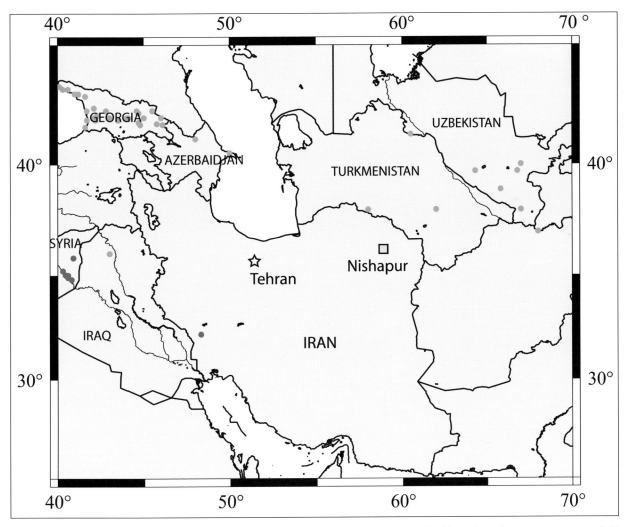

Figure 23: Extension of the geographical area where intensity data were selected for building the reference geomagnetic field intensity variation curve; Dots indicate the sites where the data with ages comprised between 800 BC and 1500 AD were obtained; in green, data obtained by Russian researchers (i.e. S. Burlatskaya, K. Burakov and I. Nachasova and co-authors; except one datum acquired by Aithen et al. in Iraq 1984); in purple, data we previously obtained in Syria and Iran (Genevey et al. 2003; Gallet et al. 2006) (© Genevey and Gallet 2010).

Our previous data obtained in Syria and Iran are reported in purple on Figure 23. They were obtained using derived protocols from the Thellier and Thellier method taking into account both the TRM anisotropy and the cooling rate effects and were constrained by strict and modern quality criteria. All other data (except one single data obtained in Iraq by Aitken and co-authors in 1984) were acquired by researchers from the Russian Academy of Sciences (namely S. Burlatskaya, K. Burakov and I. Nachasova and co-authors), Russia being a country where there has been a long tradition of archaeomagnetic activity since the late 1960s (green dots on Figure 23). These results were also acquired using procedures derived from the Thellier and Thellier method. The TRM anisotropy effect was, however, not systematically evaluated for those data and the cooling rate effect (which leads in most cases to an overestimation of the intensity values) was never assessed. Before considering these data for building a reference curve, a reasonable cooling rate correction of 3% decrease was applied to all of them. This factor was estimated from our collection of archaeological artefacts from Syria, averaging the cooling rate correction factors measured for all relevant fragments analyzed.

All the selected data were then reduced to the latitude of Nishapur (36.17°N) and finally averaged using sliding intervals of 100 years shifted by 50 years to build a regional geomagnetic intensity variation reference curve between 800 BC and 1500 AD (see the grey curves in Figure 24). At this point, it is however important to underline that the resolution of this curve is limited first by the dispersion of the data within each sliding time interval and, second, by the averaging process of the data which attenuates the amplitude of the variations and prevents us from recovering possible rapid fluctuations. Such an effect may be illustrated by comparing the intensity data that we previously obtained in Syria and Iran (purple symbols on Figure 24) with the computed curve. Both datasets exhibit the same pattern of intensity variations characterized by a strong decrease of the intensity values from ~700 BC to 100–200 AD and by a maximum in intensity at the end of the 1st millennium of the Current Era. However the Syrian data taken separately support the fact that the latter intensity peak derived from the computed curve was most probably more enhanced and centred around the 9th century.

Although we acknowledge its intrinsic limitations, the curve was hereafter tentatively used for bringing dating constraints to the 11 baked clay fragments collected from the citadel of Nishapur, which were successfully analyzed in intensity.

Our results are reported in Figure 24 where each horizontal line indicates the mean intensity value obtained for one fragment. The colour conventions considered to display the data are the same as used in Figure 14 (TL report, above): i.e. in green, – respectively in red and black –, the data obtained from the fragments associated, from TL analysis, to the group 1 – respectively group 2 and group 3. The age intervals, defined at 95%, for the three TL groups are further reported in our Figure 24. The mean intensity values obtained for the three fragments from Unit 110 of Trench 26, which were not analyzed by TL, are indicated with blue lines.

We focus first the discussion on our archaeointensity results independently of the TL constraints.

One can observe in Figure 24 three clusters of intensity values around relatively low values (~50µT, Fragments #26, #30 and #32), intermediate ones (~58µT, Fragments #24, #31, #33 and #36) and relatively high values (~64µT, Fragments #06, #07, #08 and #22). Comparing these clusters with the reference curve, we note that the lowest values appear compatible with the minimum in intensity observed at the beginning of our era. This minimum is very interesting; it is indeed a clear marker within the period covered in Figure 24 since such low values are only seen again just over thousand years later. Making the reasonable assumption that shards #26, #30 and #32 cannot be older than 1200 AD, our archaeomagnetic analysis thus suggest an age for these fragments comprised between 150 BC and 450 AD and, therefore, support the hypothesis of a pre-Islamic occupation period on the citadel of Nishapur at the beginning of the Current Era.

The four fragments displaying the relatively high intensity values, around 64µT, were unearthed in the Unit #110 (Test-pit 26), which was archeologically dated from the Islamic occupation period of the citadel. When compared to the smoothed reference curve available for this period, these values appear higher than the curve. However, as previously mentioned, the intensity peak occurring during the end of the 1st millennium AD was probably more

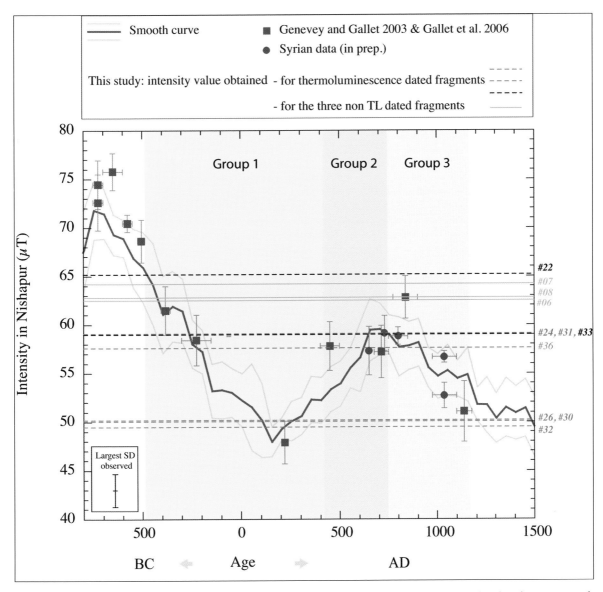

Figure 24: Geomagnetic intensity variations between 800 BC and 1500 AD deduced from selected dated archeomagnetic data obtained from relatively closeby regions to Nishapur; The grey averaged curve was built using sliding windows of 100 years shifted by 50 years. It is reported with an uncertainty envelope given by the standard errors around the successive means. Purple symbols (square and dot) indicate the intensity data that we previously obtained in Syria and Iran (Genevey et al. 2003; Gallet et al. 2006 and new Syrian data). Horizontal lines display the mean intensity results and the label at the end of each line indicates the archeomagnetic identification number. The largest standard deviation (SD) of the mean obtained for the 11 results is shown at the bottom left of the figure to indicate visually the precision of our intensity results. All standard deviations are of this order and are available in Table 10. See text for further explanations (© Genevey and Gallet 2010).

intense than the one revealed by the curve and our data are in fact in very good agreement with a previous result acquired from a group of ceramic fragments sampled at Tell Qaryat Medad in Syria associated to the Abbassid dynasty and dated between 775 and 900 AD (Genevey *et al.* 2003). Using archaeomagnetic constraints, we therefore suggest that these four fragments are dated to this period.

The situation appears more complex for the four fragments showing the intermediate intensity values around 58μT. When compared with the reference curve, these fragments may be individually either dated from a relatively large period, roughly between the middle of the 5th century and the middle of the 2nd century BC, from the period just preceding the Arabic conquest or of the Islamic Period.

It is now of interest to confront the archaeomagnetic dating constraints with that dating provided by the TL analysis.

Group 1 is defined in TL from three fragments of which two were successfully analyzed in intensity (#24 and #31). The TL age range defined at 95% for this group is rather large spanning the period comprised between 485 BC and 415 AD. Considering the archaeomagnetic constraints, we observe in Figure 24 that our data may be in agreement with the TL age range but would tend to favour the oldest portion of this age interval, between ~450 BC and ~150 BC. This would support the view of a possible old (probably non-architectural) occupation period of the site. However, let us recall that the intensity values obtained for the Fragments #31 and #24 would also be compatible with more recent periods.

Group 2 is well defined in TL, being documented by nine fragments among which only four provided reliable intensity values. Excluding Fragment #36, the archaeomagnetic constraints obtained for the three other fragments indicate that Group 2 would have in fact begun a little bit earlier than proposed by TL, at the beginning of the Current Era.

Finally the TL Group 3 corresponding to the Islamic Period is defined from six fragments. Archaeomagnetic analysis successfully performed for only two of these fragments, appear in very good agreement with the TL age but do not provide further constraints on the duration of this period.

The archaeomagnetic analysis of baked clay fragments found in the citadel of Nishapur thus allows one to confirm an occupation period of the site by the Sasanids during the first centuries after Christ and prior to the later Islamic occupation.

Our intensity results are globally coherent with the dating constraints provided by the thermoluminescence measurements performed by Zink and Porto (see above). Although a limited number of fragments were analyzed in the frame of this study, we show that combining both archaeomagnetic and TL methods provides complimentary results allowing one to refine the occupation periods of the citadel of Nishapur.

This study has shown the potential of using variations in geomagnetic field intensity as a dating tool for the Middle East region. Although the present study illustrates in several successful examples of archaeomagnetic dating based on a preliminary reference intensity variation curve, the acquisition of new archaeointensity data from well-dated artefacts is still very much needed to improve the precision and the resolution of this curve. In return, it will allow one to increase the accuracy and the reliability of the archaeointensity dating method.[13]

---

[13] We thank Maxime Le Goff for fruitful discussions and support during the experiments and Ruven Pillay for his help with the manuscript.

5. The Stratigraphical sequence

The aim of this section is to explain the stratigraphy of the main test-pits excavated on the Qohandez. This will be performed using the results acquired with the Thermoluminescence and Archaeomagnetism analyses and, therefore, in a chronological manner. The architectural structures are not analyzed here, as this is not the purpose of this study. They are, nevertheless, mentioned and a chronological sequence of the occupations is established. It is necessary for the pottery sequence and chronology to be easily read. Therefore, the most important occupation phases issuing from the stratigraphical and archaeometrical analysis will be considered. Later, in order to achieve the objectives of this study, the pottery will be presented and analyzed in a final chronological framework. The extreme heterogeneity of the site, as previously mentioned, means that the stratigraphical sequence shows different characteristics for each test-pit.

The test-pits analyzed here will not include all those on the Qohandez. The most representative among them were selected to give a general, but complete, framework of the site. Beginning with the data from these contexts, a more exhaustive discussion concerning the entire Qohandez will be made.

Test-pit B (TB)

Positioned on an artificial slope oriented north–south resulting from the agricultural exploitation of the mud brick, this test-pit (Fig. 25) was opened between the altitudes of 1197 m on the upper part and 1195.50 m on the lower. The western part of the test-pit presented a group of mud brick and pisé structures that were not well defined but certainly artificially destroyed. After a thorough examination of these structures, we proceeded to the excavation.

Period I

The surface of the natural mound was encountered at the altitude of 1191.70 m. From this point the first pottery fragments, as well as other organic elements such as small animal bones, were found. Around 60 cm of deposits of friable material had accumulated under the first occupation soil belonging to Period II. On the basis of the general study of the Qohandez pottery and layers, above all corresponding with the comparisons with T12 (test-pit not studied here but of which the pottery analyses have been performed), this phase could belong to Period I, although no fragments have been analyzed, following the relative stratigraphical sequence. This phase appears between the virgin soil and the soil SU 249 (Period II) and should have been a non-architectural phase of the Qohandez.

Period II

The interface of the layer (SU 249) presented some pottery fragments, with organic elements like animal bones and carbon. This occupation soil (Fig. 26: altitude 1192.38 m), on which was found a large storage jar (Fig. 27), is datable to Period II. On the surface of the soil a well (11), excavated down to the altitude of 1189.25 m, should be the oldest structure found here (Fig. 28). The mixed mud brick and pisé wall (1) erected to the northern part of the test-pit, oriented east–west should be associated with this first architectural phase. Another identical wall (13), parallel to the former, was erected in the southern area of the test-pit but there is no further information to confirm if it corresponds to the same architectural phase.

A series of layers was excavated that had accumulated between the two walls and rested against them. A few successions of occupation levels were found. Moreover, despite the 1.75 m

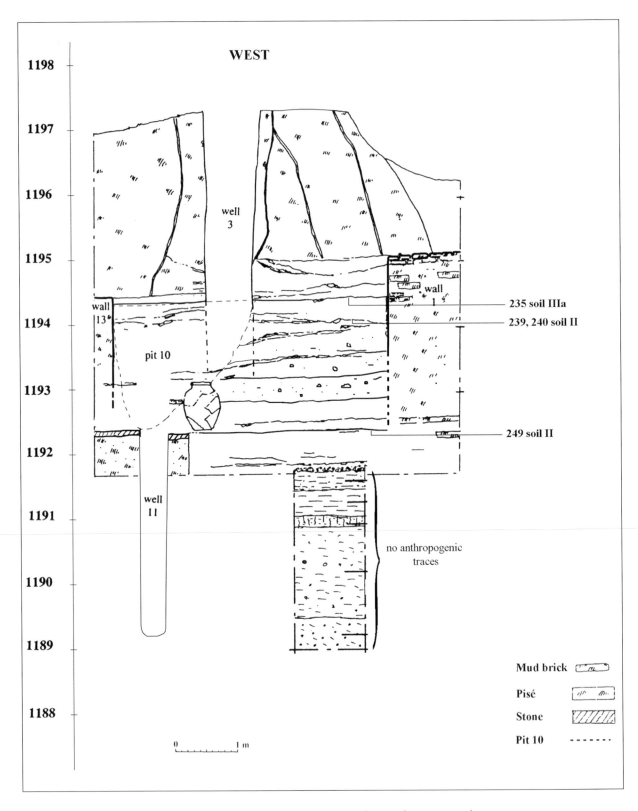

Figure 25: Nishapur, Qohandez, section of Test B (© Rante 2005).

depth of this phase, it seems that these layers accumulated rapidly. The pottery, whose assemblages show a typological constancy, and organic elements were frequent. The presence of mud brick fragments in some deep layers shows the existence of several periods of destruction. This phase precedes an important occupation soil found at the altitude of 1194.06 m. The interface of the soil SU 239–240 was rich in unidentified animal bones (Fig. 29), plaster fragments and carbonized fragments. Pottery shards were also numerous. The previously mentioned external walls should correspond with this soil. The soil belongs to Period II, the same as the previous occupation. The study of the pottery and the stratigraphical context shows that this was a long period of occupation, in which these two phases articulated two different facies. As noted at the beginning of this chapter, this part of the Qohandez lies outside the fortress excavated in the northeastern part. The function of the structures is unknown and it would probably be premature to make suggestions given to the limited available information.

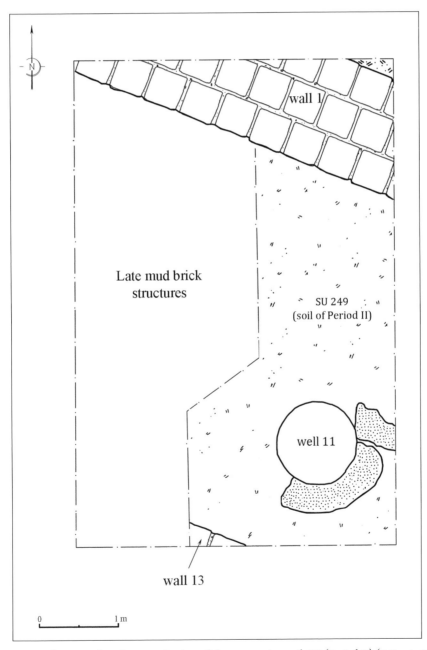

Figure 26: Nishapur, Qohandez, Test B, plan of the occupation soil 249 (Period II) (© Rante 2010).

Figure 27: Nishapur, Qohandez, Test B, large jar corresponding to the soil 249 (Period II) (© Rante 2005).

Figure 28: Nishapur, Qohandez, Test B, view of the well 11 (© Rante 2005).

SU 239-240
(soil of Period IIIa)

Pit (10)

Figure 29: Nishapur, Qohandez, Test B, view of the soil 239-240 (© Rante 2005).

Period IIIa

The occupation soil SU 235, covering a preparatory layer of around 30 cm, was found at an altitude of 1194.51 m and belongs to Period IIIa. This period corresponds to several cultural changes: it is the beginning of Islamic cultural development. The ancient architectural structures were apparently reused for several years. A deep pit (10) was excavated on the surface of this soil, SU 235, extending down to the altitude of 1192.30 m. The pit's bottom in one place cut across the top of the well belonging to the first occupation soil. In fact, some material of this phase was mixed with older material present on the surface of the well. There were numerous plaster and charcoal fragments present in this soil. The southern wall (13) was destroyed at this altitude and another wall, still oriented east–west, was constructed above it. This last wall was still existent at the beginning of the excavation. A series of layers presenting the material similar to that found previously was excavated from soil SU 235.

The large walls visible outside were cut by a well (3), whose upper limit is unknown (Fig. 30). Although the well was not completely excavated, its lower layers included some later pottery fragments. These fragments are of the same typology as those in TA.[14] One could be tempted to attribute these fragments, as well as TA, to Period IIIb due to their similarities with the material of this period. But in this case there are insufficient elements – for example, the presence of baked brick – to verify and confirm this suggestion. The cultural changes apparent amongst the construction material corresponding to Period IIIb are not only the appearance of specific pottery typologies but also the use of baked brick in the architecture.

---

[14] The stratigraphy of this test-pit is not published here, but the ceramic material is presented in Chapter IV.

Figure 30: Nishapur, Qohandez, Test B, view of the western side (© Rante 2005).

Test-pit 10 (T10)

Test-pit T10 (Fig. 31) was opened above the supposed monumental door of the northeastern fortress of the Qohandez. This mud brick structure is situated in the eastern part, between the open space platform and the internal area of the citadel. As previously noticed, this structure could be, with high probability, a monumental door of the fortress, or perhaps of the Qohandez itself. In fact, no traces of structures have been found on the whole northeastern part of the mound. Was this open space an incomplete spreading of the Qohandez mound or just an area conceived to give more space to the citadel? The question remains unanswered. Moreover, this part of the site is cultivated each year with the use of agricultural tractors; it is therefore impossible to find or recognize any structures today.

Period II

This door was constructed above a mud brick platform (Fig. 32), extending on a radius of around 15 m from the entrance limit, presenting its surface at 1195.28 m. This platform, which still exists, is composed of three ranges of mud bricks measuring 42 × 42 × 12 cm. The outside façade of the door was cleaned to trace the different parts. It was noted, first, that its central lower part was slightly projecting (2). The quality of this construction was, moreover, different to the architectural remains. After a thorough cleaning of the door base, its northeastern part revealed a quarter-circular structure of mud brick (1), preserved for few centimetres (Fig. 33). This structure, one of the door towers, incorporates another mud brick structure, now quadrangular. This latter could be a previous phase of the tower. The internal limit of the quarter-circular tower (1) reached the limit of the northern doorjamb (3), constituting a complete half of the door. The doorjamb was raised at the altitude of 1199.75 m and the

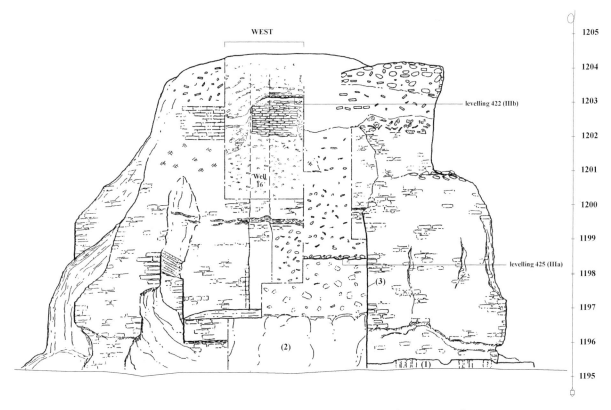

Figure 31: Nishapur, Qohandez, section of Test 10 (© Rante 2006).

Figure 32: Nishapur, Qohandez, Test 10, view of the eastern platform (© Rante 2006).

Figure 33: Nishapur, Qohandez, Test 10, view of the northern tower (quart-circular) (© Rante 2006).

Figure 34: Nishapur, Qohandez, Test 10, view of the stopping block mud brick (© Rante 2006).

beginning of the arc at the altitude of 1199.20 m. The other doorjamb, the southern one, was much more destroyed and was found to be in a fragmentary state. The arched entrance was around 5.5 m wide. The southern mud brick structure of the door is more destroyed than the northern one. This represents several walls added to the original structure. While the construction material and size were the same, the architectural links are traceable. The pottery analyses, as well as the associated construction material, date this complex to Period II, moreover demonstrating good homogeneity with the material found in TB.

The previously mentioned central structure (2) was excavated on its southern part, leaving the northern part attached to the doorjamb because of the stability of the complex. Starting from the platform, the entrance soil rises up from the exterior, showing a slight ramp; some possible steps were found, although the excavated portion was too small to confirm this. The excavation showed that this mud brick central structure was probably a stopping block of the entrance, similar to that found at the internal façade of the door (Fig. 34). This could have been an artificial mud brick block intended to stop the door during an enemy incursion. The chronology data confirms that the door was used for a long time. Comparison with other structures of the Qohandez dated to the origins of the city, suggests that the door should belong to the foundation of the Qohandez. Its destruction can probably be attributed to later than the second half of the 8th century.

Period IIIa

Stone level 425 (Fig. 31), belonging to Period IIIa and recorded at the altitude of 1198.39 m, confirms this chronological data. In fact, the presence of mud brick fragments of the same size and composition as those of the door were noticed mixed with the material belonging to the layers under level 425. The excavation of the layers above level 425 showed no mud brick fragments. The upper part of level 425 was effectively a unique embankment composed of compacted earth and pottery fragments. This embankment was intented to prop up the occupation level of the door and for this it was necessary to raise it until it covered the upper limit of the remaining door arc.

The excavation of this embankment also showed an unusual layer of compressed lenses of sand traversing the central part of the entrance (Fig. 35), but covered by this embankment. There are not any concrete suggestions concerning its function. Its chemical composition was confirmed by the analysis performed by Pascale Richardin.[15] One can only propose that it was a material used during the construction of the door, of which its position at the beginning of the arch could be proof, or perhaps a phase between the first construction and the destruction of the door.

The embankment corresponding to Period IIIa was raised for around 2.5 m, above which were found the first real occupation layers belonging to this period. The construction material employed was always mud brick, but of a different size, smaller than 27 × 27 × 6/7 cm. While severely damaged, some architectural structures corresponding to a habitat have been recognized in this area. The good quality of the mud brick construction, but above all the use of sophisticated stuccoes (unfortunately not *in situ*), indicate the high status of this locale. Moreover, the fine quality of the pottery – of which the analyses and the assemblages have established a 10th century date – has confirmed this suggestion.

Period IIIb

Stone level 422 (Fig. 31) respresents a new occupation level corresponding to Period IIIb just above these house structures, whose destruction interface was found at the altitude of 1203.13 m. Well 16, the altitude at which it was conceived being unknown, belonged to this occupation. The pottery found at the bottom of the well corresponds to the 12th–early 13th centuries.

---

[15]   Centre de Recherche et de Restauration des Musées de France, C2RMF – CNRS UMR 171.

Figure 35: Nishapur, Qohandez, Test 10, view of the silica layer (© Porto 2009).

From this period on one can find the constant use of baked brick as a construction material.

Unfortunately, there are no other elements present with which to conduct a complete study of this occupation, though it has been recorded throughout the area of the Qohandez. The zones occupied at that period in Nishapur are known from Wilkinson's excavation. It seems that the 10th century occupation of the Qohandez represents the last time in which this zone was of importance. After that, there was a movement of the population away from this oldest part and also to some extent, from Shadyakh, which, however, seems to have continued to be occupied until the Mongol invasion (cfr. Bulliet 1976; Labbaf 2006).

Test-pit 26 (T26)

Test-pit 26 (Fig. 36) was opened in a less-explored zone of the Qohandez close to Test-pit (TE) which was opened during the 2006 season by Meysam Labbaf. As this test-pit produced significant material, it was decided to continue to dig in this zone, some metres to the west, still following the profile of the slope of the artificial mound. Test-pit 26 was excavated from

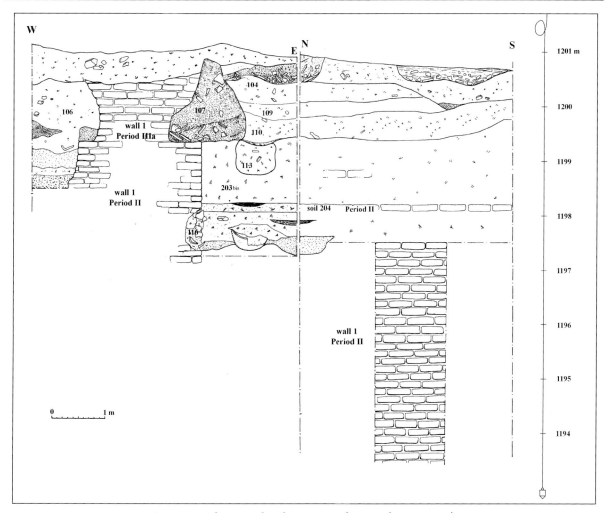

Figure 36: Nishapur, Qohandez, section of Test 26 (© Cuny 2007).

the altitude of 1201 m, and the aim, above all, was to verify the different urban and social functions of this zone, as well as to confirm the stratigraphy sequence of Test-pit 10.

Period I

As supposed from the beginning of the excavation, Test-pit 26 revealed some differences to the other test-pits. In addition, the limited size of the test-pit did not permit an architectural sequence and history of the structures to be traced. At the altitude of 1193.40 m, corresponding to the excavation limit and not to the limit of the structure, a mud brick wall (1) rising to altitude 1200.50 m and oriented north–south belongs to Period II (Fig. 37). The wall was constructed with mud bricks larger than those already noted (47 × 47 × 11 cm). The TL analysis of one pottery fragment belonging to one of the lowest layers cut by the wall (1) dates to Period I (in Tab. 2, 203 E1).[16] Another fragment, belonging to layer SU 110, was also dated to Period I (Tab. 2, 110 E4). Archaeomagnetism confirms this, but refines its dating to a period between the 1st–5th centuries AD. According to archaeomagnetism, it could also nevertheless be probable for this pottery to belong to a period between the 7th–10th centuries AD. It is important to precise that this fragment was found in SU 110, stratigraphically connected with the Islamic era. Although the former fragment (SU 203) was dated to Period I by the TL, stratigraphically it belongs to Period II.

---

[16] Archaeomagnetism rejected this fragment.

Figure 37: Nishapur, Qohandez, Test 26, view of the wall (1) (© Rosati 2007).

Period II

The previously described wall (1) belongs to this period. A preparatory level of pisé appears just above the interface of the wall (2). After a series of occupation layers leading to the wall (1), soil 204 probably shows a new redevelopment of this space. This soil is composed of a mud brick layer. The small pit (113) dug inside this preparatory level represents the last activity of Period II, as confirmed by the Thermoluminescence analyses.

Period IIIa

From the altitude of 1199.37 m, wall (1) was understood to belong to Period IIIa, though it does not present any architectural changes. The difference is probably in the occupation, since this is associated with materials, especially pottery, dated to Period IIIa. The stratigraphy of the east–west cross-section shows notable irregularity in the wall at this altitude. Layer 110, from which a variety of pottery fragments were analyzed and dated by Thermoluminescence, and layer 109, belonging to Period IIIa and originally resting against the wall (1), were therefore reused during this period. The analysis of the pottery assemblages from layer 104 shows a clear change in production and an evolution of technique.

Period IIIb

This period is the less identifiable of the Qohandez, first because these layers have been the most exposed to atmospheric agents and human activity. Moreover, the Qohandez presented evidence for limited occupation during this period.

Wall (1) could also have been reused in this period, but the total absence of baked bricks as construction material, characteristic of this phase, leaves doubt concerning this chronological attribution. A large pit (107), beginning not far from the surface, was dug into the eastern side of the wall (1). The western side of the same wall seems to have also been damaged by a poorly identified pit (106).

Test-pit 27 (T27)

Test-pit 27 (Fig. 38) was opened on the west side of the Qohandez mound. This area was less well-explored and only a test-pit carried out by Wilkinson in 1930 can be mentioned, for which there is no data. The test-pit was positioned on the upper part of the mound following an artificial slope created by bulldozers in order to bring mud bricks to the cultivated fields.

As shown by the east–west cross-section Test-pit 27 does not present any architectural structure. This was not surprising because of the situation of the test-pit just on the slope and its proximity to the mound's western limit. The first aim of this research was to also verify the stratigraphy on this side and to record the pottery sequence. Because of the variety and quantity of material, it was decided to analyze the test-pit accurately and verify the chronology with Thermoluminescence and Archaeomagnetism analyses.

Period II

Virgin soil was not reached in this excavation, it being interrupted at the altitude of 1194.60 m. No layers of Period I were found up to this occupation level. At the altitude of 1196.44 m an occupation soil of clay (516) was recognized. The pottery fragments of this layer, analyzed with Thermoluminescence and Archaeomagnetism, date to Period II. The pottery found in the layers below confirms this dating.

From this occupation level to the altitude of 1197.92 m there are no concrete elements with which to date the layers and occupation episodes because the presence of the pit at the eastern part of the test-pit was recognized only after the excavation. After the comparative study, only an attribution to a chronological meantime corresponding to Periods II and III could be suggested.

Period IIIa

The interface of layer 511, found at the altitude of 1197.92 m, was characterized by some carbonized material and lightly burnt pottery fragments. The excavation showed the presence of soil 511 and the analysis of the pottery confirmed a change in the production type corresponding to Period IIIa. The stratigraphical sequence beginning from this point is a succession of layers, almost all similarly oriented. This could be the result of different accumulations of occupation layers in a zone exposed to the citadel's limits. It could therefore be a part in which the habitation area was not developed, perhaps because it was too close to the western rampart. Layer 508, just above the soil 511, was interesting because of the numerous pottery fragments found there. Burnt fragments of cooking pots were frequent. The upper layers of Period IIIa were not diagnostic in the context of our analysis.

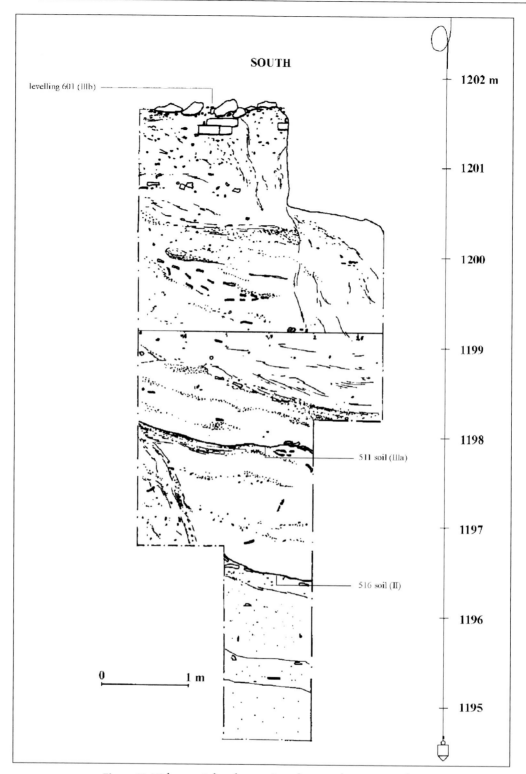

Figure 38: Nishapur, Qohandez, section of Test 27 (© Rante 2007).

Period IIIb

This period in this test-pit is poorly represented; there is no data with which to confirm the findings from other IIIb contexts. However, this period is clearly represented by level 601, discovered just below the humus layer at the altitude of 1201.57 m. As in other test-pits, the level was realized with cobbles.

6. Interpreting occcupation chronology and urban development

The aim of the present study is to specify and define that which cannot be either verified or explained by the excavation and the stratigraphy alone. Moreover, the total absence of dating material in a stratigraphical context renders this study absolutely necessary. The deficiency of these elements at the present time makes work to finalize the results of an archaeological excavation frustrating and unfinished.

The occupation framework of the Qohandez resulting from this study is therefore limited because of the absence of extensive excavation in several parts of the mound, while it is clear enough to enable us to attempt to show some socio-political and urban features occurring during the centuries at Nishapur and on the Qohandez.

As shown by this study, according to the 'synthesis' of the Thermoluminescence and Archaeomagnetism analyses, the three chronological groups concern three periods: **Period I** ~450–~150 BC (showing that between ~150 BC and ~405 AD there is an occupation lacuna); **Period II** (405[17]–785 AD); and **Period III** (745–1165 AD). Period III, after cross-referencing different data from other archaeometrical as well as archaeological analyses, was divided into two parts: Period IIIa (2nd half of 8th–early 11th centuries) and Period IIIb (11th century–1165 AD).

In this chronological framework the Qohandez, and not only the excavated areas, was completely analyzed. This means that we analyzed the areas excavated, as well as the unexcavated ones. For example, all the western area is less well known. Only Test-pit T27 provided us with some important information to raise a stratigraphy and an occupation sequence. These data have been used to formulate a hypothesis concerning the entire western area of the Qohandez and these suggestions are also compared with the surveyed material.

PERIOD I: corresponds to the first identified occupation of the Qohandez. The survey of the pottery material performed in 2009 by the Louvre and C2RMF team at Shahr-e Ark[18] showed a complete change in the techniques and typologies of pottery, confirming our data, for example the total absence at Nishapur of the grey pottery found at Shahr-e Ark and dated to the Parthian and first Sasanian period.[19] Period I is characterized by no architectural occupation, of which there are not enough elements to give more information. Pertaining to the occupation of the Qohandez, following the test-pits where the shards have been found, Period I is characterized by an occupation corresponding at least to the central and southern part of the Qohandez area.

PERIOD II: presents true differences to the previous period (Fig. 39) and corresponds with the foundation of the city. The bracket of time furnished by the TL analyses was better defined by means of archaeomagnetism and the archaeological data and should correspond to the late 4th–on the eve of the 5th centuries AD. The probable fortress of the citadel is situated between 1195 m and 1197 m in an elevated position compared to the other parts of the Qohandez, situated between 1191.70 m and 1193 m. The important difference in altitude of 3 m (1195 m and 1197 m) in such a restricted part of the city only concerns the rampart. In fact, the corridor of the archers' rooms seems to be elevated to around 2 m. The occupation of the rest of the citadel, situated 2–3 m below the fortress, appears to be uniform. It seems, therefore, that the Qohandez originally included one more elevated parts in its northeastern zone.

PERIOD IIIA: the urban and cultural changes undoubtedly occured in Period IIIa (Fig. 40). The urban changes are traceable above all in the northern part of the Qohandez. In fact, the fortress

---

[17] As previously mentioned, thanks to the Archaeomagnetism analyses, this date could be slightly more ancient than 405 AD.

[18] Achaemenian and Parthian site 10 km north-west of Nishapur recently excavated by an Iranian team directed by Mohammad Ettemadi.

[19] In addition, a close type of grey pottery belonging to the Parthian Period has been also found at Rayy (Rante 2008, 194) and Shahr-i Qumis (Hansman and Stronach 1970, 55–59).

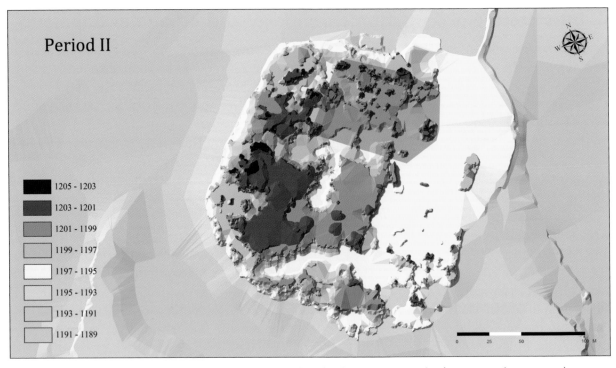

Figure 39: Nishapur, Qohandez, plan showing the urban development in Period II (© Rante and Rosati 2011).

Figure 40: Nishapur, Qohandez, plan showing the urban development in Period IIIa (© Rante and Rosati 2011).

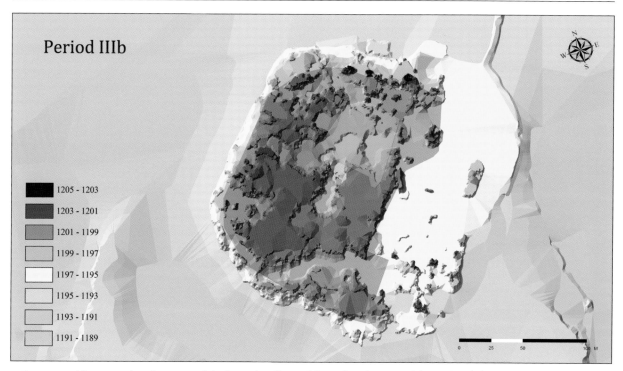

Period IIIb

1205 - 1203

1203 - 1201

1201 - 1199

1199 - 1197

1197 - 1195

1195 - 1193

1193 - 1191

1191 - 1189

Figure 41: Nishapur, Qohandez, view of the latest levelling of the Qohandez mound (Period IIIb) (© Rante and Rosati 2011).

seems to have lost its military function and the area restructured as urban space. Moreover, the excavation of the rampart side effectively showed the abandoning of its military role in the fact that the rooms and the passages for the archers were filled with layers presenting late material, probably belonging to Period IIIa. According to the pottery analyses and study of the assemblages, a cultural change seems to have appeared in the last part of Period IIIa, most probably from the 10th century. The central part of the Qohandez shows the formation of a large depression. This zone includes Test-pits TA, TB and T12 (Fig. 8). The study of the pottery material pertaining this period seems to show, here, a lesser proportion of fragments, due perhaps to a decline in use of this precise area.

The southern part of the Qohandez, the largest, in contrast shows a proportionally much more significant presence of pottery fragments. Certainly the few excavated areas cannot exactly explain the relative intensity of occupation. Our results can, however, provide a view of the general development of the citadel between the second half of the 8th and the 10th century.

Period IIIb: Period IIIb is the prolongation of Period IIIa. This has been noticed due to the proportion of fragments found on the site. The central area was still occupied by a large depression. The fortress did not require its original defensive nature. This period is characterized by the largescale levelling of the Qohandez surface. This remains visible, although a deep layer is overhung by a large stone layer constituting the streets. This was constructed in various areas of the Qohandez, but most probably not everywhere[20] (Fig. 41). The depth of the level at this time indicates the importance of the redefinition of the Qohandez. Unfortunately, there is not enough material to analyse this period in any depth. It is certain that the previously indicated urban changes testify a different function for the Qohandez; it lost its previous military purpose and became part of a larger city, perhaps preserving a religious and administrative facet.

---

[20] Test T27, and so a large part of the western side of the Qohandez, shows the clear absence of this important level.

Chapter III

Pottery Study and Analyses

(with contributions by A. Bouquillon,[1] Y. Coquinot[2] and C. Doublet[3])

1. Recording methodology

The ceramic material was systematically processed and recorded during the excavation seasons. The first count and observations were made on the site, and the recording in the excavation house, where the material discovered was carried at the end of each day of the excavation or survey.

The excavated material was recorded by Stratigraphic Unit (SU) in order to work by ceramic assemblages and, so far as possible, following the excavations in progress. The material collected during the surveys of the Qohandez was processed by squares. That collected during the surveys of the Shahrestan and of the mosque was recorded by wider areas, numbered by zones.

The ceramics from each SU, square or zone were washed, quantified by shard count, and then classified. A first recording was made in notebooks describing the composition of each assemblage: main characteristics and counting of not diagnostic and diagnostic shards, shapes, types of fabrics, glazed and unglazed material.

Shards which were systematically selected for further study or which were recorded with more details were the diagnostic ones (that is to say with a rim or a base), the glazed ones, and non-diagnostic shards when their fabric or their surface treatment seemed unusual or not previously recorded. The terminology chosen for the characterization of the shapes is deliberately broad and indicates their function when identifiable by the size and/or the fabric of the shards. Closed shapes are large storage jars, jars, jugs, pots and cooking-pots; open shapes are bowls, basins and a very few dishes. The other identified shapes are lids, beakers, lamps and lamp-stands.

The rims and bases that were drawn were identified and named by using their size, dimensions, and type of fabric. However, some of them are not obvious and fall between two types: thus some are called 'jar/jug' in the database.

The partial or complete profiles were drawn each time a new type of shape was seen. As the ceramic assemblages from the Qohandez were very fragmented in the majority of cases and very few montages/reconstructions were made, the rare complete profiles were systematically drawn even when one shape had already been illustrated.

---

[1] C2RMF, 14 Quai François Mitterrand, 75001 Paris.
[2] *Ibid.*
[3] *Ibid.*

For each drawn shard, a specific record card was created with the following data, entirely used to build the Qohandez ceramic database that was later developed:

- Provenance of the shard (test-pit name; survey area).
- Individual number of the shard made up of its SU or survey context.
- Measurements taken with rim chart and calliper.
- Shape. The complete shapes of the Nishapur wares – especially of the fine unglazed and glazed wares – were to a large extent known thanks to Wilkinson's publication. In order to help the identification work, the drawings published in 1973 throughout the book were grouped together and presented at the same scale. They formed morphological typologies, very useful during the recording of the Islamic Period material recovered. The reference of one published shape could then be added on the card for a better understanding of a partial shape.
- Visual description of the fabric (colour, quality, inclusions). The fabrics of the unglazed wares had been sampled during the first season of excavation, to develop their future codification. After the third excavation season in 2007, 16 types of fabrics had been finally classified, by the naked eye and magnifying glass (Figs 42–5). The samples selected formed the *corpus* of the different types of fabrics in terms of colour, quality and visible inclusions.
- Description of the surface treatment (technology recognized visually and decoration).
- The presence of a coating (mainly slip) was systematically notified, as was burnishing, chattering, moulding, engraving and combed, *champlevé* or applied ornaments. For the classification and description of the clayey glazed wares, Wilkinson's terminology was also partly used during the recording, especially the most peculiar types of his typology which have become well known names of glazed types, such as 'buff ware' and 'ware with yellow staining black'.
- State of preservation; especially to record the shards which were burnt or bore traces of fire.
- Each drawn shard was photographed. In addition, a representative selection of shards from each stratigraphic unit, surveyed square or zone was systematically photographed. This selection was made up of all the different ceramic types encountered in one assemblage.

Once processed, the retained shards were put in sealed bags inscribed with the year of excavation, the number or letter of the test-pit and their stratigraphic unit number. Those from the surveys were processed in the same way, with their provenance and number of square or zone. The rejected shards were put back and buried in the Qohandez.

At the end of each season, a selection of the excavated material (ceramics, glass and other finds) was taken to Mashhad for restoration and storage, under the authority of the Miras-e Farhangi branch in Mashhad.

2. Questioning the material: the ceramic analysis program

Preliminary comments

The ceramic material recorded amounts to 7312 shards: 5590 come from the excavations of the Qohandez and 1722 from the surveys of the citadel, the Shahrestan and the mosque (see Fig. 3). 1178 shards from the total amount recorded were drawn and registered in the field. This *corpus* formed the basis for the database that was later developed, in which are included the results of our research concerning the chronological sequence of the material; the characterization of the fabric groups; and the shards which were analyzed by the C2RMF.

Table 11: Nishapur unglazed ceramic shards analysed.

No. OF SHARD	No. C2RMF	PROVENANCE	VISUAL CLASSIFICATION OF FABRICS AND SURFACE DECORATIONS					
			TYPE	SUB-TYPE	FABRIC QUALITY	FABRIC COLOUR	SURFACE	COMMENTS
Unglazed clayey fabrics								
N07-106-E1	1	Qohandez T26	1	a	rather coarse	orange	beige slip	
N07-101-E1	2	Qohandez T26	1	b	rather coarse	orange	stamped, beige slip	
N07-116-E1	3	Qohandez T26	2		medium	red orange	beige slip	white inclusions
N07-101-E2	4	Qohandez T26	3	a	coarse to medium	orange	engraved, beige slip	numerous inclusions
N07-102-E1	5	Qohandez T26	3	b	medium	orange, overcooked		numerous inclusions
N07-309-E1	6	Qohandez T23	4	a	medium	beige orange/grey overcooked	beige slip	numerous inclusions
N07-301-E1	7	Qohandez T23	4	b	fine to medium	orange	beige slip	numerous inclusions, burned
N07-110-E1	8	Qohandez T26	5	a	rather fine	orange	beige slip	few inclusions visible
N07-110-E2	9	Qohandez T26	5	b	rather fine	red orange	engraved, beige pinkish slip	
N07-102-2-E2	10	Qohandez T26	5	b	rather fine	red orange	moulded, beige pinkish slip	
N07-110-E3	11	Qohandez T26	6	a	rather fine	red orange	beige pinkish slip	few inclusions visible
N07-101-9-E3	12	Qohandez T26	6	b	rather fine	orange	beige pinkish slip	few inclusions visible
N06-338-E1	13	Qohandez T18	6	c	very fine	orange	combed, thick beige slip	burned
N07-102-E3	14	Qohandez T26	7		fine	beige	thin slip	
N07-106-E2	15	Qohandez T26	8	a	rather fine	beige slightly orange	smoothed slip	
N07-104-E1	16	Qohandez T26	8	b	fine	beige	slip	
N07-102-E4	17	Qohandez T26	8	c	rather fine	beige yellowish		

VISUAL CLASSIFICATION OF FABRICS AND SURFACE DECORATIONS

No. OF SHARD	No. C2RMF	PROVENANCE	TYPE	SUB-TYPE	FABRIC QUALITY	FABRIC COLOUR	SURFACE	COMMENTS
N07-110-E4	18	Qohandez T26	8	d	fine	beige	combed/engraved	
N07-102-E5	19	Qohandez T26	9		fine	beige yellowish	slip	
N07-104-E2	20	Qohandez T26	10	a	fine	beige/grey greenish	beige slip	very hard fabric
N07-110-4-E5	21	Qohandez T26	10	b	fine	grey greenish	engraved	
N06-419-E1	22	Qohandez T10	10	c	fine	light grey	greyish slip	
N06-149-1-E1	23	Qohandez T15	10	d	fine	light grey	engraved	
N06-420-E1	24	Qohandez T10	10	e	very fine	light grey		
N07-101-E4	25	Qohandez T26	11	a	fine	beige	beige slip	very hard fabric
N07-110-E6	26	Qohandez T26	11	b	medium	grey greenish		few inclusions visible
N07-302-E1	27	Qohandez T23	11	c	rather fine	grey beige		few thick inclusions visible
N07-101-E5	28	Qohandez T26	12		rather fine	dark grey		very hard fabric
N07-101-E6	29	Qohandez T26	13	a	fine	dark grey		very hard fabric
N07-106-E3	31	Qohandez T26	14		rather fine	dark grey overcooked	beige slip	many inclusions
N07-203-E1	32	Qohandez T26 (wall)	15		medium	burned		
N07-200-E1	33	Qohandez T26 (wall)	16		medium	grey beige	beige slip	foliated aspect of the fabric

Figure 42: Nishapur, samples of clayey fabrics (visual fabric types 1-4) (© Collinet 2010).

Figure 43: Nishapur, samples of clayey fabrics (visual fabric types 5-8) (© Collinet 2010).

The ceramic study was organized in two main directions: the stratigraphic study of the assemblages (Chap. IV) and the laboratory analyses which mainly concerned the petrography and the chemical and mineralogical analyses of 67 unglazed, clayey glazed and fritware samples[4] (Tables 11–12; Figs 42–50).

The aim of this work is, on one hand, to propose a new approach for a material known since Hauser's and Wilkinson's researches, especially in terms of chronological sequence, study of the ceramic assemblages, and characterization of the fabrics. On the other hand, the study also includes material which was not known through the previous excavations, but which was

---

[4] Until then, only the main clayey glazed types of the medieval Islamic Period had already been classified visually. Wilkinson had set up a project of analyses of clay and glaze, which were planned to be published as an appendix to his volume and later as a separate work (Wilkinson 1973, xxiv). Eighteen shards and a stilt from the site (R. W. Bulliet's collection) were analysed in Berkeley by Neutron Activation, in order to define the clay composition of the glazed wares (Azarpay *et al.* 1977). More recently petrofabric of a few samples – most of them of the 15th century – were published by R. B. Mason (2004, 207–208, 225–226, 249, 263).

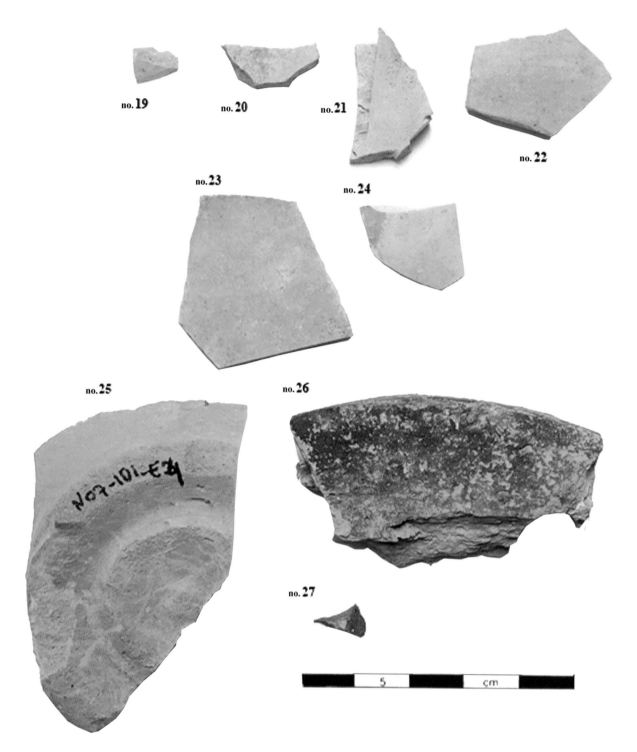

Figure 44: Nishapur, samples of clayey fabrics (visual fabric types 9–11) (© Collinet 2010).

identified and studied by the Irano-French team: essentially the pre-Islamic wares and the common unglazed wares of the Islamic Period.

   More widely, this work is an attempt to produce the most precise and newest data possible concerning a reference site in Khorasan. The Sasanian Period material, which had not previously been identified in Nishapur, is furthermore rather difficult to comprehend within a comparative study: it is a 'regionalist' material (Puschnigg, 2006, xiii). The contemporary ceramics excavated in western Iran and Iraq present quite different characteristics from those found in the eastern

Figure 45: Nishapur, samples of clayey fabrics (visual fabric types 12–16) (© Collinet 2010).

Table 12: Nishapur kiln material and glazed ceramic shards analysed.

No. of shard	No. C2RMF	Provenance	Fabric quality	Fabric colour	Surface	Comments
Kiln material						
N07-321-2-E1	34	Qohandez T23	coarse	beige orange ?	glazed	kiln stick fragment
N07-Surv-Shahr-E1	35	Shahrestan Survey	coarse	red orange	glazed (monochrome green)	kiln stick fragment
N07-Surv-Shahr-E2	36	Shahrestan Survey	coarse			kiln wall fragment
N07-Surv-Shahr-E3	37	Shahrestan Survey	coarse			kiln wall fragment
Clayey fabrics, opaque white glazes						
N06-114-1a-E1	38	Qohandez T15	very fine	pale yellow		
N07-317-11-E1	39	Qohandez T23	fine	beige orange ?		
Clayey fabrics, monochrome glazes						
N07-Surv-Shahr-E4a	40	Shahrestan Survey	very fine	red orange	turquoise glaze	
N07-Surv-Shahr-E4b	41	Shahrestan Survey	very fine	red orange	turquoise glaze	
N07-Surv-Shahr-E5	42	Shahrestan Survey	very fine	beige orange	turquoise glaze	
N07-Surv-Shahr-E6	43	Shahrestan Survey	very fine	beige orange	turquoise glaze	
N07-Surv-Shahr-E7	44	Shahrestan Survey	fine	beige orange	turquoise glaze	
N07-Surv-Shahr-E8	45	Shahrestan Survey	rather fine	beige orange	turquoise glaze	
N07-Surv-Shahr-E9	46	Shahrestan Survey	rather fine	orange	green glaze	
N07-106-E4	47	Qohandez T26	rather fine	grey	green glaze (out.) and purple (ins.)	
Clayey fabrics, polychrome glazes						
N07 surv shar 1	A, 48, 49, 50	Shahrestan Survey	rather fine	red orange	decor. yellow, black and white	
N07 surv-shahr 2 z9-16	B, 51, 52, 53	Shahrestan Survey	rather fine	beige/buff	decor. yellow, black and white	
N07 surv-shahr 3	C/H 54, 55,64, 71	Shahrestan Survey	rather fine	red orange	decor. yellow, black and white	
N07 surv shahr 4	D, 56,57	Shahrestan Survey	rather fine/medium	orange	dark green glaze	

No. OF SHARD	No. C2RMF	PROVENANCE	VISUAL CLASSIFICATION OF FABRICS AND SURFACE DECORATIONS			
			FABRIC QUALITY	FABRIC COLOUR	SURFACE	COMMENTS
N07 surv shahr 5	E, 58, 59	Shahrestan Survey	rather fine	red orange	decor. White and blue/green	
N07 T26 101-19	F, 60	Qohandez T26	rather fine	red orange	yellow glaze	
N07 T26 struct 203	G, 61, 62, 63	Qohandez T26 (wall)	rather fine	beige orange	decor. Black and white	
N07-1 T27	I, 65a, 65b	Qohandez T27	rather fine	beige/buff	very altered, brown aspect	
N07 surv shahr z 11	J, 66	Shahrestan Survey	rather fine	red orange	yellowish glaze	
N06 303-1	K, 67, 68	Qohandez	rather fine	beige/buff	green and blue glazes	
N06 420	L, 69	Qohandez T10	rather fine	beige pinkish	green glaze	
N06 418-16	M, 70	Qohandez T10	rather fine/medium	red pinkish	yellow glaze	
FRITWARES						
N07 surv shahr 3	ps1	Shahrestan Survey		white	turquoise glaze	
N07 surv shahr 2 9-23	ps2	Shahrestan Survey		white yellowish	clear glaze	
N07 surv-shahr 1	ps3	Shahrestan Survey		white	black painted under turquoise glaze	
N07 surv shahr 2	ps4	Shahrestan Survey		white	cobalt glaze	
N07 101	ps5	Qohandez T26		white	lavander glaze, lustre	
N06 419	ps6	Qohandez T10		white	turquoise glaze	
N07 surv shahr z4	ps7	Shahrestan Survey		white	turquoise glaze (2 shards sticked)	

Figure 46: Nishapur, samples of monochrome glazed shards (© Collinet 2010).

areas of Iran which, in addition, were rather poorly defined before the excavations of Tureng Tepe and Merv. The analyzed material from Nishapur thus serves to enrich and specify the *corpus* of Sasanian Period ceramics in the Khorasan region.

Concerning the Islamic Period, we now know for certain that the glazed wares contemporary with the Samanid Phase published by Wilkinson are far from being the main examples of the ceramic culture of Nishapur. Ceramics contemporary to the Saljuk and post-Saljuk Phases are also well represented in the Qohandez. In addition, new data on the material linked with the Samanid Phase can be written.

no. 39

no. 38

Figure 47: Nishapur, samples of opaque white shards (© Collinet 2010).

The program set up with the C2RMF also had as its objectives the production of the characterization and classification of the fabrics by petrography and physical chemistry analyses, and the provision of data on the surface treatment technologies. This was in order to obtain characterized ceramic groups which could then be interpreted within the ceramic assemblages and within the chronology of the site.

The choice of the samples was thus decided according to their stratigraphic position on the one hand – for the analyses programme was obviously designed to be closely linked to the stratigraphic study of the material – and, on the other hand, the *corpus* was selected in order to obtain, as far as possible, the most complete representation of the main unglazed and glazed ceramic types encountered. The interest was also to see if a connection between shape/function and fabric could be ascertained in the cases of well represented types (such as fine pale yellow jugs, storage jars or cooking pots). The shards sampled thus come from the excavations of the Qohandez, but also from the surface material collected during the surveys of the Shahrestan. A *corpus* of clayey and fritware shards was selected to be sampled and analyzed to define their petrographic, mineralogical and chemical characteristics. The selection only included ware shards and kiln fragments and sticks: architectural materials or ornaments were not represented in the selection. Some kiln fragments and rods collected in the Shahrestan and the Qohandez were also analyzed to further elucidate the products of the city, in relation to the petrography of the shards sampled and the geology of the area. The aim was to distinguish between local products and imports. Finally, and in relation to the stratigraphic study, the goal was to detect possible changes in the components of the fabrics and glazes and the technologies that could characterize chronological sequences of the site's cultural history.

The merged fabrics of any period were first characterized visually when recording the material in the field. They were distinguished according to colour, type of inclusions and quality.

Figure 48: Nishapur, samples of polychrome glazed shards (© Collinet 2010).

Sixteen main groups of clayey fabrics were defined by visual observation: they vary in colours from pale yellow, grey, pinkish and buff to orange-red, and from very fine to coarse in quality. Visually, they seemed very different and heterogeneous.

The fabrics: petrography and chemical analyses

Methods of study and analytic conditions

Three methods of examination and analyses were chosen for the study of the fabrics:

- Optical Microscopy (MO) and binocular magnifying glass observations for their petrography (47 unglazed and glazed clayey shards sampled; 7 fritwares sampled)
- PIXE (Particle Induced X-Ray Emission) on AGLAE (Accélérateur Grand Louvre d'Analyse Elémentaire) for their chemical composition (52 unglazed and glazed clayey shards; 4 kiln elements and sticks; 7 fritwares sampled)
- XRD (X-Ray Diffraction) for the mineralogical identification of 7 fritwares.

Figure 49: Nishapur, samples of fritware glazed shards analysed (© Collinet 2010).

The PIXE method is one of the best-adapted for the analysis of major and trace elements of ceramic fabrics as it allows the analysis of the clayey matrix between large-sized inclusions in order to obtain a composition the closest possible to the base clay. The analyses were carried out on a perfectly smooth and polished surface with silicium carbide (SiC) in grains of 6 μm. The chemical analyses by PIXE were carried out according to a protocol described in Calligaro *et al.* (2005): a microbeam extracted from 3MeV protons, with a diameter close to 30 μm, scans a surface of 1 mm^2. A standard of CRPG of Nancy and corresponding to a diorite was analyzed at the start and end of each day of analysis. The composition of this standard, obtained by ICP-MS and ACSP-AES, as well as the compositions obtained by PIXE, are reported in the table DRN compo standard (Table 32).

no. 36

no. 37

no. 35

no. 34

Figure 50: Nishapur, samples of kiln fragments and sticks (© Collinet 2010).

All the shards were enclosed in an epoxy resin (EMS) in order to make fine polished strips destined for petrographic observations in Optical Microscopy. This method of examination was used to identify the nature of the inclusions (natural or added) present in the clayey matrix and to characterize their texture. This examination allowed the establishment of 'petrographic groups'. The parameters retained to define these groups correspond to the nature of the mineral non-plastic inclusions of a size greater than 25 μm, in respect of the clayey matrix as well as different textural characteristics (size and morphology of grains, granulometric classification). One can thus identify most of the constituent minerals of the material and see the disposition, size and morphology of different elements present in the sample (minerals, bioclasts, etc.). It equally allows one to obtain information on the porosity of the materials (the type of porosity but also the size, distribution and morphology of pores) and its stratigraphy. The petrographic observations were carried out with an Olympus BH2 polarising microscope, under 'polarized non-analyzed' light (LPNA) and under 'polarized and analyzed' light (LPA). The observations and analyses of the fabrics were all carried out without metallization with a 'partial' vacuum pressure of 10^{-4} Torr, and an acceleration tension of 20 kV.

In order to distinguish the mineralogy of the fritware and to identify the nature of the mineral inclusions present in certain glazes, X-ray diffraction analyses were carried out. The device used was a system of X diffraction developed at C2RMF and comprising (1) a Rigaku tube of monochromatic X-rays of λ=1.54186 Angström (8042 eV) with a collimator of 200 µm. The tension used, maximum value, was 45 KV and the current 660 µA (2) a Rigaku detector 2D type imaging plate (R-AXIS IV++) (3) a stand composed of 4 axes: X, Y, Z, Phi and an independent axis: Theta. The acquisition time generally comprised between 2 and 5 minutes. The circular diffractograms were calibrated in 2Theta and took the form of linear diffractograms with the software Fit2D© v. 12.077 developed by Andy Hammersley (ESRF). The correction of the diffractograms and the identification of phases were then carried out with the help of Bruker's EVA© software.

The observations and analyses were also carried out on some shards with a scanning electron microscope coupled with an EDX (SEM-EDX) probe. The SEM used was a PHILIPS XL30 CP equipped with a tungsten filament gun and coupled with an energy-dispersion X-ray spectrometer (a system of Si(Li) detection of X-rays). This Oxford Instrument Link ISIS system allows one to make various qualitative and semi-quantitative analyses according to the energy of X-rays.

The clayey fabrics

Chemical analyses of clayey fabrics

The results of the PIXE analyses demonstrate the homogeneity of chemical composition (Tables 13–15) of the unglazed, monochrome glazed and polychrome decorated ceramic fabrics. This homogeneity was not identifiable from the visual aspect of the fabrics, which appear very diverse (Fig. 51). In fact 16 'types' of fabrics were visually distinguished before the laboratory study (Table 11; Figs 42–45). Almost all the fabrics are nonetheless very close if one does not consider the variations in silicium content of some of them. These variations are linked to the greater or lesser appearance of inclusions. This similitude of composition is also observed as much in the ceramics of the Qohandez as those of the Shahrestan. Only five or six shards diverge significantly from the average for a few elements (notably Mg and Ca/Al) (Figs 52–53): also distinct within the *corpus* of unglazed shards are samples no. 4, 7 and 12; shard B in the polychrome decorated shards (Fig. 48); and finally the two shards with an opaque white glaze (Fig. 47, nos 38 and 39).

Some shards also showed silicium content which varied significantly from the average (samples no. 4 and 12, Figs 42 and 43). For one (no. 4), it appears that the differences are due to the texture and/or the nature of the inclusions. For the other (no. 12), the petrographic observations do not allow one to know to what the differences from a mineralogical and/or textural point of view are due.

For most of the samples (>95%), the content of major elements, expressed as a mass percentage of oxides, is relatively homogeneous and comprised of the following intervals:

Na_2O: 1–2%
MgO: 3–5%
Al_2O_3: 13–17%
SiO_2: 55–60%
K_2O: 2.3–3.6%
CaO: 9–15%
Fe_2O_3: 5–9%

With the exception of two shards with an opaque white glaze (nos 38 and 39)[5] the composition of the ceramic fabrics analyzed is similar, whatever their chronology and their provenance in

---

[5] See below, p. 78–9.

Table 13: PIXE analyses of unglazed clayey shards (© C2RMF, Y. Coquinot 2010).

No. OF SHARD	No. C2RMF	Ref. PIXE	Na_2O	MgO	Al_2O_3	SiO_2	P_2O_5	SO_3	Cl	K_2O	CaO	TiO_2	MnO	Fe_2O_3	TOTAL
Unglazed clayey fabrics															
N07-106-E1	1	28aou016	1.37	3.17	14.41	56.48	0.29	0.34	0.05	2.69	14.59	0.72	0.12	5.62	100
N07-106-E1	1	04sep104	1.25	3.17	14.38	56.58	0.25	0.25	0.03	2.73	13.88	0.76	0.12	6.45	100
N07-101-E1	2	28aou017	1.47	3.76	14.71	58.08	0.15	0.26	0.03	2.92	11.10	0.96	0.13	6.28	100
N07-101-E1	2	04sep102	1.28	3.59	14.44	59.30	0.13	0.22	0.01	3.01	10.56	0.76	0.12	6.42	100
N07-101-E1	2	04sep103	1.09	3.74	14.58	57.28	0.18	0.32	0.03	2.88	12.13	0.84	0.14	6.64	100
N07-116-E1	3	28aou018	1.82	3.66	15.43	56.77	0.42	0.47	0.12	3.44	10.18	0.96	0.13	6.44	100
N07-116-E1	3	04sep105	1.56	3.71	14.85	57.21	0.30	0.48	0.15	3.33	10.34	0.79	0.13	6.99	100
N07-101-E2	4	28aou019	1.68	1.67	13.37	66.65	1.55	0.28	0.09	3.64	5.51	0.62	0.06	4.72	100
N07-101-E2	4	28aou020	1.64	2.67	13.25	68.19	0.35	0.12	0.06	3.48	4.91	0.63	0.07	4.50	100
N07-102-E1	5	28aou021	2.30	3.64	14.10	63.15	0.26	0.35	0.12	1.92	7.10	0.76	0.12	6.03	100
N07-309-E1	6	28aou022	1.75	3.27	15.31	58.04	0.30	0.33	0.03	3.02	10.50	0.79	0.10	6.41	100
N07-309-E1	6	28aou023	1.56	3.07	14.54	60.26	0.31	0.34	0.01	2.98	9.70	0.67	0.10	6.30	100
N07-301-E1	7	28aou024	0.97	1.87	16.96	60.84	0.14	0.12	0.02	3.23	8.22	0.92	0.10	6.43	100
N07-301-E1	7	28aou025	1.04	1.72	17.22	59.92	0.07	0.12	0.01	3.26	9.12	0.79	0.07	6.49	100
N07-110-E1	8	28aou026	1.40	3.90	15.10	60.84	0.42	0.31	0.10	3.37	7.30	0.73	0.11	6.25	100
N07-110-E1	8	04sep106	1.42	4.01	15.41	60.12	0.19	0.20	0.09	3.60	7.00	0.77	0.11	6.92	100
N07-110-E2	9	04sep107	1.36	3.51	16.10	58.27	0.26	0.26	0.11	3.16	8.85	0.80	0.11	7.08	100
N07-110-E2	9	28aou027	1.13	3.66	16.41	57.31	0.19	0.25	0.08	3.25	8.86	0.83	0.11	7.79	100
N07-102-2-E2	10	28aou028	1.45	3.29	14.92	58.54	0.31	0.22	0.07	3.11	10.43	0.73	0.13	6.64	100
N07-102-2-E2	10	04sep108	1.14	3.33	15.18	57.61	0.25	0.24	0.07	3.30	10.64	0.80	0.12	7.15	100
N07-110-E3	11	28aou030	1.74	3.06	15.09	57.59	0.20	1.02	0.13	3.26	10.51	0.84	0.11	6.17	100
N07-110-E3	11	04sep109	1.34	2.91	14.66	60.07	0.21	0.38	0.08	3.27	9.65	0.78	0.11	6.39	100
N07-101-9E3	12	28aou031	1.20	3.41	11.95	48.03	0.21	1.02	0.14	2.13	26.09	0.64	0.10	4.96	100
N07-101-9E3	12	04sep110	1.23	3.25	11.85	49.30	0.17	0.95	0.12	2.36	24.90	0.60	0.11	5.03	100
N06-338-E1	13	28aou032	1.63	4.09	14.02	56.36	0.11	0.60	0.42	3.07	12.25	0.79	0.12	6.40	100
N06-338-E1	13	04sep111	1.69	3.78	13.96	56.10	0.16	0.57	0.29	3.06	12.81	0.76	0.12	6.55	100
N07-102-E3	14	28aou029	1.61	3.84	15.25	57.29	0.19	0.16	0.04	3.19	10.91	0.75	0.13	6.46	100
N07-102-E3	14	04sep112	1.22	3.74	14.82	57.51	0.11	0.28	0.08	3.15	11.59	0.80	0.13	6.44	100
N07-106-E2	15	28aou052	1.50	4.12	15.07	54.41	0.26	0.12	0.11	2.95	13.54	0.83	0.12	6.76	100
N07-106-E2	15	28aou053	1.28	4.19	14.99	55.36	0.17	0.07	0.11	2.85	13.01	0.87	0.13	6.80	100
N07-104-E1	16	28aou033	1.34	4.25	14.09	55.92	0.25	0.24	0.05	2.81	13.12	1.20	0.11	6.48	100
N07-104-E1	16	04sep113	1.36	4.23	14.80	53.33	0.10	0.40	0.06	2.58	14.36	1.01	0.13	7.48	100

Sample	No.	Code													
N07-102-E4	17	28aou034	1.94	4.36	13.55	56.80	0.12	0.25	0.02	2.32	13.46	0.73	0.13	6.18	100
N07-102-E4	17	04sep114	1.77	4.55	13.87	55.45	0.13	0.25	0.03	1.87	14.51	0.72	0.14	6.57	100
N07-110-E4	18	28aou035	1.88	4.07	14.43	57.31	0.17	0.21	0.08	2.39	12.28	0.71	0.13	6.23	100
N07-110-E4	18	04sep115	1.78	4.01	14.84	55.70	0.36	0.23	0.09	2.64	12.76	0.83	0.14	6.47	100
N07-102-E5	19	28aou036	1.87	5.08	14.32	55.01	0.16	0.05	0.03	1.78	14.32	0.77	0.11	6.37	100
N07-102-E5	19	04sep116	1.93	4.55	14.15	54.89	0.23	0.12	0.03	1.91	14.64	0.70	0.13	6.60	100
N07-104-E2	20	28aou038	1.51	4.01	14.76	55.69	0.20	0.19	0.06	3.08	12.87	0.74	0.13	6.61	100
N07-104-E2	20	04sep117	1.34	4.08	15.14	56.93	0.13	0.15	0.05	3.10	11.24	0.80	0.13	6.78	100
N07-110-4-E5	21	28aou039	2.03	3.60	14.40	59.00	0.21	0.28	0.17	3.61	9.97	0.73	0.11	5.76	100
N07-110-4-E5	21	04sep118	1.75	3.75	14.62	58.06	0.14	0.24	0.13	3.39	10.85	0.71	0.12	6.09	100
N06-419-E1	22	28aou040	1.77	3.92	14.37	57.83	0.39	0.22	0.16	2.97	11.22	0.78	0.11	6.14	100
N06-149-1-E1	23	28aou041	2.30	3.46	14.45	57.41	0.88	0.24	0.06	2.19	12.32	0.70	0.11	5.73	100
N06-420-E1	24	28aou042	1.27	3.69	14.69	50.88	0.56	0.47	0.18	2.09	17.61	0.78	0.14	7.46	100
N07-101-E4	25	28aou043	1.29	3.56	14.53	58.64	0.09	0.13	0.04	2.69	11.32	0.82	0.12	6.58	100
N07-110-E6	26	28aou037	1.31	4.61	13.69	58.73	0.20	0.86	0.21	3.30	10.46	0.67	0.12	5.65	100
N07-302-E1	27	28aou044	1.24	3.69	14.49	56.83	0.23	0.10	0.05	2.77	13.17	0.76	0.13	6.37	100
N07-302-E1	27	28aou045	1.33	3.63	14.89	56.42	0.27	0.12	0.06	3.08	13.06	0.71	0.11	6.16	100
N07-101-E5	28	28aou046	1.41	3.58	16.18	57.94	0.14	0.02	0.01	2.80	10.22	0.72	0.10	6.74	100
N07-101-E6	29	28aou047	1.40	3.62	15.43	57.26	0.17	0.15	0.03	3.10	11.12	0.76	0.13	6.71	100
N07-100-E1	30	28aou048	1.46	3.39	16.50	56.67	0.19	0.15	0.04	3.07	10.55	0.82	0.15	6.88	100
N07-100-E1	30	28aou049	1.40	3.64	15.79	58.08	0.18	0.19	0.03	3.08	9.58	0.75	0.12	7.04	100
N07-106-E3	31	28aou050	1.59	3.48	14.83	58.84	0.15	0.07	0.02	2.58	11.30	0.78	0.13	6.09	100
N07-106-E3	31	28aou051	1.88	3.44	14.81	59.50	0.13	0.00	0.03	2.68	10.79	0.71	0.11	5.78	100
N07-106-E3	31	04sep119	1.46	3.20	13.99	60.70	0.00	0.05	0.02	2.48	11.17	0.69	0.12	6.00	100
N07-203-E1	32	28aou009	1.07	3.04	16.75	56.30	0.26	0.38	0.10	3.29	9.19	1.05	0.10	8.33	100
N07-203-E1	32	28aou010	1.21	2.77	15.80	57.56	0.28	0.24	0.07	3.17	9.58	1.11	0.16	7.90	100
N07-200-E1	33	28aou011	1.40	3.73	15.47	56.61	0.41	0.24	0.14	3.62	10.55	0.79	0.12	6.77	100
N07-200-E1	33	28aou012	1.03	3.44	15.52	57.16	0.42	0.28	0.14	3.53	10.80	0.79	0.09	6.67	100

Chemical composition in oxyde volume %. Compositions normalized at 100%
In red: at the limit of detection level. Dash: under detection limit

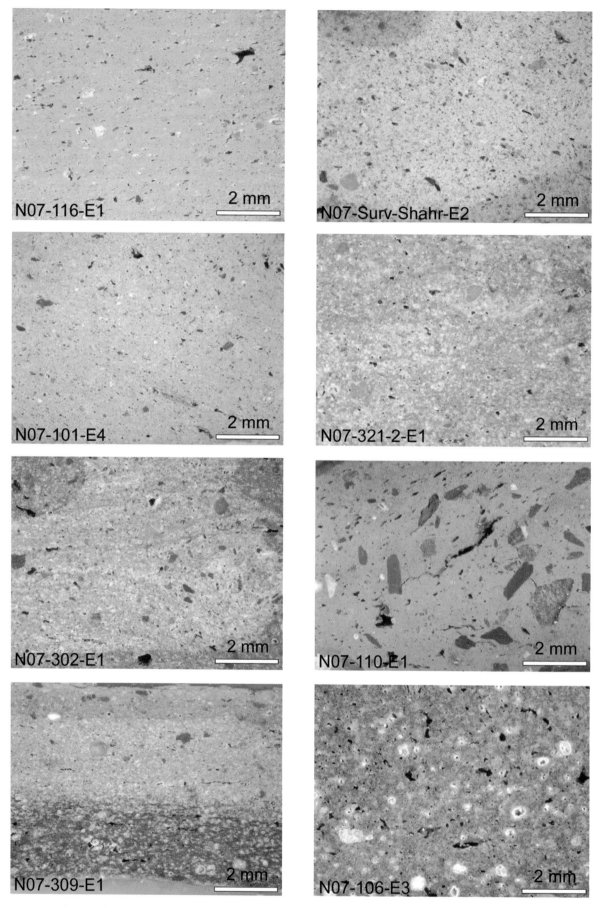

Figure 51: Nishapur, clayey fabrics: photographs under binocular magnifying glass of polished shards (© C2RMF, Y. Coquinot 2010).

Table 14: PIXE analyses of kiln material (© C2RMF, Y. Coquinot 2010).

No. of shard	No. C2RMF	Ref. PIXE	Na$_2$O	MgO	Al$_2$O$_3$	SiO$_2$	P$_2$O$_5$	SO$_3$	Cl	K$_2$O	CaO	TiO$_2$	MnO	Fe$_2$O$_3$	NiO	CuO	ZnO	Rb$_2$O	SrO	ZrO$_2$	Total
KILN MATERIAL																					
Fabrics																					
N07-Surv-Shahr-E1	34	28aou005	1.86	3.99	14.71	56.36	0.14	1.53	0.34	2.79	11.25	0.76	0.12	6.00	0.010	0.008	0.017	0.012	0.083	0.018	100
N07-Surv-Shahr-E1	34	28aou006	1.51	4.34	13.54	56.28	0.16	2.21	0.70	2.94	10.73	0.76	0.13	6.54	0.010	0.008	0.019	0.011	0.093	0.024	100
N07-321-2-E1	35	28aou003	1.25	3.83	14.56	56.34	0.33	0.14	0.02	2.73	13.41	0.73	0.13	6.40	0.009	0.006	0.019	0.012	0.085	0.027	100
N07-321-2-E1	35	28aou004	1.26	3.30	14.45	58.58	0.33	0.16	0.01	2.90	11.97	0.73	0.12	6.05	0.008	0.006	0.018	0.017	0.074	0.026	100
N07-Surv-Shahr-E2	36	28aou013	2.76	3.35	13.41	57.84	0.11	0.49	0.20	2.37	13.36	0.62	0.14	5.22	0.007	0.010	0.015	0.010	0.075	0.027	100
N07-Surv-Shahr-E2	36	28aou014	2.73	3.56	13.36	54.80	0.19	0.70	0.25	2.80	15.13	0.73	0.15	5.45	0.009	0.012	0.016	0.011	0.080	0.023	100
N07-Surv-Shahr-E2	36	04sep120	2.26	3.32	13.75	57.54	0.12	0.43	0.18	3.02	12.87	0.73	0.14	5.48	0.007	0.013	0.014	0.015	0.079	0.034	100
N07-Surv-Shahr-E3	37	28aou007	1.36	2.73	12.53	55.07	0.55	0.68	0.02	2.46	18.67	0.60	0.10	5.09	0.007	0.011	0.014	0.009	0.085	0.016	100
N07-Surv-Shahr-E3	37	28aou008	1.54	2.98	12.40	58.64	1.04	1.11	0.00	2.28	14.55	0.57	0.10	4.63	0.005	0.025	0.013	0.007	0.084	0.024	100
VITREOUS PHASE																					
N07-Surv-Shahr-E2	36	28aou015	15.46	4.33	3.18	61.57	0.33	0.29	0.64	3.48	8.77	0.20	0.39	1.21	0.004	0.034	0.009	0.005	0.091	0.021	100
N07-Surv-Shahr-E2	36	04sep121	10.68	4.23	2.61	62.01	2.65	0.39	0.54	3.67	10.63	0.18	0.75	1.37	0.004	0.057	0.013	0.006	0.178	0.018	100
N07-Surv-Shahr-E2	36	04sep122	14.42	4.38	3.41	61.37	0.14	0.33	0.55	3.36	9.67	0.23	0.33	1.63	0.004	0.051	0.009	0.006	0.082	0.027	100
N07-Surv-Shahr-E2	36	04sep123	15.49	4.11	3.35	63.50	0.20	0.29	0.70	3.94	5.89	0.23	0.42	1.69	0.006	0.063	0.009	0.007	0.087	0.024	100
N07-Surv-Shahr-E2	36	04sep124	15.59	3.53	3.03	60.83	0.26	0.33	0.58	3.49	10.71	0.12	0.57	0.82	0.002	0.031	0.006	0.006	0.079	0.017	100

Chemical composition in oxyde volume %. Compositions normalized at 100%
In red: at the limit of detection level. Dash: under detection limit

Table 15: *PIXE of clayey glazed wares (© C2RMF, Y. Coquinot 2010).*

No. of shard	No. C2RMF	Ref. PIXE	Na$_2$O	MgO	Al$_2$O$_3$	SiO$_2$	P$_2$O$_5$	SO$_3$	Cl	K$_2$O	CaO	TiO$_2$	MnO	Fe$_2$O$_3$	NiO	CuO	ZnO	Rb$_2$O	SrO	ZrO$_2$	Total
Clayey fabrics with opaque white glazes																					
N06-114-1a-E1	38	01dec037	1.64	6.20	10.94	47.16	0.44	0.14	0.16	0.77	25.33	0.68	0.14	6.27	0.022	0.005	0.011	0.003	0.069	0.015	100
N06-114-1a-E1	38	01dec038	1.66	6.30	11.10	47.37	0.52	0.14	0.18	0.78	24.41	0.71	0.15	6.55	0.023	0.005	0.012	0.003	0.068	0.015	100
N07-317-11-E1	39	01dec016	1.15	6.19	13.04	52.89	0.29	0.64	0.06	1.72	15.71	0.79	0.18	7.22	0.035	0.007	0.012	0.005	0.048	0.016	100
N07-317-11-E1	39	01dec017	1.30	6.30	12.98	52.16	0.41	0.77	0.06	1.56	16.06	0.78	0.17	7.34	0.036	0.008	0.011	0.005	0.049	0.019	100
Clayey fabrics with monochrome glazes																					
N07-Surv-Shahr-E4a	40	01dec048	1.52	3.50	16.09	56.56	0.18	0.70	0.05	3.44	9.86	0.75	0.17	6.98	0.009	0.061	0.017	0.011	0.063	0.024	100
N07-Surv-Shahr-E4a	40	01dec049	1.44	3.47	15.78	56.70	0.12	0.80	0.07	3.45	9.62	0.81	0.16	7.40	0.009	0.070	0.019	0.014	0.054	0.023	100
N07-Surv-Shahr-E4b	41	01dec041	1.26	2.75	14.04	57.62	0.20	1.10	0.04	2.97	13.00	0.68	0.14	6.02	0.008	0.055	0.017	0.014	0.057	0.021	100
N07-Surv-Shahr-E4b	41	01dec042	1.34	2.96	14.57	57.13	0.23	1.03	0.05	2.73	12.39	0.77	0.15	6.50	0.007	0.050	0.017	0.013	0.061	0.012	100
N07-Surv-Shahr-E5	42	01dec019	1.79	3.24	14.76	56.86	0.18	0.23	0.10	2.67	12.61	0.74	0.14	6.47	0.007	0.097	0.017	0.009	0.056	0.033	100
N07-Surv-Shahr-E5	42	01dec020	1.87	3.21	15.01	56.57	0.16	0.15	0.08	2.59	12.59	0.84	0.14	6.56	0.007	0.100	0.019	0.011	0.055	0.030	100
N07-Surv-Shahr-E6	43	01dec022	1.81	4.18	14.94	56.10	0.10	0.82	0.07	2.23	12.16	0.73	0.16	6.48	0.008	0.118	0.018	0.010	0.056	0.023	100
N07-Surv-Shahr-E6	43	01dec025	1.85	3.91	14.91	56.35	0.10	0.72	0.06	2.22	12.21	0.81	0.15	6.47	0.008	0.123	0.019	0.008	0.059	0.028	100
N07-Surv-Shahr-E7	44	01dec026	1.86	3.87	12.75	56.35	0.17	0.77	0.05	1.80	16.09	0.67	0.14	5.23	0.009	0.084	0.014	0.006	0.083	0.044	100
N07-Surv-Shahr-E7	44	01dec029	1.97	3.66	12.39	58.87	0.15	0.26	0.17	1.93	14.01	0.66	0.15	5.59	0.009	0.063	0.013	0.007	0.067	0.012	100
N07-Surv-Shahr-E8	45	01dec030	1.67	3.67	14.23	58.13	0.17	0.31	0.03	2.19	12.68	0.82	0.13	5.84	0.008	0.010	0.014	0.010	0.071	0.025	100
N07-Surv-Shahr-E8	45	01dec031	1.81	3.67	14.08	58.59	0.26	0.33	0.03	2.36	12.43	0.66	0.14	5.50	0.007	0.011	0.014	0.011	0.078	0.015	100
N07-Surv-Shahr-E9	46	01dec044	1.41	3.55	14.65	57.56	0.24	0.11	0.14	2.48	12.48	0.75	0.15	6.30	0.007	0.087	0.017	0.007	0.047	0.015	100
N07-Surv-Shahr-E9	46	01dec045	1.42	4.02	15.53	55.31	0.28	0.62	0.07	2.50	12.46	0.74	0.15	6.66	0.007	0.106	0.019	0.009	0.070	0.044	100
N07-Surv-Shahr-E9	46	01dec046	1.45	3.91	14.82	56.62	0.27	0.56	0.07	2.52	12.03	0.77	0.16	6.58	0.008	0.115	0.017	0.011	0.057	0.022	100
N07-106-E4	47	01dec034	1.56	3.32	15.33	56.54	0.19	0.02	0.09	2.66	12.73	0.87	0.18	6.39	0.008	0.024	0.014	0.011	0.045	0.026	100
N07-106-E4	47	01dec035	1.50	3.25	15.14	56.61	0.21	0.01	0.11	2.29	13.04	1.00	0.16	6.58	0.008	0.011	0.014	0.009	0.040	0.019	100

CLAYEY FABRICS WITH POLYCHROME GLAZES

N07 surv shar 1	A	12mai059	1.24	3.87	13.67	57.20	0.14	0.31	0.07	2.59	13.86	1.18	0.11	5.58	0.009	0.008	0.016	0.012	0.080	0.027	100
N07 surv shar 1	A	12mai060	1.33	4.09	14.69	56.97	0.18	0.28	0.08	2.72	12.91	0.79	0.11	5.71	0.008	0.008	0.014	0.015	0.075	0.018	100
Nish06 303-1	K	12mai061	1.25	4.41	14.84	57.26	0.45	0.52	0.06	2.78	11.78	0.69	0.11	5.57	0.007	0.158	0.010	0.010	0.076	0.027	100
Nish06 303-1	K	12mai062	1.16	4.30	14.64	57.30	0.77	0.62	0.05	2.43	11.34	0.81	0.15	6.14	0.006	0.160	0.010	0.009	0.073	0.024	100
N07 surv shahr 5	E	12mai063	1.16	3.77	16.86	57.56	0.19	0.20	0.02	3.08	9.40	0.84	0.11	6.67	0.009	0.006	0.016	0.013	0.060	0.035	100
N07 surv shahr 5	E	12mai064	1.19	3.81	16.85	57.37	0.37	0.33	-	3.05	9.15	0.78	0.14	6.84	0.008	0.007	0.016	0.009	0.066	0.018	100
N07 surv shahr 3	C	12mai065	1.32	3.82	15.23	61.47	0.13	0.11	-	2.63	8.85	0.75	0.11	5.48	0.006	0.005	0.012	0.007	0.048	0.014	100
N07 surv shahr 3	C	12mai066	1.20	3.33	14.45	65.56	0.68	0.18	-	2.58	7.36	0.58	0.08	3.93	0.005	0.003	0.008	0.008	0.039	0.009	100
N07 T26 struct 203	G	12mai067	0.91	4.09	14.63	58.80	0.33	0.30	0.12	2.66	11.76	0.66	0.09	5.58	0.006	0.003	0.011	0.009	0.033	0.016	100
N07 T26 struct 203	G	12mai068	0.90	3.98	16.42	55.86	0.29	0.42	-	1.98	13.61	0.68	0.08	5.71	0.005	0.003	0.010	0.006	0.039	0.017	100
N07 T26 101–19	F	12mai069	1.29	4.21	15.26	58.36	0.54	0.71	-	3.10	9.72	0.77	0.13	5.80	0.010	0.005	0.013	0.010	0.052	0.014	100
N07 T26 101–19	F	12mai070	1.10	4.45	14.87	58.10	0.43	0.57	0.02	3.23	9.74	0.76	0.12	6.50	0.009	0.005	0.014	0.007	0.051	0.017	100
N07 surv shahr 2 z 9–16	B	12mai071	1.38	6.07	13.93	56.62	1.13	1.84	-	2.11	11.07	0.55	0.12	5.08	0.013	0.009	0.011	0.005	0.055	0.007	100
N07 surv shahr 4	D	12mai072	1.18	3.95	16.04	57.40	0.53	0.34	0.02	3.08	10.09	0.73	0.13	6.38	0.008	0.007	0.018	0.008	0.062	0.017	100
N07 surv sharh zone 11	J	12mai073	0.92	3.85	17.59	58.35	0.23	0.15	0.08	3.64	6.60	0.86	0.15	7.45	0.009	0.005	0.016	0.012	0.050	0.027	100

Chemical composition in oxyde volume %. Compositions normalized at 100%

In red: at the limit of detection level. Dash: under detection limit

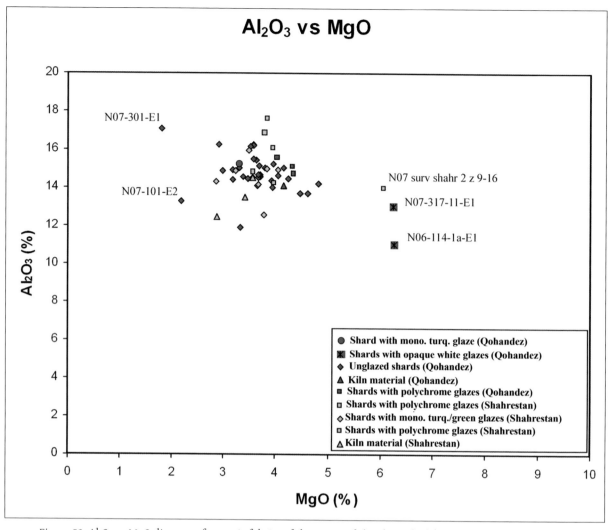

Figure 52: Al₂O₃ vs MgO diagram of ceramic fabrics of the group of shards studied (© C2RMF, Y. Coquinot 2010).

the site (lower town or citadel). The fabric of unglazed ceramics is similar to that of glazed ceramics (monochrome and polychrome) and to those of kiln sticks. The composition of the ceramics in general, unglazed and glazed, including kiln fragments, is divided between a more aluminous pole (17% Al$_2$O$_3$) and a calcic pole (CaO >15% for SiO$_2$ <51%), without it being possible to establish a clear boundary between these two 'extremes'. For the great majority of the shards, the homogeneity of the composition of the different fragments analyzed and the presence of 10–15% CaO leads one to think that it could be the same basic clayey material, which could come from a marl or a calcareous silt. The minor variations could be explained by the different preparation of the fabrics, according to the envisaged product, by the differences in texture and notably the relative percentage of inclusions of a diameter greater than 20 μm and the clayey matrix. Shard B (Fig. 48), with polychrome decoration, is distinguished from the others only by its magnesium content. The composition of the clayey fabrics supposedly produced at Nishapur is relatively rare in the literature. Nevertheless, those reported by R. B. Mason are similar to those obtained in this work (Mason, 2004, p. 207–208).

The composition of the fabrics with an opaque white glaze (nos 38 and 39) is close to that of Iraqi fabrics (Mason, 2004, p. 32 and tab. 3.3 p. 34. Also see Hedges, 1976; Hedges and Moorey, 1975; Bouquillon *et al.*, 2008). These have relatively similar composition – at the very least for a certain number of elements – and are easily distinguishable from the fabrics of Nishapur

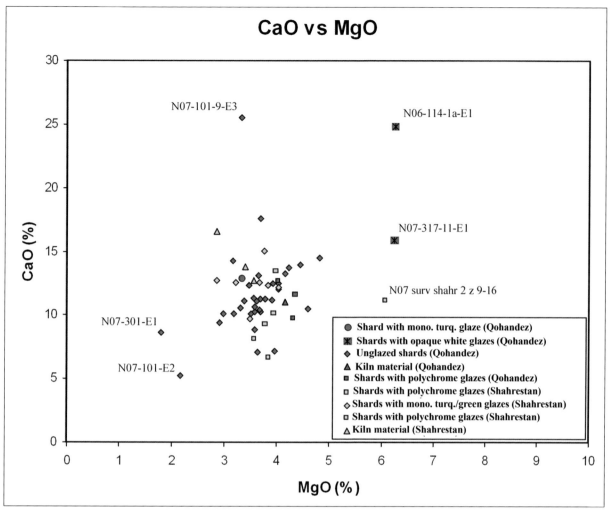

Figure 53: CaO vs MgO diagram of ceramic fabrics of the group of shards studied. Each point represents the average of the compositions obtained for each sample (© C2RMF, Y. Coquinot 2010).

or even the Iranian fabrics whose composition has been reported in the literature (Mason, 2004, p. 32 and tab. 3.3 p. 34; tab. 6.3 p. 133). They are more magnesian (% MgO >5.5 and often >6%), more calcic (% CaO >16% and for most >18%) and less potassic (0.4<% K_2O <1.5). The composition of the fabric of the two shards with opaque white glaze nonetheless differs from one another in calcium and silica content. This difference arises in part from the nature of the percentage of inclusions. In fact, the fine fabric of sample no. 38 contains less than 1% inclusions of a diameter greater than 20 μm (quartz only) while the average fabric of sample no. 39 contains 7–8% quartz and plagioclase calco-sodic feldspars (+1–3% of other minerals). However, these differences rather reflect the different Iraqi production sites, which also suggest the composition of the glazes.

PETROGRAPHY OF THE CLAY FABRICS

Forty-seven shards of clay fabric were subjected to petrographic study (Figs 42–45, 50; Tables 11–12), in thin sections observed in optical microscopy. This type of examination must first allow the establishment of petrographic groups based on the nature of the inclusions and the determination of the texture of the fabrics. Secondly, it must allow one to identify the production site and the source of the raw materials of the ceramics examined. The results were compared with those of the chemical analyses. Research into the provenance of the geological materials

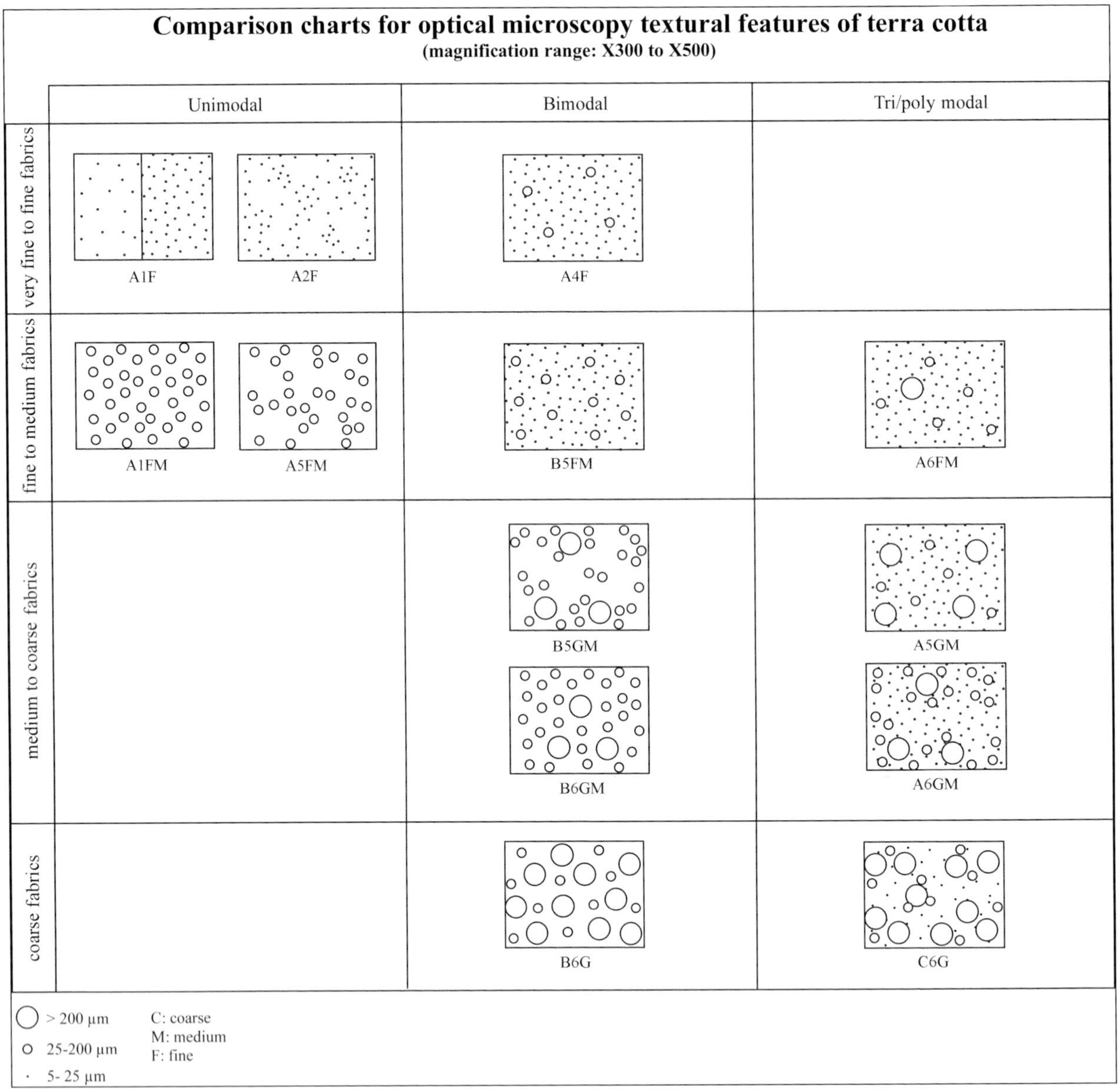

Comparison charts for optical microscopy textural features of terra cotta
(magnification range: X300 to X500)

Figure 54: textural classification of the fired earths used in this work. Symbols: C: coarse; M: medium; F: fine; FM: fine to medium; MC: medium to coarse; R: regular distribution; I: irregular distribution (© C2RMF, Y. Coquinot 2010, Collinet and Rante 2011).

used to make the fabrics was carried out from geological maps compiled by geologists of Iran's oil company.[6] This permitted the characterization of the nature of the inclusions of a size greater than 20 μm and the texture of the ceramic fabrics. A textural classification in optical microscopy was established and used in order to codify and compare the different textures encountered (Fig. 54).

A difficulty is generally encountered in connecting the petrographic groups to the production site, as the texture of the fabric is often linked to the size and usage of the piece. The construction processes (such as purification or the addition of a temper) vary according to these two demands. The quantity and nature of the inclusions can thus reflect the degree of purification of the clayey material, but equally the quantity and the type of temper added. Thus, a very fine fabric only containing small grains of monocrystalline quartz and a coarse fabric containing monocrystalline quartz and fragments of volcanic rock can have been made from the same 'clay' and in the same workshop. The petrographic groups thus reflect, in part, the technology employed.

---

6   Geological map of Iran at 1/1,000,000 online: http://www.ngdir.ir/ThematicGeology/Geology.asp?#Nod

Table 16: Chemical composition (%) in oxyde volume of the glass inlcusion in sample no. 39 (© C2RMF, Y. Coquinot 2010).

COMPOSITION	GLASS		GLASS + DIOPSIDE	
(% VOLUME)	INCLUSION 1	INCLUSION 2	INCLUSION 3	INCLUSION 4
Na$_2$O	4.44	3.36	4.12	4.73
MgO	3.12	2.23	4.70	5.31
Al$_2$O$_3$	1.80	2.97	1.28	1.24
SiO$_2$	69.26	72.08	69.68	68.50
K$_2$O	5.71	6.76	5.32	5.77
CaO	4.71	5.73	10.42	9.81
MnO	n.a.	n.a.	0.87	0.60
Fe$_2$O$_3$	n.a.	n.a.	0.21	0.71
PbO	10.97	6.87	3.40	3.32
TOTAL	100	100	100	100

The most differentiating factor in the establishment of groups nevertheless remains the nature of inclusions. The results of petrographic observations are in agreement with the results of the chemical analyses. Save for a few shards, a relatively good homogeneity in the nature of the inclusions may be noted. Apart from all geographical and chronological considerations, 11 types of inclusions were identified and are listed below (Tables 17–18; Figs 55–58):

- plagioclase feldspars
- fragments of metamorphic rocks: meta-arenites (quartzite/quartzo-phyllade≈schist), meta-siltites or meta-pelites (= very fine schist)
- monocrystalline quartz
- polycrystalline quartz (can correspond to a fragment of quartzite)
- fragments of andesite
- brown amphibole crystals (calco-magnesian amphibole)
- clinopyroxene crystals
- potassic feldspars (perthite, orthose and microcline)
- micas (biotite and muscovite)
- fragments of chert (= silex)
- fragments of sandstone, siltite or pelite (detritic sedimentary rocks)
- carbonated fragments (vein of calcite or limestone)
- glass with acicular diopside crystals

For the shards studied as a whole, the inclusions were largely sub-angular. Some among them, infrequently, were nonetheless sub-rounded, for example sample no. 35. The textures were rather varied (Fig. 54). The medium to coarse and coarse fabrics in general show more fragments of rock than the fine fabrics. In the latter, fragments of andesite are rare while minerals coming from this same volcanic rock can be very much present and the composition similar. This suggests the use of the same 'clay', but with a difference in preparation.

The petrographic characteristics of the fabrics allowed a distinction to be drawn between four large groups (Tables 17–18):

- Group A: comprises the great majority of the shards examined (42 out of 47 (89%)). Fabrics with inclusions coming from volcanic rocks and the conjoint presence of either plagioclase feldspar and andesite, or plagioclase feldspar and amphibole. The ceramics in this group can also contain fragments of metamorphic rocks (metapelite or meta-arenite), micas, quartz, clinoptroxenes and potassic feldspars.

Petrographic group A is sub-divided into two sub-groups:

Table 17: Petrography of the clayey fabrics (© C2RMF, Y. Coquinot 2010).

No. of shard	No. C2RMF	Fabric type (visual classification) (classement visuel)	Petrographic group	Petrographic sub-group	% of inclusions Ø > 25 μm	Inclusions		Fragment of andesite	Fragment of metamorphic rock
						Feldspars			
						Plagioclase	Potassic		
Unglazed clayey fabrics									
N07-106-E1	1	1	A	Aa	5–10%	+++		+	ma: (+)
N07-101-E1	2	1	A	Aa	5–10%	+		+	ma/mp: (+)
N07-116-E1	3	2	A	Aa	5–10%	+		(+)	(ma + ms): ++
N07-101-E2	4	3	A	Aa	10–20%	+++	(+)	++++	ma: (+)1
N07-102-E1	5	3	A	Aa	15–20%	+++		+++	ma: +; mp: +
N07-309-E1	6	4	A	Aa	12–15%	+++		+++	ma et mp: (+)
N07-301-E1	7	4	A	Aa	7–12%	++	(+)	(+)	
N07-110-E1	8	5	B	-	7–12%	(+)			ma: +; mp: ++
N07-110-E2	9	5	A	Ab	5–10%	+			ma : +
N07-102-2-E2	10	5	A	Aa	10–15%	+		+	ma: (+); mp: (+)
N07-110-E3	11	6	A	Aa	5–10%	+	(+)	+	ma: (+)
N07-101-9E3	12	6	A	Ab	7–12%	+			
N06-338-E1	13	6	A	Aa	10–15%	+		(+)	
N07-102-E3	14	7	A	Aa	5–10%	+		+	
N07-106-E2	15	8	A	Aa	5–7%	+		(+)	ma: (+)
N07-104-E1	16	8	A	Aa	3–7%	+		(+)	ma: (+)
N07-102-E4	17	8	A	Aa	15–20%	+		(+)	ms/mp: (+)
N07-110-E4	18	8	A	Aa	5–10%	++		(+)	
N07-102-E5	19	9	A	Aa	5–10%	+		(+)	ma: (+)
N07-104-E2	20	10	A	Aa	8–12%	+		(+)	ma: (+)
N07-110-4-E5	21	10	A	Aa	7–12%	+	(+)	(+)	ma: +; mp: (+)
N06-419-E1	22	10	A	Aa	10–15%	++		(+)	ma: (+)
N06-149-1-E1	23	10	A	Aa	10–20%	+		(+)	ma/ms: (+)
N06-420-E1	24	10	A	Ab	3–8%	(+)	(+)		
N07-101-E4	25	11	A	Aa	8–12%	+++		+	
N07-110-E6	26	11	B	-	6–12%	+	(+)		ma et mp: ++
N07-302-E1	27	11	A	Aa	10–15%	++	(+)	+	
N07-101-E5	28	12	A	Aa	5–15%	+++		(+)	ma: (+)
N07-101-E6	29	13	A	Aa	5–10%	++	(+)	+	ma: (+)
N07-100-E1	30	13	A	Aa	10–15%	++++	(+)	+	ma: (+)
N07-106-E3	31	14	A	Aa	10–15%	++++	(+)	++	
N07-203-E1	32	15	B	-	15–20%	(+)			mp: +++
N07-200-E1	33	16	A	Aa	2–5%	+++		+	

Inventory of identified inclusions and estimation of the temper %
?: not classified; ++++ very common; +++ common; ++ rather common; + not very common; (+) rare (=trace). cpx : clinopyroxène
Petrographic sub-groups: Aa = volcanic rocks and feldspars; Ab = numerous fragments of metamorphic rocks and quartz; Ac = feldspars and amphibole, without volcanic rock fragments

MICA BIOTITE (b) MUSCOVITE (m)	AMPHIBOLE	CPX	QUARTZ MONOCRYSTALLINE (m)/ POLYCRYSTALLINE (p)	chert	FRAGMENT CALCAREOUS (CAL)/ CALCITE (c)	CALCITE 2DARY	IRON OXYDES AGGREGATE	IRON OXYDES DIFFUSE	PELITE (P)/ SILTITE (S)/ SANDSTONE (g)	GLASS
m: (+)	+		(m + p): +			+	+	+		
m: (+)	+	(+)	(m + p): +			++				
m: +			(m + p): +			+	+	+++		
	(+)			(+)				++		
m: +	(+)					++	(+)			
m: (+)	+		+	(+)		+++		++	s: (+)	
m: (+)	+	+	(+)			++		++++		
m: (+)			+			+	+	+++		
	(+)		(+)			(+)				
m: +	+	(+)	(+)			+		++		
m: (+)	(+)	(+)	(m + p): +			(+)	+	++	s (+)	
m: (+)	++	+	+			+	++	+		
m: (+)	(+)	(+)	+							
	(+)	(+)		(+)		++	+	++		
	(+)		+	(+)			+	+	p: (+)	
	(+)		+			+	+			
m: (+)	(+)	(+)	++			+				
+	+	(+)	+							
+	(+)	(+)	+			+	+			
	(+)	(+)	+			+	+	+		
m: (+)	(+)		+				+	(+)	g: (+)	
		(+)	m +; p: +				+			
m: (+)	(+)	(+)	m: ++; p: (+)				+			
(+)	++						+			
	+	(+)	+			+	++	++		
		(+)	++			++			p/s: +	
	+		++							
	(+)	(+)	+			+	++			
	(+)		+			++		++		
			+			++	+	++		
			+				++			
	(+)		(+)		(+)	+	+	+++	s: +	
	(+)	(+)	++		(+)	+++	+			

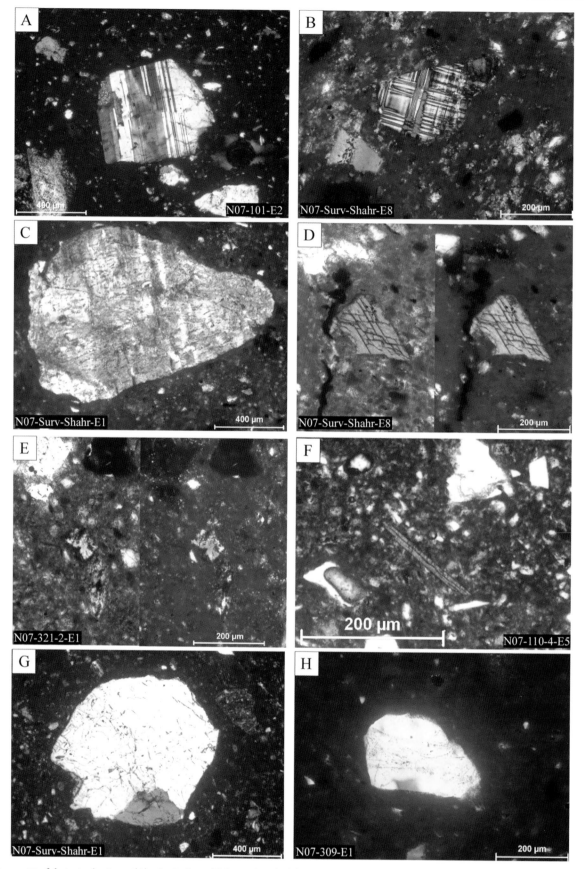

Figure 55: fabric inclusions. (A) plagioclase feldspar (LPA); (B) potassic feldspar (microcline) (LPA); (C) potassic feldspar (orthose or perthite) (LPA); (D) brown hornblende (=amphibole) (left: LPNA; right; LPA); (E) clinopyroxene (left: LPNA; right: LPA); (F) biotite rod (LPNA); (G) grain of polycrystalline quartz (=quartzite) (LPA); (H) grain of monocrystalline quartz (LPA) (© C2RMF, Y. Coquinot 2010).

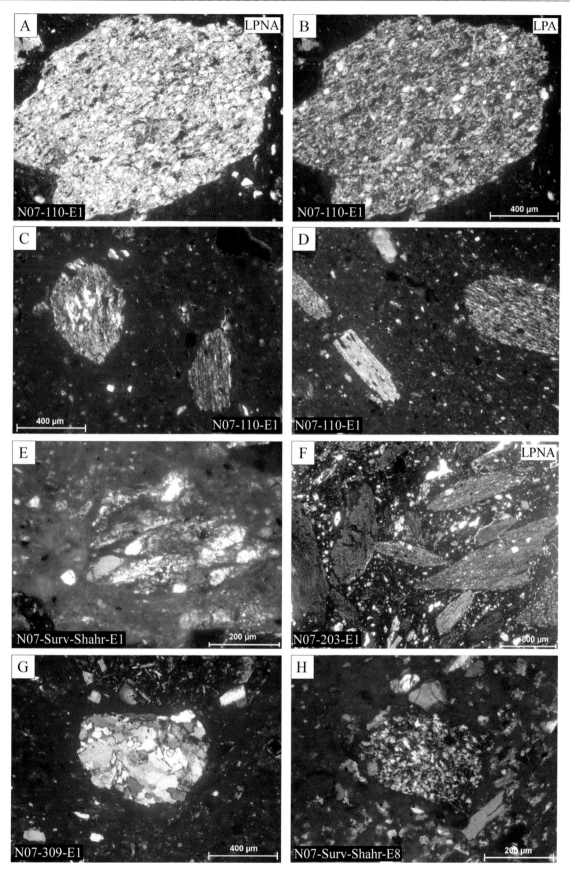

Figure 56: fragments of metamorphic rocks. (A) and (B) fragments of metapelite (≈metasiltite); (C) fragments of metapelite (=mica schist) with, for the fragment on the left, quartz veinule; (D) left: fragment of mica schist, right: fragment of metapelite (≈schist); (E) fragment of meta-arenite (≈coarse schist); (F): fragments of weakly metamorphosed pelite; (G) fragments of quartzite; (H) fragments of metasiltite (quartzite) (© C2RMF, Y. Coquinot 2010).

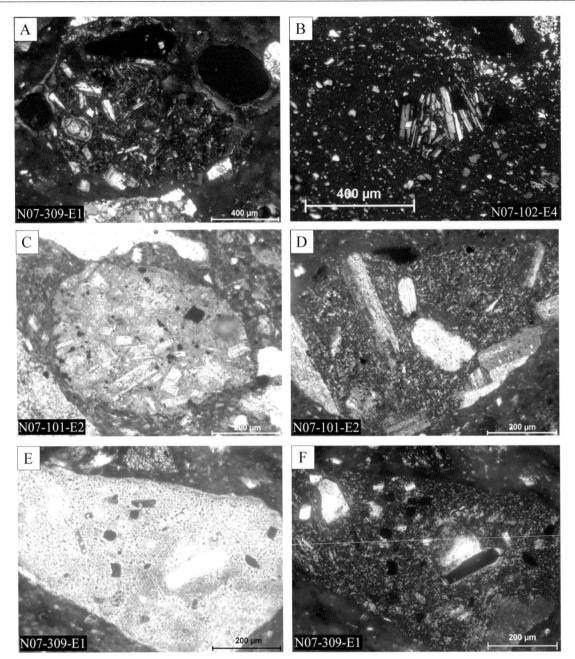

Figure 57: fragments of felsic volcanic rock of the andesite type. (A) inclusion of porphyritic andesite showing plagioclase phenocrystal and a groundmass of small plagioclase and glass; (B) inclusion of felsic volcanic rock corresponding to an andesite with microlithic texture; (C) inclusion of felsic volcanic rock with essential andesine needles and magnetite in the groudmass composed of glass and small plagioclase crystals; (D) inclusion of felsic volcanic rock corresponding to an andesite with a holohyaline mesostase and plagioclase phenocrystals; (E-F): inclusion of felsic volcanic rock with plagioclase phenocrystals and magnetite and holohyaline groudmass texture (© C2RMF, Y. Coquinot 2010).

(Aa): characterized by the presence of fragments of andesite;

(Ab): characterized by the absence of fragments of andesite and the presence of plagioclase feldspars and amphibole;

- Group B: fabrics with numerous fragments of metamorphic rocks and without fragments of andesite. The other inclusions it having been possible to observe in these fabrics corresponding to quartz, potassic feldspars, micas, amphibole or fragments of sedimentary detritic rocks (pelite or sandstone). Group B is comprised of three unglazed shards (nos 8, 26 and 32),

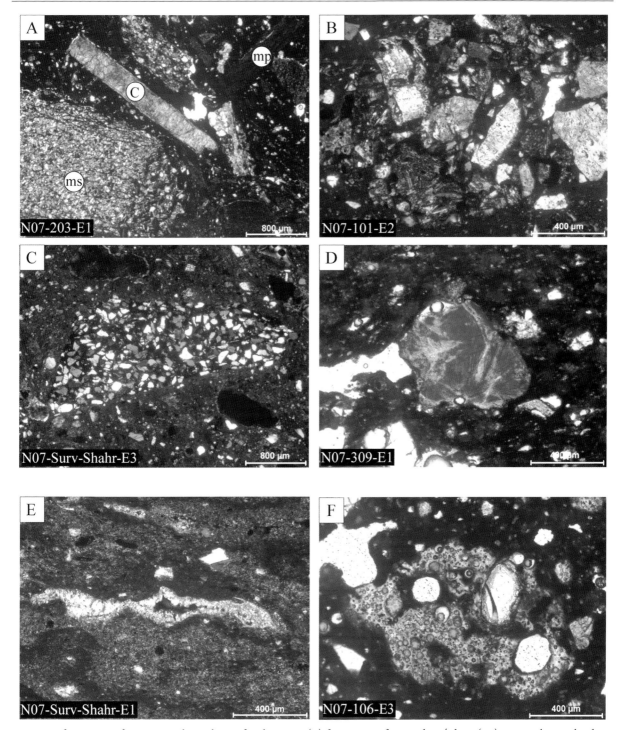

Figure 58: fragments of various rocks and specific elements. (A) fragments of metasiltite/siltite (ms), metapelite and calcite veinule (C); (B) fragment of sandstone very rich in inclusions resulting from felsic volcanic rocks; (C) fragment of fine sandstone; (D) fragment of chert (≈silex); (E) secondary calcite; (F) vitrified range of the clayey matrix (© C2RMF, Y. Coquinot 2010).

containing numerous fragments of metamorphic rocks. These latter do not, however, present the same facies in each of the samples.

The two samples with white opaque glaze represent two petrographic groups very distinct from Groups A and B;

- Group C: fabric with quartz only (shard no. 38).
- Group D: fabric with fragments of glass (shard no. 39).

The fine fabrics present very little temper (1–10%) and this is generally well-classified (= one sole granulometric class for the inclusions of a diameter greater than 20 µm). One can note that the relative proportion of quartz grains in comparison to the feldspar grains and fragments of rock is much higher in this type of fabric. The 'coarser' fabrics, which however remain poor in large inclusions (>500 µm), are richer in plagioclase feldspars and above all in rock fragments, notably in fragments of volcanic and metamorphic rocks. The volcanic rocks are of the felsic type, with an intermediate composition. According to the texture (porphyric with microlitic or hyaline mesostase) and the nature of the feldspars (andesite, sometimes zoned), it is andesite. The presence of clinopyroxenes, brown amphibole and plagioclase feldspars in the matrix leads to the same interpretation.

Certain samples demonstrate the presence of secondary calcite (pedogenic cement). This secondary calcite, present in a more or less significant manner in the fabrics, could partly explain the variability of their calcium content.

On the other hand, the shards present differences from a textural point of view, notably as far as concerns their size, dispersion or the relative proportion of different types of inclusions. A textural classification was carried out in order to be able to visualize the texture of each fabric and thus be able to compare the texture of the shards with one another (Fig. 54).

Petrographic groups C and D (shards with opaque white glaze, nos 38 and 39) significantly differ from the other shards in certain petrographical characteristics. They are also very different to one another. Shard no. 38 presents a very fine fabric with inclusions of monocrystalline quartz. It is related to the petrography of Basra as defined by R. B. Mason (Mason and Keall 1991; Mason 2004, 200–201). The other (no. 39) shows a fine to medium fabric with inclusions of quartz, biotite, amphibole, plagioclase feldspars, fragments of volcanic rocks and (relict) vitreous inclusions rich in acicular diopside crystals (Fig. 59). These fragments of plumbiferous glass were used as a temper. They represent approximately 3–4% of the inclusions. The diopside crystals visible in these fragments of glass present a centripetal disposition and are visibly crystallized from the glass-fabric interface. This appears to have played the role of the nucleation surface. Gaps have also been observed in most of these inclusions. They could be the result, at least partly, of the crystallization of the diopside and/or an alteration of the glass.

The diopside crystals were certainly formed during heating, at a temperature of above 800°C (Karamanov and Pelino 2006), while the viscosity of the glass had become sufficiently elevated for a demixing and crystallization. These latter were not present in the vitreous inclusion at the time when it was added to the clay. The diopside was probably crystallized from elements of the vitreous phase, which consequently must have become poorer in these elements, but maybe also from certain elements in the argilocarbonated matrix. Two analyses of glass located between the diopside crystals were carried out at SEM-EDS in as well as two comprehensive analyses (glass + diopside). The results have been reported in Table 16. These compositions are close to those of the fragments of glass in a sample published by Mason and Tite, from Nippur in Iraq (Mason and Tite 1994, table 1, p. 81, sample Ni.H304.3). Vitreous inclusions with acicular diopside crystals, cristobalite/trydimite or wollastonite were identified in certain Iraqi fabrics from the sites of Nippur and Samarra. They appear present only in the petrographic facies 'Samarra 2', defined by Mason and Tite and hypothetically linked to Baghdad (Mason, 2004, 32, 211 and pl. 3.1 p. 246; Mason and Tite 1994, p. 80).

Among the unglazed samples, one can note the presence of four shards with an 'overfired' fabric, in which the argilo-calcerous matrix and certain fragments of volcanic rock were partially vitrified (nos 28, 29, 30 and 31). The fabrics of these shards present similar petrographic characteristics (nature of the inclusions and texture). Despite their different macroscopic appearance to the other shards, the may be grouped in sub-group Aa due to the presence of inclusions of andesite.

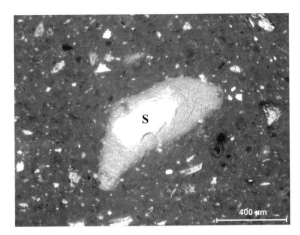

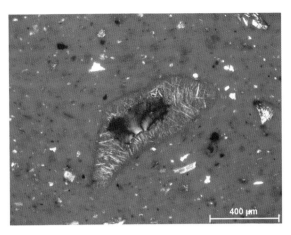

(A) glass with acicular diopside crystals (LPNA)
S: space

(B): LPA

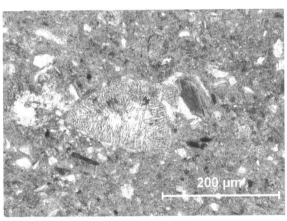

(C): acicular diopside crystals with a centripetal
disposition (LPNA)

(D): (LPA)

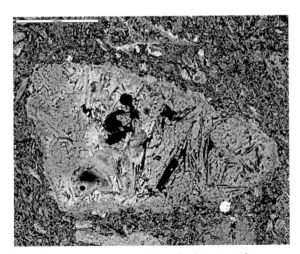

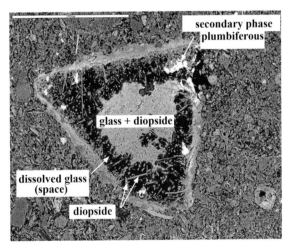

(E): vitreous inclusions with acicular crystals
(SEM image in BSE mode)

(F): very altered vitreous inclusion with diopside
acicular crystals and plumbiferous neoformation
(lead carbonate ?) (SEM image in BSE mode)

Figure 59: fragments of glass in inclusions in sample no. 39. (A) glass with acicular diopside crystals (LPNA); S: space; (B): LPA; (C): acicular diopside crystals with a centripetal disposition (LPNA); (D): (LPA); (E): vitreous inclusions with acicular crystals (MEB image in BSE mode) (© C2RMF, Y. Coquinot 2010).

Table 18: Petrography of kiln material and clayey glazed wares (© C2RMF, Y. Coquinot 2010) – Continued on opposite page.

No. of shard	No. C2RMF	Petrographic group	Petrographic sub-group	% of inclusions Ø > 25 μm	Feldspars Plagioclase	Feldspars Potassic	Fragment of andesite	Fragment of metamorphic rock
Kiln material								
N07-321-2-E1	34	A	Aa	5–10%	++		+	
N07-Surv-Shahr-E1	35	A	Aa	10–15%	++++		+++	ma: (+); mp: +
N07-Surv-Shahr-E2	36	A	Aa	8–12%	+++		+	
N07-Surv-Shahr-E3	37	A	Aa	8–12%	++	(+)	+	ma: (+); ms: (+)
Clayey fabrics, opaque white glazes								
N06-114-1a-E1	38	C	-	2–4%	(+)			
N07-317-11-E1	39	D	-	5–10%	+++		(+)	
Clayey fabrics, monochrome glazes								
N07-Surv-Shahr-E4a	40	A	Aa	8–10%	++		(+)	ma: (+)
N07-Surv-Shahr-E4b	41	A	Aa	3–8%	+		(+)	ma: (+)
N07-Surv-Shahr-E5	42	A	?	5–10%	+			
N07-Surv-Shahr-E6	43	A	Aa	7–10%	+++		(+)	ma: +
N07-Surv-Shahr-E7	44	A	Aa	10–12%	++	(+)	+	ma: +
N07-Surv-Shahr-E8	45	A	Aa	10–12%	++	(+)	(+)	ma: (+)
N07-Surv-Shahr-E9	46	A	Aa	4–8%	+		(+)	ma: (+)
N07-106-E4	47	A	Aa	8–12%	+	(+)	+	ma +

Inventory of identified inclusions and estimation of the temper %
?: not classified; ++++ very common; +++ common; ++ rather common; + not very common; (+) rare (=trace). cpx: clinopyroxène
Petrographic sub-groups: Aa = volcanic rocks and feldspars; Ab = numerous fragments of metamorphic rocks and quartz; Ac = feldspars and amphibole, without volcanic rock fragments

Unglazed shard no. 32 contains numerous angular fragments of pelite (= lutite) and of weakly metamorphosed siltite/fine sandstone and, in a lesser proportion, sparitic calcite corresponding to the fragments of veinlets. No fragment of andesite was observed in this sample. The composition of this shard is, on the other hand, not very different to the average composition of the other shards.

The fritwares

Chemical analyses of the fritwares

Seven fritware shards (nos ps1–ps7; Figs 49 and 60) were examined under a binocular magnifying glass. The shards studied had a white fabric, lightly yellowed in one sample (no. ps2). This coloration is due either to the presence of impurities or a greater proportion of glass and crystals of a size less than 50 μm. Shard no. ps3 also shows brown-orange zones resulting from the diffusion of impurities from the soil (iron oxides and other insoluble elements) in the sample. Sample no. ps7 presents itself in the form of two shards joined by a glaze. The two have an 'exterior' glaze of a slightly different colour.

MICA BIOTITE (B) MUSCOVITE (M)	AMPHIBOLE	CPX	QUARTZ MONOCRYSTALLYNE (m)/ POLYCRYSTALLINE (p)	CHERT	FRAGMENT CALCAREOUS (CAL)/ CALCITE (c)	CALCITE 2DARY	IRON OXYDES		PELITE (p)/ SILTITE (s)/ SANDSTONE (g)	GLASS
							AGGREGATE	DIFFUSE		
m: (+)	(+)	+	+			++	++			
	+		+			+++	+	+++		
m: (+)	+		+							
m: (+)	+	(+)	++					+	g: (+)	
							+			
b: + m: (+)	+		m: +; p: (+)				+(+)			+
(+)	(+)		m: +; p: (+)				+	+++		
(+)		(+)	+				+	++		
	(+)		(+)				++	++		
(+)	+		+							
(+)	+(+)	(+)	m: +; p: (+)				+			
(+)	+	(+)	m: +; p: +	+++		+?	+			
(+)	(+)		m: +				+	++		
(+)	(+)		m: +			(+)	++			

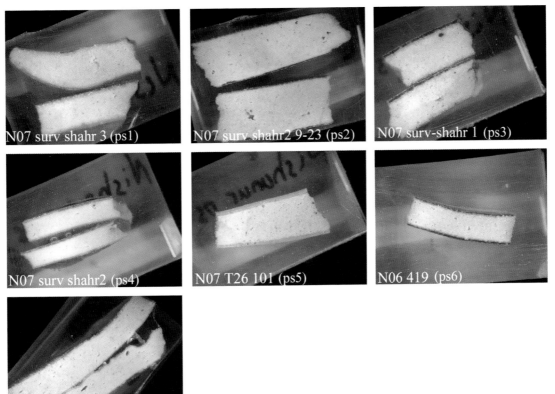

Figure 60: photographs of fritware shards enclosed in resin and polished (© C2RMF, Y. Coquinot 2010).

N07 surv shahr 3 (ps1)
N07 surv shahr2 9-23 (ps2)
N07 surv-shahr 1 (ps3)
N07 surv shahr2 (ps4)
N07 T26 101 (ps5)
N06 419 (ps6)
N07 surv shahr z4 (ps7)

Table 19: PIXE analyses of fritwares shards (© C2RMF, Y. Coquinot 2010) – Continued on opposite page.

No. of shard	No. C2RMF	Ref. PIXE	Na$_2$O	MgO	Al$_2$O$_3$	SiO$_2$	P$_2$O$_5$	SO$_3$	Cl
N07 surv shahr 3 pt1	ps 1	11fev016	3.45	1.19	5.74	84.96	0.08	0.32	0.03
N07 surv shahr 3 pt2	ps 1	11fev017	3.40	1.09	5.77	84.66	0.04	0.29	-
N07 surv shahr2 9-23 pt 1	ps 2	11fev030	3.49	1.22	5.88	85.28	-	0.26	0.19
N07 surv-shahr 1 pt1	ps 3	11fev007	2.52	0.83	4.49	89.05	-	0.13	0.07
N07 surv-shahr 1 pt2	ps 3	11fev008	2.70	0.90	4.81	88.53	-	0.11	0.06
N07 surv shahr2 pt 1	ps 4	11fev024	3.31	1.17	5.69	85.23	-	0.31	0.28
N07 T26 101 pt1	ps 5	11fev010	2.35	0.94	3.58	90.54	-	0.23	0.04
N07 T26 101 pt2	ps 5	11fev011	2.47	1.15	3.82	89.61	-	0.22	0.05
N06 419 pt 1	ps 6	11fev027	3.05	1.04	5.55	86.00	0.03	0.35	0.07
N07 surv shahr z4 pt1	ps 7	11fev020	2.49	0.94	4.02	88.88	-	0.22	0.11
N07 surv shahr z4 pt2	ps 7	11fev021	2.38	0.92	4.03	89.04	-	0.24	0.11

Chemical composition in oxyde volume %. Compositions normalized at 100%
In red: at the limit of detection level. Dash: under detection limit

The results of the PIXE analyses (Table 19) show a good homogeneity of chemical composition. Nevertheless, two groups could potentially be distinguished by Na$_2$O, Al$_2$O3, SiO$_2$ and Fe$_2$O$_3$ content (Fig. 61):

• Group 1: composed of samples ps1, ps2, ps4 and ps6.
• Group 2: composed of samples ps3, ps5 and ps7.

Petrography and mineralogical composition of the fritwares

The shards are all composed of monocrystalline sub-angular to angular grains of quartz and, in a small proportion of feldspars (plagioclase + potassic?), small diopside crystals, fragments of quartzite (rare), cristobalite and a vitreous phase (Table 20; Fig. 62). Some rare sticks of very 'altered' biotite were observed in two shards (ps3 and ps5). Some 'phantoms' of fragments of glass, recognisable by the particular presence and disposition of diopside crystals, were identified. They are pseudomorphic structures corresponding to small fragments of glass (which were added to sand in the form of a glass frit), which were partially melted and crystallized during the firing of the fabric. They were therefore recognizable by the presence of small diopside crystals tracing the contours of the original fragment of glass (Fig. 63). Secondary calcite, pedogenic, was also observed in weak proportions (<0.5%). Cristobalite and diopside were generally present between the grains of quartz, generally in the vitreous phase, playing the role of binder. Shard ps3 also contains a fragment of sub-rounded andesite with a diameter of 500 μm (Fig. 64). The great majority of the grains are angular and relatively elongated. In the seven samples, the majority of the monocrystalline quartz grains (60–80%) are rather limpid. The others contain fluid inclusions and thus appear less clear. Some of the grains also show an undulant extinction (10–20%).

X-ray diffraction analysis of the seven shards revealed an identical mineral composition: quartz (>80%), diopside, cristobalite and feldspars (plagioclase and potassic?) (Figs 65a–g).

The relative proportions of these four phases were not able to be directly determined from the diffractograms but, knowing the nature of all the mineral phases present, chemical analyses of the fabrics were used to estimate the modal composition with the aid of the Excel equation solver. A 'macro' permitted us to empirically determine the modal composition of the sample (Table 21) from:

• the overall chemical analysis of the sample
• the analysis of SEM images (estimation of the volumic percentage of the vitreous phase)

K$_2$O	CaO	TiO$_2$	MnO	Fe$_2$O$_3$	NiO	CuO	ZnO	Rb$_2$O	SrO	ZrO$_2$	PbO	Total
0.99	2.27	0.15	0.01	0.64	0.019	0.038	0.002	0.0009	0.017	0.011	0.133	100
0.97	2.65	0.31	0.02	0.66	0.008	0.036	0.003	0.0014	0.014	0.005	0.150	100
1.19	1.71	0.13	0.02	0.62	0.022	0.003	0.002	0.0014	0.013	0.008	0.026	100
1.01	1.21	0.09	0.01	0.61	0.012	0.031	0.002	0.0011	0.010	0.005	0.000	100
1.05	1.19	0.09	0.02	0.56	0.029	0.030	0.002	0.0010	0.011	0.005	0.001	100
1.26	1.97	0.14	0.01	0.56	0.007	0.002	0.002	0.0011	0.015	0.007	0.057	100
0.99	0.88	0.08	0.01	0.39	0.010	0.002	0.002	0.0008	0.013	0.007	0.002	100
0.93	1.20	0.09	0.01	0.46	0.017	0.003	0.002	0.0015	0.012	0.013	0.002	100
1.29	1.50	0.11	0.01	0.66	0.005	0.063	0.003	0.0019	0.011	0.009	0.286	100
0.99	1.62	0.09	0.03	0.58	0.005	0.034	0.002	0.0016	0.017	0.004	0.012	100
1.00	1.67	0.05	0.03	0.52	0.010	0.029	0.002	0.0016	0.014	0.006	0.007	100

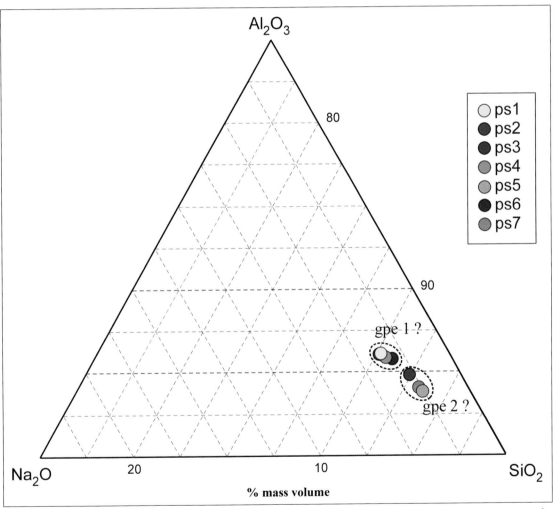

Figure 61: fritware compositions reported in a triangular Na$_2$O-Al$_2$O$_3$-SiO$_2$ diagram (© C2RMF, Y. Coquinot 2010).

- the chemical composition and density of each mineral phase. The density of the minerals is used to pass from a percentage in surface (volume) to a percentage in mineral mass
- the qualitative mineralogical composition established by X-ray diffraction
- the composition of the vitreous phase present in the fabric

Table 20: Petrography characteristics of fritwares (© C2RMF, Y. Coquinot 2010).

| No. of shard | No. C2RMF | INCLUSIONS | | | | | | | | TEXTURE % grains + glass (in volume) | Ø size (3 classes) | | | MORPHOLOGY |
| | | QUARTZ | | FELDSPARS | | FRAGMENT OF ANDESITE | CRISTOBALITE | DIOPSIDE | GLASS | | 5–20 µm | 20–200 µm | 200–500 µm | |
		MONOCRYSTALLINE	POLYCRYSTALLINE (= QUARTZITE)	PLAGIOCLASE	POTASSIC									
N07 surv shahr 3	ps 1	+++++	tr	+	tr		++	(+)	++	50–70	+++	+++++	(+)	angular
N07 surv shahr2 9–23	ps 2	++++++	tr	+	tr		++	(+)	++	50–70	+++	++++++		angular
N07 surv-shahr 1	ps 3	++++++	tr	+	tr	tr	++	(+)	++	50–70	++++	+++++		angular
N07 surv shahr2	ps 4	++++++	tr	+	tr		++	(+)	++	50–70	+++	++++++		angular
N07 T26 101	ps 5	++++++	+	+	tr		++	(+)	++	50–70	++++	+++++		angular
N06 419	ps 6	++++++	(+)	+	tr		++	(+)	++	50–70	+++	++++++		angular
N07 surv shahr z4	ps 7	++++++	tr	+	tr		++	(+)	++	50–70	++++	+++++	(+)	angular
(+): < 5%; tr: trace (<0,5%)														

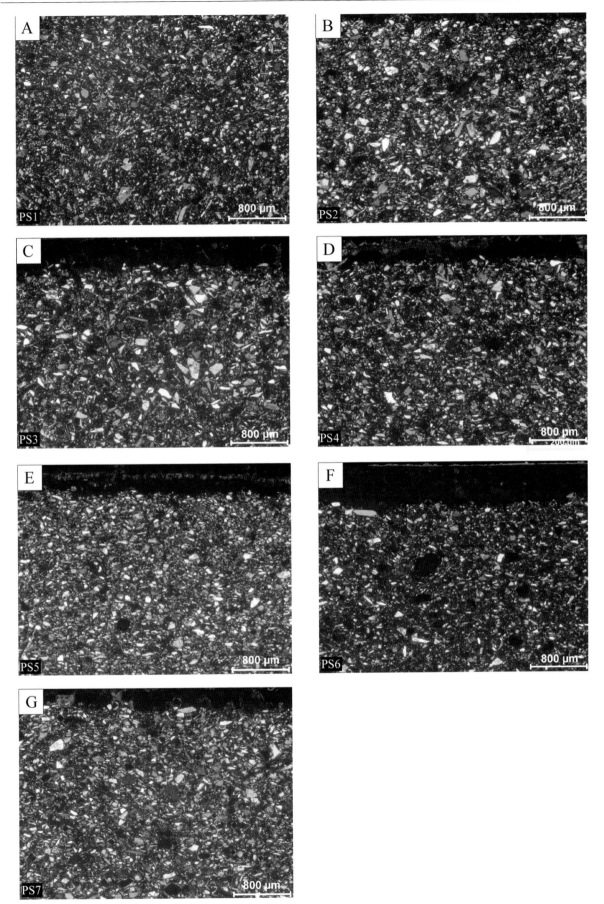

Figure 62: Fritware petrofabric. Characterized by numerous angular clear quartz, a few feldspar, diopside, cristobalite and an intergranular glassy matrix (© C2RMF, Y. Coquinot 2010).

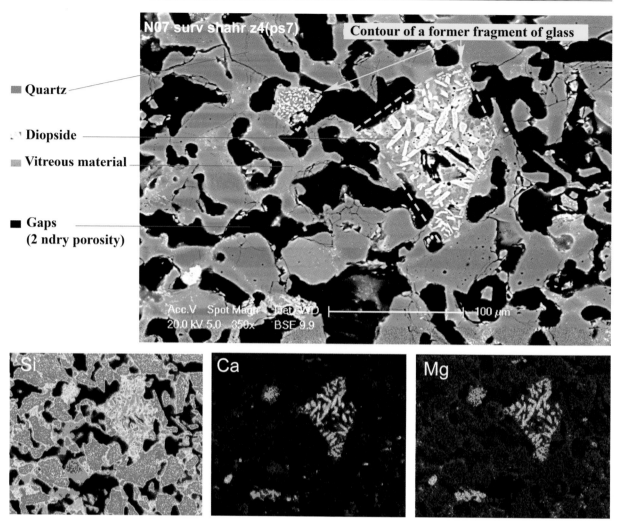

Figure 63: 'Phantoms' of fragments of glass in shard no. ps7. In the BSE image and the elementary cartographies can be seen diopside crystals which were crystallized during heating (to more than 800°C), at the time of the softening of the glass (© C2RMF, Y. Coquinot 2010).

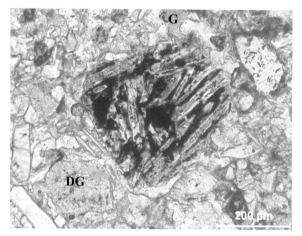

A: fragment of volcanic rock in sample ps3 (LPNA);DG: diopside +glass; G: glass

B: fragment of andesite (in the centre) in ps3 (LPA)

Figure 64: Photographs of the fritware shards enclosed in resin and polished. A: fragment of volcanic rock (in the centre) in no. ps3 (LPNA); DV: diopside +glass; G: glass. B: fragment of andesite (in the centre) in no. ps3 (LPA) (© C2RMF, Y. Coquinot 2010).

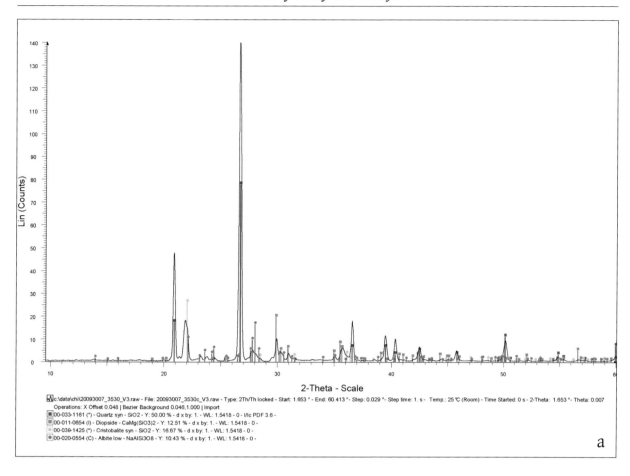

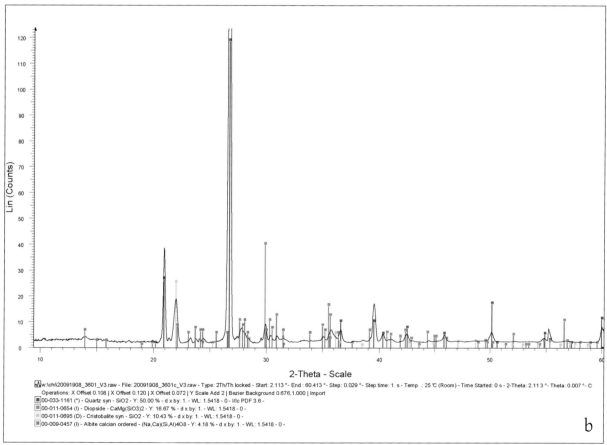

Figures 65a and b: Diffractograms of fritware (© C2RMF, Y. Coquinot 2010).

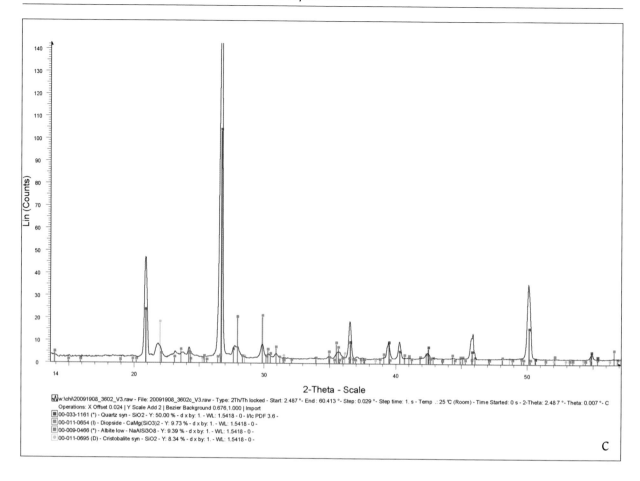

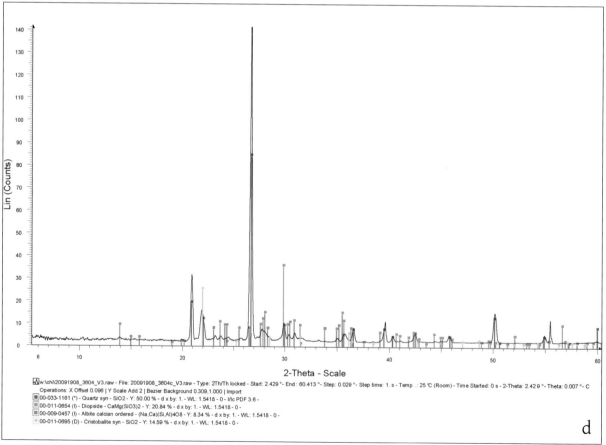

Figures 65c and d: diffractograms of fritware (© C2RMF, Y. Coquinot 2010).

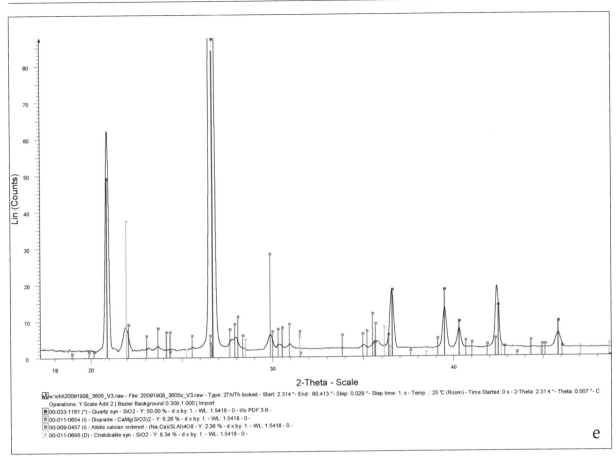

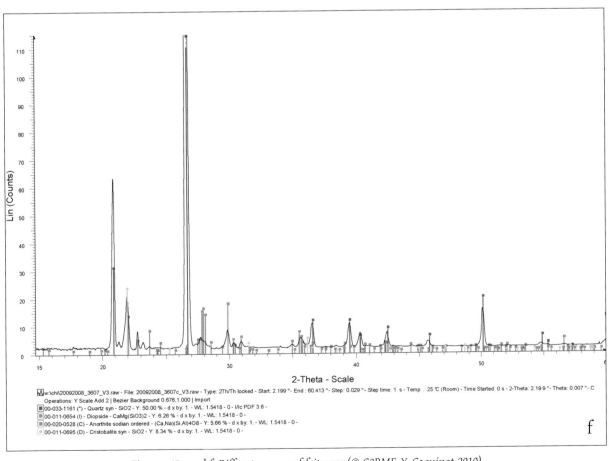

Figures 65e and f: Diffractograms of fritware (© C2RMF, Y. Coquinot 2010).

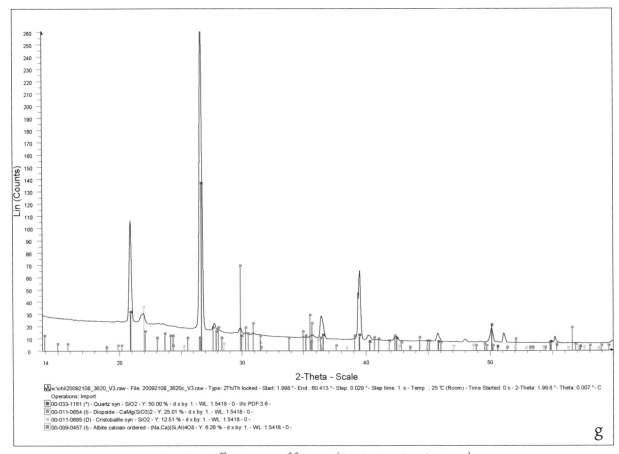

Figure 65g: Diffractograms of fritware (© C2RMF, Y. Coquinot 2010).

Table 21: Mineralogical composition of fritwares (© C2RMF, Y. Coquinot 2010).

% VOLUME	ps 1	ps 2	ps 3	ps 4	ps 5	ps 6	ps 7	ERROR
Quartz	64	64	65	67	65	65	67	± 8
Plagioclases	8	8	6	6	5	6	5	± 2
Cristobalite	10	10	11	7	8	8	11	± 3
Orthose	1	1	1	1	1	4	1	± 0,5
Diopside	3.6	3.6	2.6	3.6	2.6	3	2.6	± 0,5
Glass	13	13	15	15	18	13	13	± 4
Calcite secondary	0.2	0.2	0.2	0.2	0.2	0.2	0.2	± 0,05

Estimation based on the chemical composition, on the SEM images and on the analyses in X-ray diffraction
The incidental inclusions as the andesite fragment in ps3 or the micas have not been taken in account in this estimation

The average structural formulae of all the mineral phases identified in the fabrics were approximated by taking the standard compositions reported on the site Webmineral.com, namely:

Quartz: SiO_2
Cristobalite: SiO_2
Diopside: $CaMgSi_2O_6$
Plagioclase feldspars: anorthite ($CaAl_2Si_2O_8$) and albite ($NaAlSi_3O_8$)
Potassic feldspars (orthose): $KALSi_3O_8$

Table 22: Composition of the vitreous phase in the fritwares (© C2RMF, Y. Coquinot 2010).

Composition	Na_2O	MgO	Al_2O_3	SiO_2	SO_3	K_2O	CaO	Fe_2O_3	CuO	PbO
%	5.8	0.43	11.6	75.5	0.27	3.7	1.6	1.1	0.14	0
Interval Type	0.3	0.05	0.7	1	0.05	0.3	0.2	0.2	0.06	-

Mica (biotite): rare (<0.5%) and unreported

Secondary calcite: $CaCO_3$

Glass: a fictional 'structural formula' and average to be determined, in the form of a sum of oxides, from the compositions obtained at SEM-EDS (Table 22), namely:

$$1.96\ Na_2O + 0.11\ MgO + 2.38\ Al_2O_3 + 13.16\ SiO_2 + 0.82\ K_2O + 0.3\ CaO + 0.14\ Fe_2O_3$$

Very few petrographic studies of Iranian siliceous ceramics have been carried out until now. The principal existing data are that reported by R. B. Mason. The results of these studies show the presence of volcanic rock in the fabrics of Nishapur but also in the fabrics from various Iranian production centres and presenting different petrographic facies.[7] He also defined that of Nishapur, from samples datable to the 15th–16th centuries: 'large angular grain of felsic volcanic, polycristalline quartz', '50% clear to very cloudy quartz, mostly in the sub-cloudy area'; '3–5% of a felsitic volcanic and associated plagioclase and microcline feldspar', 'the grainsize distribution is mostly of the 'fine' profile but there are samples with a 'very fine' profile, all having largest grainsizes above 0.2 mm in diameter' (Mason and Golombek 1996, 38; table 3.6 p. 42; figs 3.9–10 p. 41; Mason 1995, fig. 2, 314, 315–317). The production sites of fritwares of the Iranian world are not always well-identified. Among all those mentioned by Mason, the majority have a local geology with volcanic rocks (Rayy, Termez, Sirjan, Nishapur, Samarkand). These volcanic rocks are also of the same type, felsitic and andesitic, and one is therefore unlikely to be able to discern the production centres due to the nature of the fragments of volcanic rocks present in the fabrics.

The petrographic results obtained at C2RMF indicate that the feldspars, a glass frit and possibly calcite must have been added to the quartz sand to make these ceramics. These components allowed the formation during heating of a vitreous phase which had bound the grains of quartz together (Fig. 63). The diopside, identified in XRD, was most certainly formed during heating, at over 800°C, from the glass frit but maybe also from the calcite and clay if these latter were added to the quartz sand, separately or mixed in the form of a marl or calcareous clay. The plagioclase feldspars, of the albite type (high temperature form), and anorthite, could correspond to unmelted inclusions or be formed during heating/cooling. If the calcite or a calcareous clay had been added to the quartz sand to make the fabric, this would have disappeared in favour of diopside and gehlenite from 850–900°C and the gehlenite would then have disappeared in favour of the diopside-anorthite association around 1000–1100°C.

The very angular form of the grains of quartz indicates that they are not of a fluviatile origin. The quartz sand used to make fritwares comes from the fine milling of monocrystalline blocks of quartz or of large-crystalled quartzites.

The glazed wares: physical and chemical analyses

Methods of study and analytical conditions

Among the 67 samples studied, 31 bore traces of glazed decoration (Figs 66–69) and constituted the body of this study (Table 23; Figs 46–50). The samples were divided into five different batches according to the typology of the material but not including any chronological

---

[7] 'Safavid-1-Mashhad', 'Safavid-2', 'Safavid-3 Kerman?', 'Tabriz (?)', 'Samarkand (?)', 'Dragon', 'Safavid-4 Shahreza' and 'Rayy-3', Mason and Golombek 1996, 32–46; 2003; Mason 2003, table 1, 273; 2004, 210.

Table 23: Glazed samples analysed (© C2RMF, A. Bouquillon 2010).

Type	No. of shard	Provenance	No. C2RMF	Glaze/decoration analysed
Opaque white glaze on clayey fabric	N06-114-1a-E1	Qohandez, T15	38	White glaze
	N07-317-11-E1	Qohandez, T23	39	White glaze
Monochrome glazes on clayey fabric	N07-Surv-Shahr-E4a	Shahrestan, survey	40	Altered green glaze
	N07-Surv-Shahr-E4b	Shahrestan, survey	41	Altered green glaze
	N07-Surv-Shahr-E5	Shahrestan, survey	42	Green glaze
	N07-Surv-Shahr-E6	Shahrestan, survey	43	Altered green glaze
	N07-Surv-Shahr-E7	Shahrestan, survey	44	Blue-green glaze
	N07-Surv-Shahr-E8	Shahrestan, survey	45	Green glaze
	N07-Surv-Shahr-E9	Shahrestan, survey	46	Green glaze
	N07-106-E4	Qohandez, T26	47	Green glaze
Polychrome decorations on clayey fabric	N07 surv shahr 1	Shahrestan, survey	A 48	Yellow glaze
			A 49	Black glaze
			A 50	White glaze
	N07 surv-shahr 2 z9-16	Shahrestan, survey	B 51	Yellow glaze
			B 52	Black glaze
			B 53	White glaze
	N07 surv-shahr 3	Shahrestan, survey	C 54	White glaze (outside)
			C 55	Yellow glaze (inside)
			C 71	Black glaze
	N07 surv shahr 4	Shahrestan, survey	D 56	Dark green glaze
			D 57	Green ? glaze
	N07 surv shahr 5	Shahrestan, survey	E 58	Blue-green glaze (engraved)
			E 59	White glaze (outside)
	N07 101–19	Qohandez, T26	F 60	Yellow glaze
	N07 wall 203	Qohandez, T26	G 61	White glaze (outside)
			G 62	Black glaze (inside)
			G 63	White glaze (inside)
	N07 3	Qohandez	H 64	Black glaze
	N07-1	Qohandez, T27	I 65	? 2 samples
	N07 surv Shahr z 11	Shahrestan	J 66	?
	N06 303-1	Qohandez	K 67	Blue-green glaze (inside)
			K 68	Green glaze (outside)
	N06 420	Qohandez, T10	L 69	Green glaze
	N06 418-16	Qohandez, T10	M 70	Yellow glaze
Glazes and pigments on fritwares	N07-Surv-Shahr-3	Shahrestan, survey	ps1	Blue-green glaze
	N07-Surv-Shahr-z9-23	Shahrestan, survey	ps2	White glaze
	N07-Surv-Shahr-1	Shahrestan, survey	ps3	Black painted, turquoise glase
	N07-Surv-Shahr-2	Shahrestan, survey	ps4	Dark blue glaze
	N07-101	Qohandez, T26	ps5	Blue glaze, lustre
	N06-419	Qohandez, T10	ps6	Blue glaze
	N07-Surv-Shahr-z4	Shahrestan, survey	ps7	Blue glaze

Table 24: PIXE analyses of monochrome clayey wares (© C2RMF, A. Bouquillon 2010).

No. of shard	No. C2RMF	Ref. PIXE	Na₂O	MgO	Al₂O₃	SiO₂	SO₃	Cl	K₂O	CaO	TiO₂	MnO	Fe₂O₃	CuO	NiO	ZnO	Rb₂O	SrO	SnO₂	PbO	Total
Opaque white glaze on clayey fabric																					
N06-114-1a-E1	38	01dec039	5.83	2.99	1.11	60.51	-	0.58	4.34	4.11	0.09	0.37	0.62	0.06	0.002	0.014	0.013	0.100	10.34	8.92	100.00
N06-114-1a-E1	38	01dec040	5.35	2.95	1.65	65.22	-	0.62	3.87	4.89	0.15	0.32	0.73	0.02	0.002	0.010	0.006	0.070	10.16	3.98	100.00
N07-317-11-E1	39	01dec018	3.10	1.58	1.30	49.92	-	0.55	1.73	2.39	0.07	0.04	0.35	0.02	0.010	0.013	-	0.026	6.69	32.22	100.00
Monochrome glaze on clayey fabric																					
N07-Surv-Shahr-E4a	40	01dec050	2.26	1.32	1.20	38.58	-	0.65	1.47	2.54	0.09	0.03	0.33	1.91	0.008	0.003	-	0.014	6.55	43.06	100.00
N07-Surv-Shahr-E4b	41	01dec043	2.32	2.11	1.69	42.14	-	0.54	1.15	3.56	0.12	0.03	0.88	1.68	0.013	0.007	0.009	-	3.75	39.99	100.00
N07-Surv-Shahr-E5	42	01dec021	2.05	1.63	1.25	41.32	-	0.53	1.22	3.28	0.13	0.03	0.70	2.24	0.009	0.007	-	0.023	4.34	41.23	100.00
N07-Surv-Shahr-E6	43	01dec023	2.56	1.16	0.98	43.35	-	0.58	1.66	2.36	0.07	0.03	0.33	1.95	0.007	0.005	-	0.011	4.62	40.33	100.00
N07-Surv-Shahr-E6	43	01dec024	2.54	1.21	1.03	42.29	-	0.58	1.62	2.56	0.09	0.03	0.45	2.02	0.008	0.010	-	0.025	4.86	40.66	100.00
N07-Surv-Shahr-E7	44	01dec027	10.86	3.80	2.93	66.05	-	0.93	4.98	5.76	0.15	0.04	1.16	3.11	-	0.014	0.017	0.063	-	0.14	100.00
N07-Surv-Shahr-E7	44	01dec028	11.47	3.74	2.89	67.14	-	0.68	4.27	5.90	0.14	0.05	1.17	2.29	0.001	0.014	0.014	0.059	-	0.17	100.00
N07-Surv-Shahr-E8	45	01dec032	3.13	3.41	5.27	72.29	-	0.38	2.68	8.56	0.21	0.09	2.09	1.75	0.003	0.014	0.011	0.101	-	0.02	100.00
N07-Surv-Shahr-E8	45	01dec033	10.04	3.69	2.98	68.74	-	0.61	3.92	6.89	0.13	0.08	1.47	1.30	0.001	0.008	0.011	0.087	-	0.02	100.00
N07-Surv-Shahr-E9	46	01dec047	0.52	1.08	2.77	32.29	-	0.35	0.94	3.25	0.18	0.05	1.49	1.96	0.012	0.035	0.007	-	2.36	52.71	100.00
N07-106-E4	47	01dec036	3.19	1.63	1.88	47.80	-	0.19	2.11	4.26	0.13	0.05	1.50	0.88	0.009	0.017	0.004	0.023	2.97	33.36	100

Chemical composition in oxyde volume %. Compositions normalized at 100%
In red: at the limit of detection level. Dash: under detection limit

consideration: ceramics with clayey fabrics and monochrome glazes (7), ceramics with clayey fabrics and polychrome decorations (13), kiln sticks bearing traces of glaze (2), clay ceramics with opaque white glaze (2) and fritware shards (7). From visual observation, the monochrome glazes on clayey fabrics are most often in the range of blues and greens, sometimes uncoloured, allowing the colour of the fabric to show through. The polychrome decorations present rather varied colours: green, yellow, black, blue and white.

The glazes were studied with two successive techniques, PIXE and SEM (Scanning Electron Microscopy). Millimetric flakes were removed with a scalpel from the accessible zones, the edges of the shard or on the perimeter of a hole. They were enclosed in Epoxy resin and then planed with a diamond-tipped grinding wheel in order to bring a transversal section of the flake to the surface, allowing one to have all the stratigraphy of the sample of the clay of the fabric on the surface of the glaze. These sections were polished to ¼ μm with the aid of diamond pastes of decreasing granulometries (6 μm, 2 μm; ¼ μm). After observation with the binocular magnifying glass or optical microscope, the samples were metallized with carbon for examination and analysis by SEM-EDS on the same device as was used for the fabrics (in a vacuum pushed with an acceleration tension of 20kV). The information obtained is on the microstructure of the materials and on the overall or selective elementary chemical composition (Figs 73–75).

The fritware shards and those with opaque white glaze were first of all analyzed by PIXE (Tables 24; 30); for each sample, the analysis was applied to two distinct zones of 500 μm × 500 μm. The elementary chemical composition of these two scanned zones at times shows rather significant differences; certain elements presenting variations in content, sometimes ranging from simple to double. These differences are perhaps due to the presence of mineral inclusions concentrated in certain zones of the glaze, but most certainly to problems of alteration, signalled by hairline cracks, surface deposits, irisations and discolorations or even loss of material.

It is therefore necessary to perform micro-sampling on each shard and to study them by SEM-EDS in order to observe the microstructure of the glaze and to access, while it is still present, the clean part in order to obtain a credible chemical analysis of the general composition ('gene' on the table of results) and of that of the vitreous phase (PV on the same tables).

The shards analyzed allow the differentiation of three 'groups' on the basis of glazes. The local productions constitute the most abundant group. They comprise glazes rich or very rich in lead (from 30–60% PbO), whether monochrome or polychrome. They are most often put on clayey fabrics of similar composition, containing constituents compatible with the local geology.

These productions, even if they present a certain homogeneity in the great characteristics of their composition, show an important diversity in colorants and the processes of colouring.

Monochrome glazes on clayey fabrics

The ceramic clayey fabrics with monochrome glazes analyzed (Fig. 46) are similar (see above), composed of a marl of approximately 12% CaO, 3.5% MgO, 55% SiO_2, 14% Al_2O_3 and 6% Fe_2O_3. However, the coexistence of two types of glazes in the studied *corpus* implies two types of production.

Glazed on both faces, these ceramics all present very strong degrees of alteration, whether on the surface, the interface or also in the thickness of the glass. Certain samples were not able to provide an area to analyse, the alteration covering the totality of the glaze (samples nos 40 and 46). The related colours systematically fall within the ranges of green on the exterior and green or white on the interior. These eight translucent monochrome glazes show textural differences in optical microscopy (Figs 66, 73). Certain among them, for example, are poor in inclusions (such as sample no. 44), and other very rich (sample no. 45, presenting a percentage of inclusions of around 20–30% in volume). The inclusions on the whole correspond to diopside

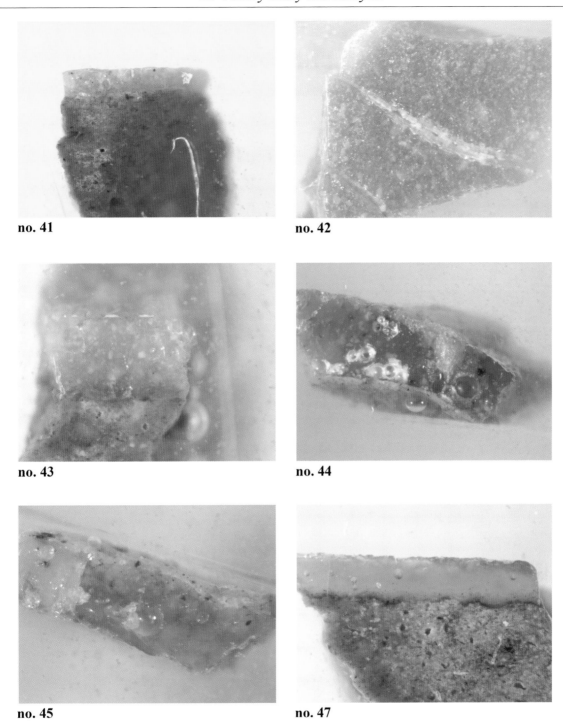

no. 41

no. 42

no. 43

no. 44

no. 45

no. 47

Figure 66: photographs under a binocular magnifying glass of samples of monochrome glazes (© C2RMF, A. Bouquillon 2010).

($CaMgSi_2O_6$), crystallized in the form of small rods or more compact crystals. The analyses in X-ray diffraction also show the presence of a little unmelted quartz (Fig. 67). Two groups of green monochrome ceramics are distinct due to the composition of the glazes (Table 25).

- The most significant correspond to plumbiferous glazes (35–40% PbO) and slightly opacified (3–7% SnO_2). This accounts for 4 to 6 shards studied (nos 41–43 and 47). Nevertheless, the alkaline content, in the order of 5% (Na_2O+K_2O) are perhaps under-evaluated because of the alteration of the glazes, these elements being in fact easily leached during the burial. The

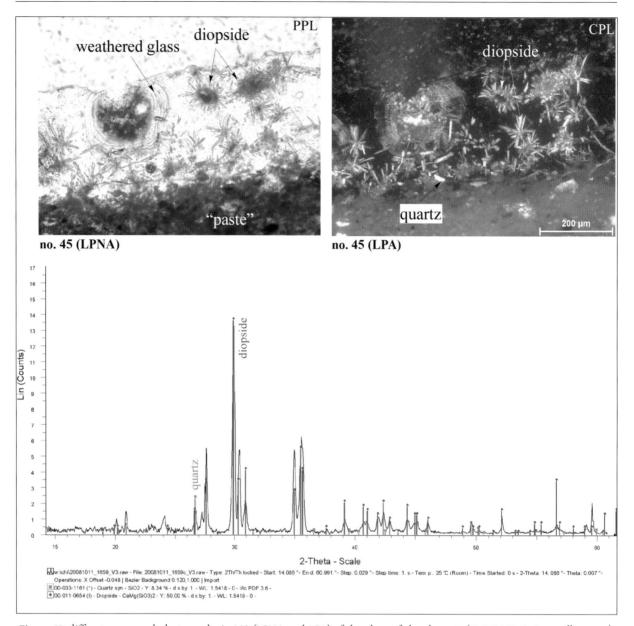

Figure 67: diffractogram and photographs in MO (LPNA and LPA) of the glaze of shard no. 45 (© C2RMF, A. Bouquillon 2010).

content in colorant elements (copper and iron) varies according to the desired shade of the glaze. Let us nevertheless note that in the glaze of sample no. 42 the copper/arsenic association perhaps reveals the use of an arsenified copper as a source of colorant. The inclusions of tin oxides are distributed in a heterogeneous manner; other inclusions of crystals of calcium and magnesium silicates, sometimes with very clear lozenge forms (diopside?), are characteristic of minerals neoformed during the cooling of the glazes during their last firing. These glazes have a thickness of around 100–150 µm. In certain samples (no. 42), the fabric/glaze interface is particularly well-developed; the crystals are feldspars of potassium. The information obtained by PIXE on the monochrome glazes (Table 24), must be considered as semi-quantative because of the alteration of the glazes but confirm that this was highlighted with the SEM. In addition they show that samples 40 and 46, which were not able to be studied by section, belong to the group of plumbo-stanniferous glazes.

Table 25: Elementary chemical composition of monochrome glazes (SEM) (© C2RMF, A. Bouquillon 2010).

No. C2RMF		Na₂O	MgO	Al₂O₃	SiO₂	P₂O₅	SO₃	Cl	K₂O	CaO	TiO₂	MnO	Fe₂O₃	CuO	As₂O₃	SnO₂	PbO
41	gene	2.64	0.93	0.77	40.79	0	0	0.4	1.85	2.48	0.15		0.29	1.92		6.58	41.2
	E-t	0.05	0.1	0.13	0.09	0	0	0.09	0.11	0.05	0.04		0.05	0.04		0.28	0.6
	pv	2.79	0.87	0.47	42.57	0	0	0.53	1.89	2.14	0.05		0.19	2.17		1.75	44.58
	E-t	0.05	0.11	0.06	1.21	0	0	0.14	0.16	0.2	0.05		0.07	0.16		0.34	1.29
42	gene	2.1	1.28	0.84	44.08	0	0	0.26	1.5	2.81	0.08		0.53	2.2	1.03	5.5	37.77
	E-t	0.18	0.12	0.05	1.03	0	0	0.09	0.05	0.48	0.08		0.1	0.24	0.76	2.02	1.69
	pv	2.12	1.33	0.85	47.22	0	0	0.27	1.61	2.98	0.11		0.46	2.28	1.55	1.38	37.85
	E-t	0.09	0.12	0.08	0.51	0	0	0.06	0.08	0.5	0.01		0.14	0.05	0.93	0.13	1.24
43a	gene	2.24	1.05	0.99	43.31	0	0	0.23	2.17	3.62	0.23	0	0.72	1.38		6.33	37.73
	pv	2.28	1.14	0.94	47	0	0	0.23	2.37	3.67	0.22	0.05	0.76	1.67		1.58	38.09
	E-t	0.14	0.16	0.27	0.6	0	0	0.08	0.09	0.23	0.1	0.06	0.22	0.21		0.32	0.94
43b	gene	2.88	1.19	1.11	46.07	0	0	0.51	2.08	3.23	0.09	0.05	0.72	2.01		4.31	35.76
	E-t	0.1	0.04	0.28	0.3	0	0	0.1	0.04	0.37	0.03	0.04	0.21	0.15		0.19	0.86
	pv	2.94	1.27	0.75	48.25	0	0	0.42	2.06	3.17	0.17	0.03	0.45	2.24		2.05	36.21
	E-t	0.05	0.18	0.14	2.55	0	0	0.23	0.05	0.69	0.13	0.03	0.3	0.23		0.59	1.17
44	gene	11.03	3.23	2.45	67.07	0	0.38	0.54	5.56	5.96	0.23		1.14	2.4			
	E-t	0.17	0.09	0.37	0.34	0	0.02	0.04	0.05	0.47	0.11		0.14	0.38			
45	gene	9.83	3.54	4.27	65.75	0.01	0.31	0.64	4.3	7.94	0.19		1.98	1.25			
	E-t	0.14	0.54	1.8	1.1	0.01	0.07	0.08	0.32	0.73	0.06		0.36	0.29			
	pv	10.23	3.33	3.01	68.2	0.05	0.27	0.59	4.65	6.58	0.13		1.66	1.29			
	E-t	0.9	0.24	0.11	2.15	0.08	0.13	0.25	0.25	1.12	0.1		0.16	0.3			
47	gene	3.19	1.52	1.65	48.04	0	0	0.09	2.47	5.02	0.2		1.82	1.45		2.99	31.39
	E-t	0.06	0.06	0.18	0.74	0	0	0.11	0.05	0.13	0.08		0.13	0.12		0.52	0.29
	pv	3.19	1.52	1.74	48.55	0	0	0.03	2.46	4.96	0.05		1.76	1.37		2.29	31.94
	E-t	0.12	0.05	0.27	0.47	0	0	0.04	0.11	0.14	0.07		0.11	0.29		0.48	1.23

SEM results in % of oxyde volumes
gene: general composition; pv: vitreous phase; E-t: type interval

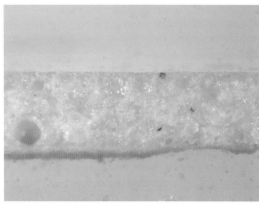 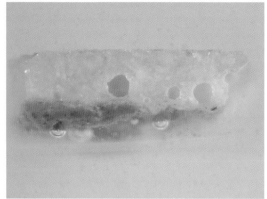

no. 38   **no. 39**

Figure 68: photographs under a binocular magnifying glass of samples of opaque white glazes (© C2RMF, A. Bouquillon 2010).

Table 26: Elementary chemical composition of opaque white glazes (SEM) (© C2RMF, A. Bouquillon 2010).

No. C2RMF		Na_2O	MgO	Al_2O_3	SiO_2	P_2O_5	SO_3	Cl	K_2O	CaO	TiO_2	MnO	Fe_2O_3	SnO_2	PbO
38	gene	5.63	3.15	1.39	63.56	0	0.13	0.6	5.16	5.7	0.11	0.33	1.06	8.27	4.93
	E-t	0.2	0.23	0.11	2.12	0	0.17	0.06	0.07	0.24	0.04	0.07	0.45	2.03	0.59
	pv	6.11	3.06	1.69	67.68	0	0.18	0.76	5.75	5.65	0.09	0.37	0.8	2.89	5.24
	E-t	0.18	0.17	0.68	0.15	0	0.05	0.1	0.1	0.47	0.07	0.06	0.05	0.95	0.87
39	gene	3.12	1.54	1.33	49.12	0	0.07	0.42	3.03	3.22	0.07	0.03	0.4	6.81	30.85
	E-t	0.02	0.06	0.13	1.72	0	0.12	0.1	0.18	0.28	0.05	0.06	0.15	1.82	0.53
	pv	3.26	1.49	1.29	51.88	0	0	0	3.22	2.98	0.09	0.03	0.29	1.76	33.71
	E-t	0.09	0.02	0.43	0.77	0	0	0	0.13	0.19	0.07	0.04	0.1	0.23	1.25

SEM results in % of oxyde volumes
gene: general composition; pv: vitreous phase; E-t: type interval

- Two samples (nos 44 and 45) are distinguished by a calco-alkaline glaze completely free of lead and tin (Na2O≈10%, K20≈5% and CaO≈7%), more siliceous and more aluminous. The microstructures of the glazes differ from one sample to another. In one of the samples (no. 45), numerous crystals neoformed of diopside are distributed throughout the thickness of the glaze and create in it an opacification or at least an opalescence which is difficult to estimate with the naked eye given the level of alteration. The second sample (no. 44) nevertheless presents a totally homogenous glaze, without inclusions.

WHITE OPAQUE GLAZES ON CLAYEY FABRICS

Two samples (Fig. 47) are covered with a white-coloured glaze, apparently opaque. The two clayey fabrics are not similar (see above) and the two pieces are not comparable from the point of view of the glaze either. If they do both contain the same chemical elements, the proportions are completely different (Table 26). Glaze 39 is much more plumbiferous (more than 30% PbO). The chemical composition of the glaze obtained by PIXE and SEM (Table 24) confirms that this shard belongs to the group known as 'Samarra 2', defined by R. B. Mason: it is in fact very close to those ceramics with opaque white glaze coming from Samarra and Nippur (Mason and Tite 1994, table 2 p. 82), of which the fabric is like that one characterized by the presence of glass inclusions (see above). The X-ray diffraction analysis of the glaze also allowed the identification of the presence of cassiterite as an opacifier as well as other phases able to correspond to quartz, cristobalite, diopside and lead silicate (Fig. 74).

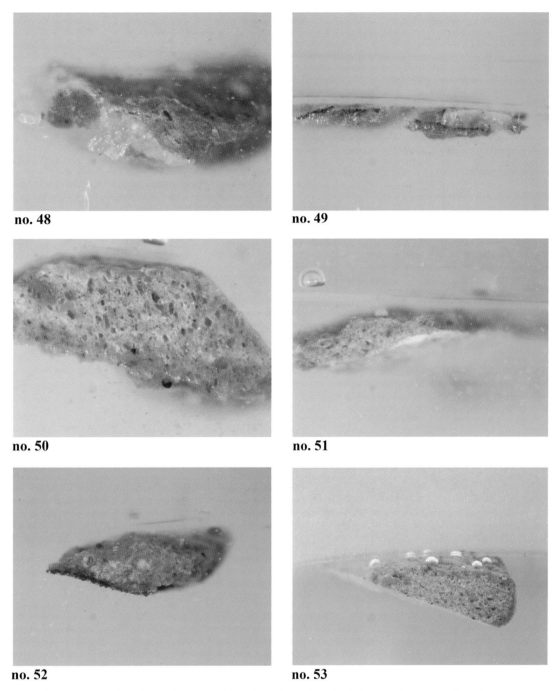

no. 48

no. 49

no. 50

no. 51

no. 52

no. 53

Figure 69a: photographs under a binocular magnifying glass of samples of polychrome glazes (© C2RMF, A. Bouquillon 2010).

The glaze of no. 38 is much less plumbiferous (less than 5% PbO), more alkaline and more siliceous, but also rich in cassirite micro crystals (more than 10% SnO_2). These elements are also characteristic of the opaque white glazes analyzed by Mason and Tite, considered to have been produced at Basra, but which nonetheless contain less tin oxide.[8] These differences in the clayey fabric and in the glaze therefore seem attributable to different workshop recipes, and using distinct supply sources of raw materials.

---

[8] Mason and Tite 1997, table 2 p. 45.

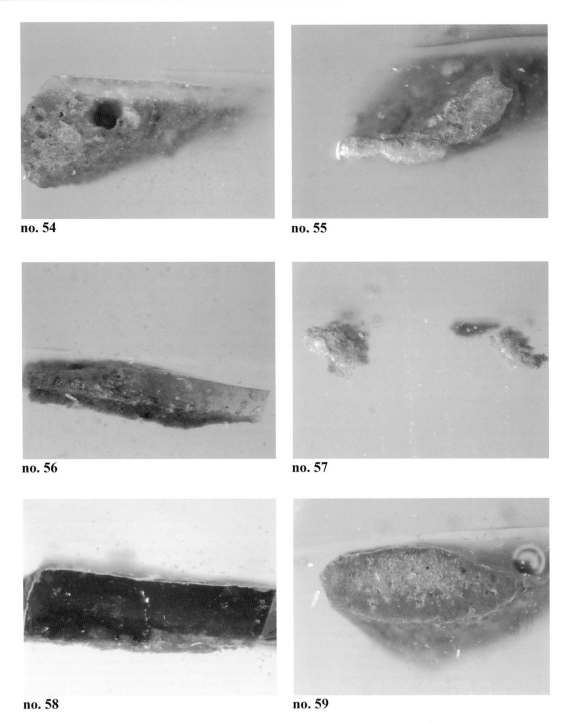

no. 54

no. 55

no. 56

no. 57

no. 58

no. 59

Figure 69b: photographs under a binocular magnifying glass of samples of polychrome glazes (© C2RMF, A. Bouquillon 2010).

POLYCHROME DECORATIONS ON CLAYEY FABRICS

The fabrics of these ceramics are relatively homogeneous (see above). All the glazes (Fig. 48, Table 29) are largely plumbiferous (more than 50% PbO). However, the polychromy leads to a great complexity in the colouring techniques and in the palette of pigments used: the differences thus arise in the technique of decoration and in the types of colorant. Two types of decoration were distinguished: those consisting of glazes coloured to the core, and those whose colour is linked to the interaction of the transparent glaze with an underlying slip. The glazes analyzed are very altered, and in a certain number of cases it was not possible to perform the analysis

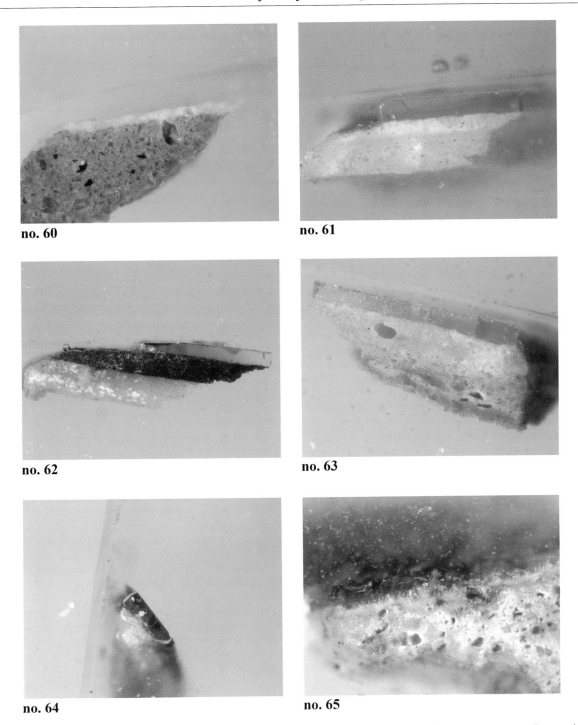

no. 60   no. 61

no. 62   no. 63

no. 64   no. 65

Figure 69c: photographs under a binocular magnifying glass of samples of polychrome glazes (© C2RMF, A. Bouquillon 2010).

well either because the sample did not present sufficient glaze (nos 50, 53, 59, 65, 65b, 57) or because the glass was corroded to the core (nos 51, 52, 49, 68, 55, 60).

Yᴇʟʟᴏᴡ ᴅᴇᴄᴏʀᴀᴛɪᴏɴs (ɴᴏs 60, 48, 70, 55)

At least three different yellows can be distinguished by eye: one very acidic and rather pale, another warmer one and a third with light coloration but which has preserved its brilliance. These aspects correspond to the different types of coloration. The first (samples nos 60/F and 48/A) is a yellow pigment of lead and tin, obtained from a base of tin and marked by a slight

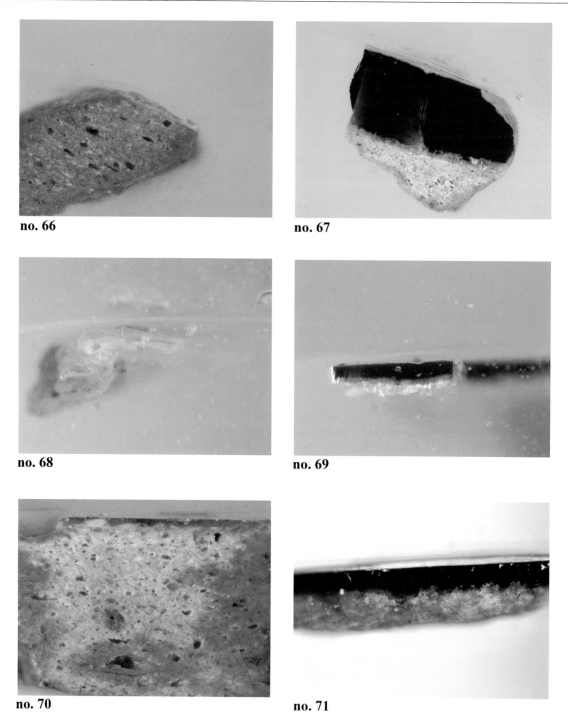

no. 66

no. 67

no. 68

no. 69

no. 70

no. 71

Figure 69d: photographs under a binocular magnifying glass of samples of polychrome glazes (© C2RMF, A. Bouquillon 2010).

augmentation of lead. The second (sample no. 70/M), seems to have been obtained from chrome (0.6% Cr_2O_3). While the lead content is very significant (65%), this shard nonetheless seems to have too deep a yellow for the coloration not to have been brought about by lead oxide. The X-ray microdiffraction analysis of the sample did not provide results allowing the determination of the exact nature of the colorant, only diopside and lead feldspars having been highlighted (Fig. 71). The third sample (no. 55) does not contain yellow pigment: it was applied on a white slip and it is its richness in lead oxide (55%) which gives it this straw-yellow colour. These results were confirmed by the PIXE analyses carried out on shards A, B and C and on sample 70.

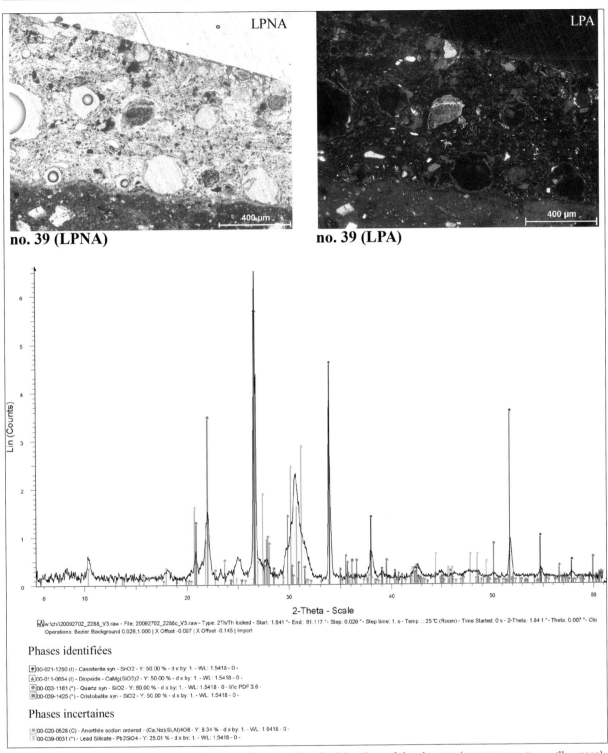

Figure 70: *diffractogram and photographs in MO (LPNA and LPA) of the glaze of shard no. 39 (© C2RMF, A. Bouquillon 2010).*

In the *corpus* analyzed, the yellow was obtained according to three different procedures:[9] in the form of lead and tin yellow, chrome yellow and by a transparent glaze coloured by an excess of lead (no. 55). The lead and tin yellow is little used in Western glazes and in glass. However, Kaczmarczyk and Hedges (1983, 82) mention the existence of such colours very early, around 330–350 AD, and maybe even from the 1st century, in the glass production of the Middle East.

---

[9] Mason (2004, 263, pl. C.11) describes a 'yellow-field ware' of the 'buff ware' type where the yellow is obtained with antimony.

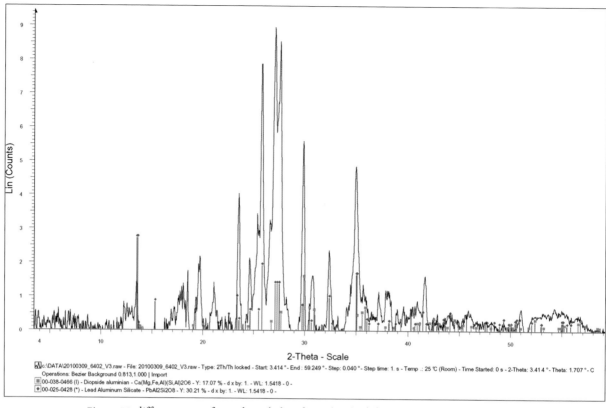

Figure 71: diffractogram of sample 70 (taken from shard M) (© C2RMF, A. Bouquillon 2010).

On the other hand, concerning the chrome-based yellow, all the authors are in agreement in dating the appearance of this pigment in Europe to the end of the 18th century or more certainly to the beginning of the 19th (Kühn and Curra 1986, 187–200). The use of chrome in the glazes, therefore, would be much older in Khorasan. According to our analyses, this use is not at all accidental and it obviously points to a recipe employing the coloration possibilities of this metallic element. In fact, the simultaneous presence of chrome and lead reinforces the yellow colour (Brongniart 1877). The existence of numerous chrome deposits in proximity to the site of Nishapur, on one hand (Yaghubpur 2006), and its use in the black tints analyses on the other, suggest that the potters of Nishapur had clearly used it much earlier than European artisans.

WHITE DECORATIONS (NOS *54, 61, 63, 66*)

These are uncoloured glazes placed on a white slip (Table 27), and in one case a whitish glaze. These glazes are homogeneous, with neither crystals nor bubbles. Only one sample (no. 54, shard C/H) contains a few grains of unmelted silica. Nos 61 and 63 (which correspond to the external and internal faces of shard G) have the same composition: approximately 54% PbO, 39% SiO_2, 2.5% Al_2O_3, 2% (Na_2O+K_2O) and 1% CaO. The glaze of no. 54 has a similar composition, with slightly more aluminium (3.9% as opposed to 2.5%) and less potassium (0.5% as opposed to 1.5%). It is perhaps another clay which was added to the mixture.

The glaze of no. 66 (shard J) is, on the other hand, very different: it is more plumbiferous (67% PbO) and less aluminous (<1% Al_2O_3); it contains almost 1% iron oxide and 0.3% copper oxide and is thus probably not perfectly white. It is the only one analyzed not to have been applied on a slip.

Table 27: Estimated composition of 2 white slips (sample no. 62) (© C2RMF, A. Bouquillon 2010).

	Na_2O	Al_2O_3	SiO_2	K_2O	CaO	MnO	Fe_2O_3	PbO
Middle slip		13%	70%	4%	2%		<1%	9%
Lower slip	<1%	14%	68%	4%	1%	<1%	<1%	10%

Table 28: Elementary chemical composition of black slip (sample no. 62) (© C2RMF, A. Bouquillon 2010).

	Na_2O	MgO	Al_2O_3	SiO_2	P_2O_5	SO_3	Cl	K_2O	CaO	TiO_2	Cr_2O_3	MnO	Fe_2O_3	PbO
Moyenne	**0.73**	**0.43**	**12.03**	**41.67**	**0.1**	**0.12**	**0.08**	**4.22**	**4.26**	**0.59**	**0.05**	**10**	**17.15**	**8.58**
écart-type	0.14	0.2	0.55	6.21	0.1	0.18	0.03	0.18	5.93	0.06	0.05	1.53	1.24	0.17

Elementary chemical composition in % of oxyde volume
The content in clacium oxyde is very heterogeneous

BLACK DECORATIONS (NOS 71, 64, 62, 52)

The procedures observed in the *corpus* analyzed to obtain black also show the diversity of the known techniques and the coexistence of opaque blacks based on manganese and transparent blacks obtained by a fine transparent glaze placed on a base of black slip. In addition to the colorations in the vitreous mass, the technique of coloured slips was also used. The use of magnesiochromite in the raw materials of the black slips analyzed confirms that the potters of Nishapur used the local resources to the maximum extent (Fig. 78).

In the case of sample nos 71 and 64 (shard C/H) the glaze is black, probably opaque, and is applied on a white slip. In the composition of this glaze one finds chrome associated with vanadium, both concentrated in small crystals rich in chrome, magnesium, iron and aluminium (magnesiochromite). X-ray microdiffractometry, which should have enabled us to identify precisely the crystals of sample 64, did not produce results, probably due to the small size of the sample. These crystals had already been identified on two fritware shards: no. ps3, with a blue glaze close to a black decoration, and ps7, with painted black underglaze decoration (see below). Sample no. 62 (shard G) is very different. The black glaze is more traditional, transparent, slightly coloured by manganese and iron oxides (c. 0.5% MnO and 0.5% Fe_2O_3); it is applied on a black slip, itself placed on two layers of similar white partially vitrified slip (Table 28).

Sample no. 52 (shard B) is too altered for the glaze to be analyzed; one can nonetheless notice in electronic microscopy the presence of grains very rich in manganese in the corroded layer, leading one to suppose that it also a glaze or a pigment coloured by iron and manganese oxides.

GREEN GLAZES (NOS 69, 56, 58, 67)

The green is obtained by the addition of copper, as is normal. Nevertheless, the presence of associated zinc leads one to suppose either a contamination by this element or a joint provision of copper and zinc, which is possible if the potters used a recycled alloy (such as brass) as a source of copper employed as a colorant.[10]

---

[10] This type of practice is frequent since antiquity, in which one finds associations of copper and tin in the glaze, proof of the use of bronze as a colorant, for example in certain Egyptian blues or certain glazes (Kaczmarczyk and Hedges 1983, 63). One should nevertheless be prudent. Hedges and Moorey (1975) noticed such an association in the pre-Islamic glazes of Kish and Nineveh in Iraq, and if they put forward the hypothesis of the use of metal alloy shavings as a source of copper, they will overcome the problem of the relative proportions of Zn (Pb and Sn) and copper.

Table 29: Elementary chemical composition of polychrome glazes (SEM) (© C2RMF, A. Bouquillon 2010).

Group	No. C2RMF		Na₂O	MgO	Al₂O₃	SiO₂	P₂O₅	SO₃	Cl	K₂O	CaO	TiO₂	V₂O₅	Cr₂O₃	MnO	Fe₂O₃	CoO	CuO	ZnO	SnO₂	PbO
Yellow glazes	60		-	-	-	-	-	-	-	-	-	-	-	-	-	-	-	-	-	-	-
	70	gene	0.48	0.39	2.66	28.02	0	0.27	0.35	0.76	0.71	0.24		0.61	0.01	0.76		0.02			64.57
		E-T	0.12	0.05	0.07	0.83	0	0.17	0.06	0.01	0.15	0.12		0.02	0.01	0.02		0.02			0.67
	48	gene	0.07	0.1	0.39	25.07	0	0.64	0.27	0.06	0.97			0.08	0.1	0.28	0.05	0.1	0.12	3.38	68.24
		E-T	0.03	0.07	0.1	1.76	0	0.32	0.06	0.02	0.14			0.08	0.09	0.12	0.05	0.11	0.18	2.29	0.82
		pv	0.07	0.12	0.37	28.62	0	0.58	0.2	0.1	0.92			0	0.08	0.18	0.08	0.11	0.15	0.46	67.96
		E-T	0.12	0.11	0.07	1.7	0	0.23	0.17	0.06	0.28			0	0.02	0.19	0.11	0.03	0.13	0.32	0.81
	55	gene	0.07	0.09	4.19	38.46	0	0.33	0.02	0.54	0.63			0.05	0.09	0.5		0.1		0.03	54.89
		E-T	0.03	0.08	0.48	0.7	0	0.29	0.04	0.04	0.01			0.04	0.07	0.05		0.17		0.06	0.42
Clear glazes	63	gene	0.6	0.07	2.38	39.15	0	0.39	0.11	1.47	0.72	0.08				0.19					54.84
		E-T	0.03	0.05	0.07	0.16	0	0.35	0.09	0.05	0.04	0.05				0.08					0.48
	61	gene	0.66	0.22	2.51	38.63	0	0.61	0.13	1.54	1.31					0.47					53.91
		E-T	0.08	0.06	0.07	0.24	0	0.35	0.07	0.06	0.1					0.18					0.48
	54	gene	0.1	0.21	3.91	39.94	0	0.45	0.1	0.46	0.91	0.1				0.69					53.13
		E-T	0.09	0.07	0.44	0.84	0	0.39	0.1	0.08	0.14	0.06				0.11					1.37
	66	gene	0.18	0.28	0.92	28.19		0.51	0	0.66	1.13	0.06			0.1	0.92		0.32			66.73
		E-T	0.05	0.04	0.19	0.47		0.14	0	0.12	0.09	0.08			0.11	0.08		0.11			0.68
	64	gene	0.15	0.55	4.65	36.07	0	0.22	0.1	0.65	0.46	0.08	0.13	1.68	0.06	1.74					53.46
		E-T	0.05	0.36	0.41	0.75	0	0.16	0.09	0.13	0.03	0.07	0.16	0.65	0.1	0.19					0.49
	62	gene	0.55	0.2	2.45	39.74	0	0.35	0.14	1.13	0.77	0.04			0.52	0.43					53.54
		E-T	0.06	0.09	0.29	1.04	0	0.12	0.04	0.13	0.14	0.07			0.21	0.17					1.74
Black glazes	71	gene	0.05	3.24	4.98	27.9	0	0	0	0.4	0.41	0.02		13.86	0.02	3.88		0.1			45.14
		E-T	0.03	1.94	0.57	4.11	0	0	0	0.08	0.09	0.02		8.66	0.02	1.1		0.09			8.14
		pv	0.13	0.33	4.58	35.41	0	0	0	0.69	0.58	0.13		0.21	0.01	1.54		0.02			56.36
		E-T	0.1	0.05	0.32	2.03	0	0	0	0.06	0.05	0.08		0.14	0.02	0.25		0.04			1.87
		gr Cr Mg Al	0.01	19.8	12.3	0.21	0	0.03	0	0.03	0.07	0.09		60.46	0.19	6.48		0.27			0.06
		Fe	0.03	1.08	1.84	0.05	0	0.06	0	0.03	0.02	0.03		2.52	0.15	1.09		0.07			0.08

	C1	C2	C3	C4	C5	C6	C7	C8	C9	C10	C11	C12	C13	C14	C15
56 gene	0.27	0.9	3.15	30.33	0	0.55	0.2	0.7	3.88	0.19	0.08	2	0.92		56.83
E-T	0.17	0.25	0.62	0.68	0	0.19	0.06	0.12	0.76	0.07	0.07	0.39	0.18		2.88
pv	0.38	0.34	3.31	29.75	0	0.43	0.13	0.71	2.8	0.22	0.06	1.89	1		58.98
E-T	0.1	0.1	0.88	0.65	0	0.2	0.03	0.2	0.27	0.07	0.11	0.34	0.09		2.08
58 gene	0.23	0.43	1.85	27.57	0	0.73	0.05	0.29	1.33	0.18	0.03	0.91	3.62	0.68	62.08
E-T	0.07	0.08	0.55	0.74	0	0.14	0.06	0.12	0.13	0.03	0.04	0.04	0.35	0.21	0.96
67 gene	0	0.25	0.42	24.93	0	0.28	0.04	0.27	1.71	0.04		0.36	4.63	0.11	66.97
E-T	0	0.07	0.05	0.32	0	0.1	0.07	0.08	0.03	0.04	0.04	0.04	0.1	0.09	0.35
69 gene	0.77	0.4	3.92	32.35	0	0.12	0.12	1.14	1.4	0.23		0.73	3.44		55.38
E-T	0.06	0.04	0.26	0.43	0	0.21	0.09	0.16	0.18	0.02		0.13	0.36		0.07

Green glazes

SEM results in % of oxyde volumes
gene: general composition; pv: vitreous phase; E-T: type interva

The glazes of samples nos 69 (shard L), 58 (shard E) and 67 (shard K) are very transparent, very homogeneous and for the most part without either bubbles or crystals. The compositions differ: samples nos 69 and 56 (shard D) contain 55–57% PbO as against 62% and 67% for nos 58 and 67. K_2O varies from 0.3% to 1.1% and CaO from 1.4% to 3.9%. The aluminium content varies greatly: from 0.2% for no. 67 to 3.9% for no. 69. Nonetheless, on the basis of major chemical elements one can propose to group samples nos 56 and 69 on one hand (shards D and L) and nos 58 and 67 (shards E and K) on the other.

The four glazes are coloured by copper oxide whose content ranges from 0.9% to 4.6%. It is to be noted that rare tin microcrystals exist in sample no. 58. These small grains perhaps signal that the copper, the main colorant element, was introduced in the form of bronze shavings. In glaze no. 67 the copper appears to be linked to zinc, which would thus be brass. Variable mixtures of Cu/Mn/Sn or Zn with greater or lesser amounts of iron explain, at least in part, the nuances observed, although it must always be borne in mind that the alteration by burial is very marked and that the copper is mobile through leaching, sometimes causing a discoloration of the glaze.

Glaze no. 56 appears lighter and apparently presents a slightly more opalescent aspect, probably due to the very numerous small crystals of calcium silicate and magnesium (diopside?) scattered during the vitreous phase.

These glazes have very little developed interfaces, except in no. 69 which presents very long crystals of 'lead feldspars'. These crystallizations would be linked to a cooling speed slower than that of the other shards (Molera *et al.* 2001).

Glazes on fritware

The majority of the glazes are much altered (Fig. 49). Their colours are between blue-green and dark blue; shards ps2 and ps5 are uncoloured. The relative homogeneity revealed by analysis of the fabrics (more than 85% of silica, a little sodium (3% on average of Na_2O) and approximately 5% aluminium) is not found in the composition of the glazes. These allow the shards to be divided into at least three groups:

- Shards ps1 and ps4 have glazes of the alkalino-plumbiferous type: they contain 7–10% PbO and approximately 7% Na_2O; calcium is around 5%. These glazes are thick (~300 µm for shard ps4) and they are

Table 30: PIXE analyses of glazes and decorations of fritwares (© C2RMF, A. Bouquillon 2010).

No. of shard	No. C2RMF	Ref. PIXE	Na₂O	MgO	Al₂O₃	SiO₂	P₂O₅	SO₃	Cl	K₂O	CaO	TiO₂
BrillA (standard)		11fev003	13.93	2.65	1.01	67.66	0.046	0.19	0.10	2.62	4.57	0.87
N07 surv shahr 3 gl pt1	ps1	11fev018	11.84	3.56	1.18	62.41	0.086	0.20	0.75	1.36	3.50	0.06
N07 surv shahr 3 gl pt2	ps1	11fev019	12.10	3.60	1.20	62.64	0.000	0.18	0.65	1.31	3.28	0.08
N07 surv shahr2 9-23 gl pt 1	ps2	11fev031	5.88	2.50	2.45	82.67	0.211	0.23	0.08	1.87	2.19	0.08
N07 surv shahr 1 gl pt1	ps3	11fev009	10.72	3.87	3.12	68.47	0.267	0.39	0.25	2.31	5.40	0.08
N07 surv shahr2 gl pt 1	ps4	11fev025	14.20	3.72	2.29	68.18	0.166	0.39	0.92	1.90	4.68	0.16
N07 surv shahr2 gl pt 2	ps4	11fev026	14.57	4.09	2.21	68.84	0.153	0.51	0.70	1.69	4.14	0.10
NO7 T26 101 gl pt1	ps5	11fev012	6.35	3.36	4.04	72.49	0.195	0.41	0.24	2.59	7.15	0.15
NO7 T26 101 gl pt2	ps5	11fev013	5.50	3.69	4.98	71.93	0.376	0.46	0.28	2.63	7.12	0.14
NO7 T26 101 gl + lustre pt1	ps5	11fev014	3.34	2.69	3.10	77.75	0.000	0.16	0.09	3.32	5.44	0.16
NO7 T26 101 gl + lustre pt2	ps5	11fev015	3.51	2.88	3.10	76.90	0.149	0.14	0.08	3.20	5.54	0.18
N06 419 gl pt 1	ps6	11fev028	8.21	2.49	1.30	53.41	0.000	0.00	0.48	0.31	3.69	0.00
N06 419 gl pt 2	ps6	11fev029	7.71	2.34	1.15	50.66	0.000	0.00	0.33	0.43	3.60	0.01
N07 surv shahr z4 gl entre 2	ps7	11fev022	15.26	4.31	1.40	66.32	0.168	0.30	0.78	1.84	5.58	0.05
N07 surv shahr z4 gl surface	ps7	11fev023	9.41	3.45	2.90	71.83	0.227	0.32	0.48	2.13	5.63	0.07

Chemical composition in oxyde volume %. Compositions normalized at 100%
In red: at the limit of detection level. Dash: under detection limit

completely transparent (less than 0.5% SnO_2 does not cause opacification), but they present strong degrees of alteration on the surface and around the bubbles, and at the fabric/glaze interface for shard ps1.

- Shard ps6 presents a plumbiferous glaze opacified with tin oxide (25% PbO–7.5% SnO_2). Its contents, very different to the others, imply another manufacturing technique. The glaze, very thick (~400 μm), is quite well preserved. It is homogeneous, with neither bubbles nor crystals except for cassiterite (SnO_2).

- Shards ps2, ps3, ps5 and ps7 offer very siliceous glazes (almost 70% SiO_2). They are sodic and calcic, magnesian, coloured by iron or cobalt sometimes associated with copper. All these glazes are transparent, coloured in the mass, and most of the time quite well-preserved. The more elevated aluminium and lime quantity favour a greater durability of the glass (Newton 1989). Shards ps2 and ps3 present neoformed diopside crystals (calcium and magnesium silicates). These crystallizations are perhaps due to different thermodynamic conditions at the time of firing. Shard ps3 shows the same general characteristics as the other glazes of this group, but reveals the presence of small grains rich in metallic elements (Cr, Fe, Cu and also Mg and Al) encircled with a ring of diopside. These scattered grains could come from the black glaze of the very close band of decoration where the black is not painted under the glaze; it is a border of solid black glaze.

MnO	Fe$_2$O$_3$	CoO	NiO	CuO	ZnO	As$_2$O$_5$	Rb$_2$O	SrO	Ag$_2$O	SnO$_2$	Sb$_2$O$_5$	BaO	PbO	Total
0.99	1.03	0.173	0.022	1.21	0.05	0.003	0.009	0.120	0.003	0.228	1.927	0.520	0.07	100
0.04	0.63	0.006	0.010	1.65	0.01	0.000	0.003	0.046	0.007	0.250	0.000	0.000	12.38	100
0.03	0.65	0.004	0.011	1.66	0.02	0.000	0.000	0.046	0.000	0.172	0.000	0.000	12.36	100
0.03	1.21	0.007	0.007	0.05	0.02	0.000	0.004	0.033	0.000	0.000	0.000	0.000	0.47	100
0.04	1.07	0.009	0.000	3.77	0.02	0.009	0.002	0.063	0.000	0.017	0.008	0.000	0.12	100
0.04	1.87	0.267	0.009	0.03	0.01	0.269	0.002	0.064	0.000	0.000	0.000	0.000	0.85	100
0.04	1.72	0.207	0.008	0.02	0.00	0.223	0.003	0.051	0.000	0.000	0.031	0.056	0.64	100
0.04	2.19	0.183	0.003	0.23	0.02	0.122	0.004	0.062	0.000	0.000	0.000	0.169	0.01	100
0.04	2.22	0.182	0.002	0.20	0.02	0.151	0.004	0.067	0.000	0.000	0.000	0.000	0.01	100
0.04	1.36	0.107	0.000	1.50	0.02	0.037	0.004	0.048	0.705	0.000	0.000	0.131	0.01	100
0.04	1.82	0.129	0.000	1.73	0.02	0.051	0.003	0.047	0.460	0.020	0.000	0.000	0.01	100
0.03	0.51	0.004	0.007	1.36	0.01	0.000	0.001	0.022	0.000	7.160	0.000	0.000	21.02	100
0.03	0.59	0.004	0.008	1.47	0.01	0.000	0.000	0.023	0.000	7.663	0.024	0.000	23.94	100
0.05	0.71	0.006	0.003	2.84	0.00	0.016	0.002	0.074	0.006	0.023	0.000	0.000	0.26	100
0.04	0.75	0.004	0.001	2.41	0.01	0.005	0.000	0.063	0.006	0.026	0.036	0.000	0.21	100

Sample ps7 is distinctive as it is constituted of two shards joined together by a glaze. The analysis demonstrates that the glaze has an identical composition on each fragment. One of the two shards presents crystals on the fabric-glaze interface which appear white in the SEM images (Fig. 72, Table 31) and black in the petrographic image (Fig. 76). They are mainly composed of Cr (~60%), Mg (~13%), Al (~7%), Fe and Cu. This could be a black underglaze decoration based on magnesiochromite (see above). The composition and the technology of this decoration painted in black under a turquoise glaze is similar to those of Iranian shards assigned to the 12th century, examined and reproduced by R. B. Mason and M. S. Tite (Mason *et al.* 2001, 198–200, fig. 4, 199).

Shards ps4 and ps5, and perhaps ps7, present glazes coloured with cobalt (detected by EDS). To refine the data, we have, despite alterations, more specifically studied the glazes with the aid of the AGLAE accelerator, by PIXE, to more certainly identify the presence of this element and of those with which it is associated (Table 30).

Cobalt exists in samples ps4 and ps5 but can also be detected, in weaker concentrations, undetectable by SEM, in ps3. On the other hand, it was not measured in the surface layers of ps7. The cobalt is associated with arsenic and iron in ps4 and ps5, but not in ps3, where cobalt and zinc appear to be linked.

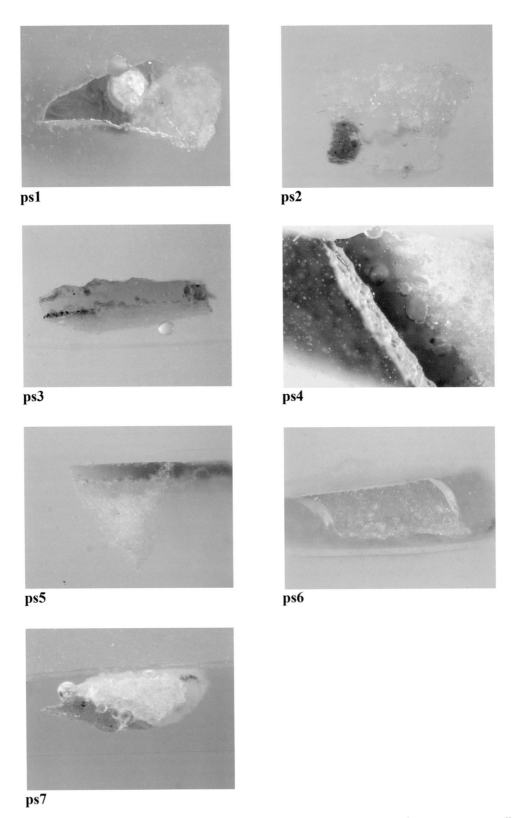

ps1

ps2

ps3

ps4

ps5

ps6

ps7

Figure 72: photographs under a binocular magnifying glass of samples of glazes on fritware (© C2RMF, A. Bouquillon 2010).

Table 31: *Elementary chemical composition of glazes on fritwares (SEM) (© C2RMF, A. Bouquillon 2010).*

No. C2RMF		Na_2O	MgO	Al_2O_3	SiO_2	P_2O_5	SO_3	Cl	K_2O	CaO	TiO_2	Cr_2O_3	MnO	Fe_2O_3	CoO	CuO	SnO_2	PbO
ps1	gene	8.75	3.25	0.94	65.66	0	0.03	0.77	1.77	4.25	0.05		0.11	0.79		1.86	0.38	11.38
	E-T	0.28	0.13	0.08	0.51	0	0.05	0.12	0.05	0.12	0.04		0.1	0.04		0.09	0.18	0.33
ps2	gene	11.2	4.18	1.82	71.76	0	0.29	0.61	2.25	5.74	0.1			1.28				0.76
	E-T	0.38	0.08	0.05	0.72	0	0.1	0.21	0.05	0.37	0.04			0.1				0.11
ps3	gene	12.56	3.36	1.38	67.9	0	0.34	0.62	2.89	5.83	0.06		0.06	1.25		3.48		0.28
	E-T	0.22	0.11	0.02	0.54	0	0.07	0.09	0.07	0.18	0.02		0.03	0.1		0.29		0.16
ps4	gene	11.71	4.07	1.46	64.02		0.17	0.37	1.93	6.24	0.16			2.85	0.68			6.35
	E-T	0.09	0.22	0.02	0.19		0.07	0.03	0.03	0.2	0.01			0.15	0.1			0.44
ps5	gene	11.64	3.34	1.89	69.94		0.37	0.48	2.07	8.25	0.1		0.07	1.62	0.2	0.03		
	E-T	0.22	0.11	0.01	0.86		0.06	0.05	0.06	0.17	0.06		0.09	0.35	0.05	0.02		
ps6	gene	6.1	2.02	0.95	50.56	0	0	0.4	1.43	3.22	0.09		0.03	0.72		1.72	7.47	25.31
	E-T	0.03	0.04	0.05	0.47	0	0	0.04	0.02	0.08	0.08		0.03	0.08		0.09	0.21	0.48
ps7 — face a	gene	12.55	3.15	1.28	70.75	0	0.42	0.63	2.51	5.32	0.1		0.03	0.76	0.04	2.28		0.18
	E-T	0.26	0.06	0.18	0.78	0	0	0.1	0.04	0.25	0.04		0.03	0.07	0.07	0.31		0.06
ps7 — face b	gene	12.74	3.03	1.38	70.05	0	0.33	0.95	2.57	6.02	0.08		0.03	1.54	0	1.01		0.26
	E-T	0.47	0.39	0.17	0.55	0	0.08	0.09	0.15	0.95	0.03		0.03	1.05	0	0.37		0.11
ps7 — interface side a	gene	13.25	3.58	1.08	67.79	0	0.43	0.63	2.52	6.32	0.07	0.03	0.06	0.8	0.04	3.01	0.17	0.21
	E-T	0.26	0.09	0.09	0.49	0	0.09	0.13	0.02	0.04	0.04	0.04	0.02	0.03	0.06	0.09	0.03	0.22
ps7 — interface side b	gene	12.88	3.65	1.1	67.87	0.05	0.39	0.48	2.42	6.81	0.08	0.04	0.06	0.87	0	2.88	0.13	0.25
	E-T	0.24	0.13	0.14	0.13	0.07	0.07	0.17	0.01	0.51	0.02	0.04	0.08	0.08	0	0.17	0.19	0.03

SEM results in % of oxyde volumes
gene: general composition; pv: vitreous phase; E-t: type interva

Table 32: Standard DRN composition.

	Ref. PIXE	Na₂O	MgO	Al₂O₃	SiO₂	P₂O₅	SO₃	Cl	K₂O	CaO	TiO₂	MnO	Fe₂O₃	NiO	CuO	ZnO	Rb₂O	SrO	ZrO₂	PbO	TOTAL
DRNi1	11fev001	3.07	4.20	18.37	54.54	0.25	0.42	0.04	1.62	6.80	1.05	0.21	9.40	0.001	0.005	0.017	0.009	0.053	0.011	0.002	100.09
DRNi2	11fev002	2.95	4.11	18.20	55.07	0.14	0.39	0.04	1.67	6.91	1.01	0.21	9.26	0.002	0.004	0.020	0.009	0.057	0.007	0.001	100.05
DRNf	11fev060	2.97	4.00	18.07	54.05	0.36	0.43	0.06	1.60	6.99	1.10	0.21	10.13	0.001	0.005	0.015	0.011	0.054	0.014	0.002	100.06
DRNi	01dec001	2.94	4.04	18.00	54.13	0.18	0.41	0.04	1.74	7.10	1.08	0.22	10.09	0.001	0.005	0.020	0.012	0.060	0.024		100.094
DRNi	01dec002	2.90	3.90	17.63	55.25	0.15	0.42	0.04	1.65	7.03	1.10	0.22	9.69	0.000	0.004	0.016	0.011	0.059	0.014		100.091
DRNf		2.83	4.02	18.17	54.16	0.25	0.30	0.05	1.68	7.16	1.07	0.22	10.08	0.001	0.005	0.017	0.007	0.061	0.013		100.086
DRNi	04sep100	2.55	3.94	17.84	54.57	0.17	0.33	0.05	1.73	7.24	1.14	0.25	10.16	0.001	0.005	0.019	0.009	0.061	0.056		100.12
DRNi	04sep101	2.74	4.01	17.87	54.15	0.22	0.34	0.05	1.70	7.29	1.12	0.24	10.24	0.002	0.005	0.020	0.008	0.062	0.010		100.08
DRNf	04sep125	2.78	3.98	17.80	54.66	0.15	0.29	0.05	1.71	7.07	1.22	0.22	10.03	0.002	0.005	0.019	0.008	0.062	0.016		100.07
DRNf	04sep126	2.83	4.04	17.94	54.21	0.15	0.43	0.04	1.69	7.26	1.10	0.23	10.05	0.001	0.004	0.021	0.012	0.065	0.012		100.09
DRNi	28aou001	2.88	4.08	18.09	54.42	0.20	0.12	0.04	1.67	6.82	1.05	0.25	10.01	0.002	0.004	0.022	0.009	0.057	0.008		99.73
DRNi	28aou002	2.88	4.00	18.06	54.77	0.22	0.38	0.04	1.64	6.98	1.04	0.25	9.43	0.004	0.005	0.017	0.002	0.060	0.009		99.78
DRNf	28aou056	2.95	4.11	18.24	54.37	0.21	0.35	0.06	1.69	6.96	1.01	0.27	9.44	0.002	0.004	0.017	0.010	0.061	0.018		99.75
DRNi1	12mai001	2.70	3.83	17.71	55.61	0.15	0.66	0.05	1.66	6.84	1.10	0.22	9.49	0.002	0.004	0.021	0.007	0.057	0.008		100.11
DRNi2	12mai002	2.96	3.93	18.23	54.66	0.00	0.57	0.11	1.61	6.88	0.98	0.21	9.82	0.002	0.004	0.021	0.009	0.053	0.006		100.04
DRNf1	12mai084	3.01	4.08	17.87	54.63	0.09	1.19	0.04	1.61	6.95	1.00	0.21	9.25	0.002	0.003	0.020	0.009	0.051	0.016		100.03
DRNf2	12mai085	2.81	4.23	17.87	55.10	0.15	0.58	0.03	1.59	6.85	0.99	0.21	9.55	0.002	0.003	0.024	0.005	0.048	0.001		100.03
DRNf3	12mai086	2.93	4.19	18.26	54.76	0.29	0.57	0.04	1.58	7.01	1.03	0.22	9.09	0.003	0.005	0.018	0.009	0.053	0.009		100.07

DRN: composition of the standard given by the CRPG of Nancy (analyses ICP-MS)

% OXYDE VOLUMES

Na2O	MgO	Al2O3	SiO2	P2O5	K2O	CaO	TiO2	MnO	Fe2O3	H2O+	H2O-	CO2	Total majors
2.99	4.4	17.52	52.85	0.25	1.7	7.05	1.09	0.22	9.7	2.22	0.25	0.1	100.34

ppm

S	Cl	Cu	Zn	Ni	Sr	Sn	Pb
350	400	50	145	15	400	2	55

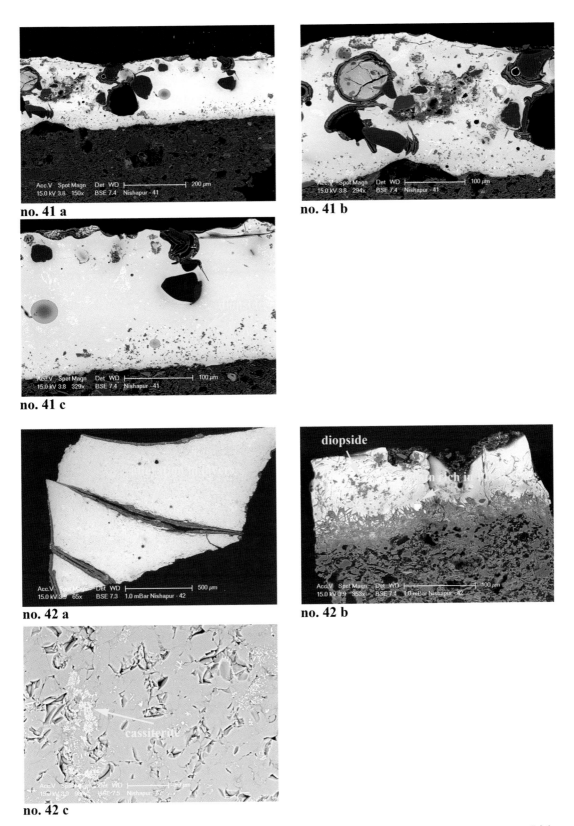

no. 41 a

no. 41 b

no. 41 c

no. 42 a

no. 42 b

no. 42 c

Figure 73a: images of samples of glazes in scanning electronic microscopy (retrodiffused electrons, composition mode) (© C2RMF, A. Bouquillon 2010).

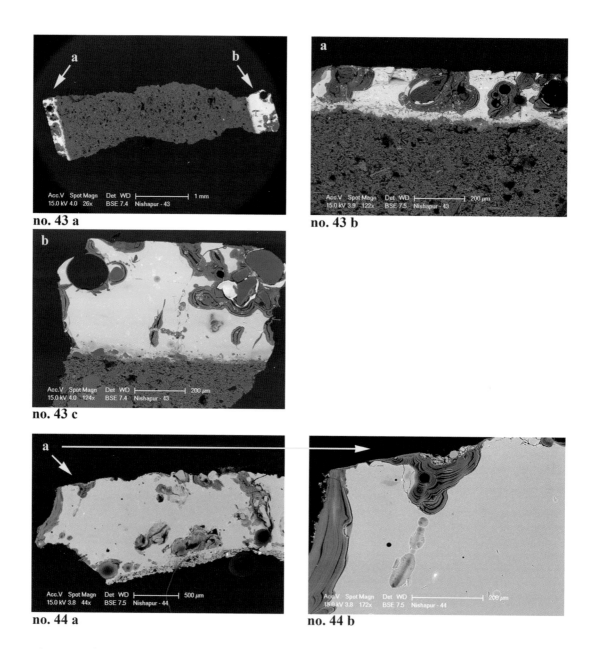

no. 43 a

no. 43 b

no. 43 c

no. 44 a

no. 44 b

Figure 73b: images of samples of glazes in scanning electronic microscopy (retrodiffused electrons, composition mode) (© C2RMF, A. Bouquillon 2010).

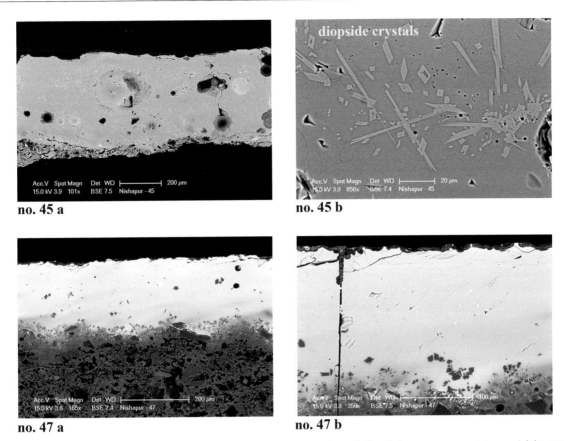

no. 45 a   no. 45 b

diopside crystals

no. 47 a   no. 47 b

Figure 73c: images of samples of glazes in scanning electronic microscopy (retrodiffused electrons, composition mode) (© C2RMF, A. Bouquillon 2010).

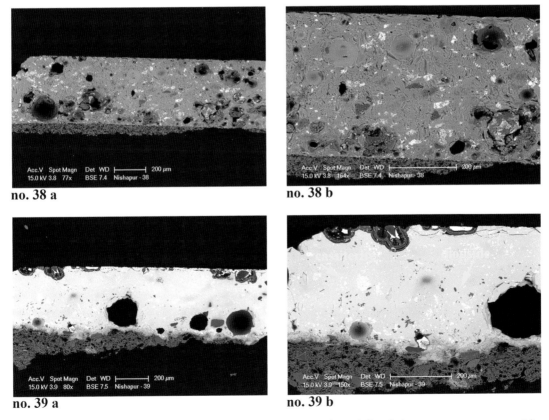

no. 38 a   no. 38 b

no. 39 a   no. 39 b

Figure 74: images of samples of glazes in scanning electronic microscopy (retrodiffused electrons, composition mode) Opaque white glazes. White grains: cassiterite; black grains: diopside (© C2RMF, A. Bouquillon 2010).

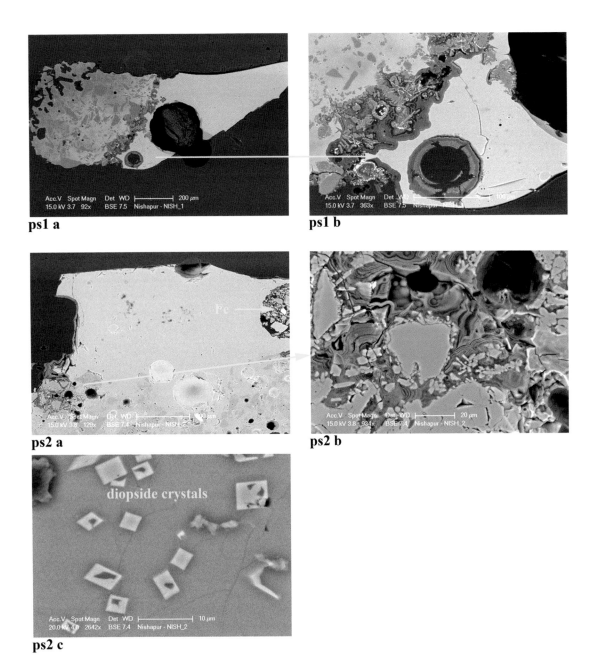

Figure 75a: Fritware shard: images of samples of glazes in scanning electronic microscopy (retrodiffused electrons, composition mode). Diopside crystals (Si Ca Mg); Detail of a grain rich in Cr Mg Fe Cu Al (© C2RMF, A. Bouquillon 2010).

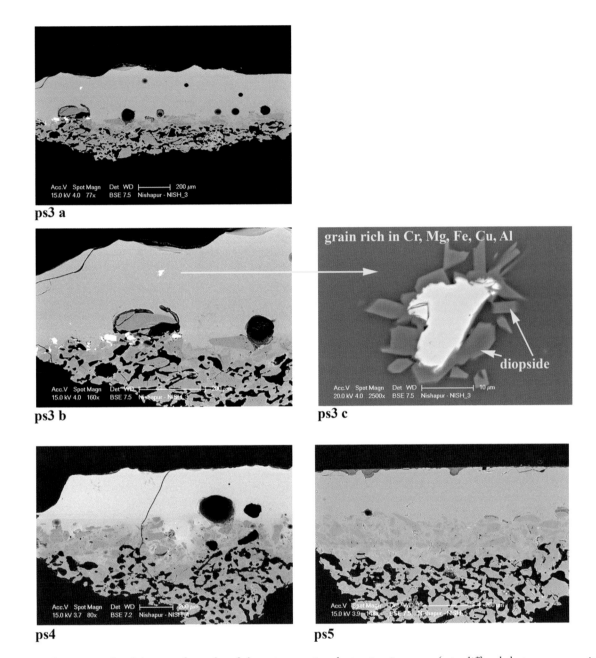

Figure 75b: Fritware shard: images of samples of glazes in scanning electronic microscopy (retrodiffused electrons, composition mode). Diopside crystals (Si Ca Mg); Detail of a grain rich in Cr Mg Fe Cu Al (© C2RMF, A. Bouquillon 2010).

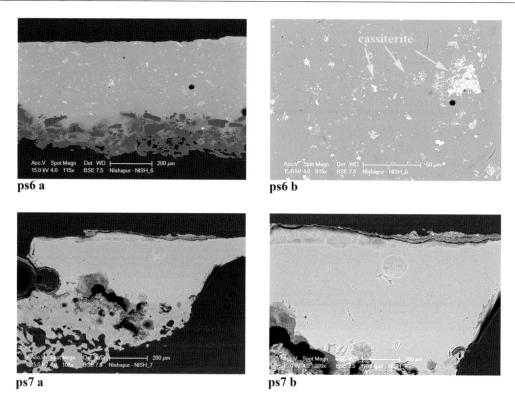

ps6 a   ps6 b

ps7 a   ps7 b

Figure 75c: Fritware shard: images of samples of glazes in scanning electronic microscopy (retrodiffused electrons, composition mode). Diopside crystals (Si Ca Mg). Detail of a grain rich in Cr Mg Fe Cu Al (© C2RMF, A. Bouquillon 2010).

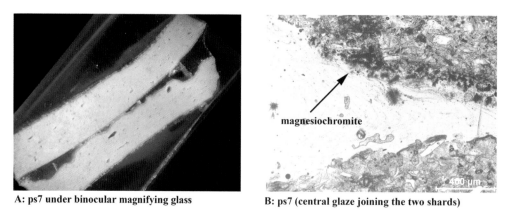

A: ps7 under binocular magnifying glass   B: ps7 (central glaze joining the two shards)

Fig. 76: (A) view under binocular magnifying glass of the polished surface of sample no. ps7; (B) view through optic microscope (LPNA) of the translucent blue glaze joining the two shards of no. ps7 (© C2RMF, A. Bouquillon 2010).

Where were the ceramics made?

Production sites of the clayey ceramics and provenance of the materials

According to R. B. Mason, two Iranian production sites show that the fired clay contains fragments of volcanic rock and minerals issuing from these rocks: Nishapur and Sirjan (Mason, 2004, 207–208). In addition, the ceramics containing inclusions of volcanic rock were probably made in Samarkand and also in several Iraqi sites (Mason, 2004, 210–214). In the fabrics from Nishapur and Sirjan, Mason notes the presence of two types of volcanic rock: basaltic and felsic. According to this author, the ceramic produced at Samarkand would only contain the felsic type, and that in very low quantities (<1%). One can also note that, according to this study, the ceramics produced at Sirjan and Nishapur do not contain fragments of metamorphic rock, which contradicts the analysis of the shards carried out at C2RMF. For Mason, the fabrics of Sirjan and Nishapur are essentially distinguished by the morphology of inclusions: sub-angular to angular for Nishapur and more rounded for Sirjan. Mason notes the presence of nine types of inclusion in the clayey ceramics of Nishapur: quartz, plagioclase feldspar, potassic feldspar of the microcline type, amphibole, clinopyroxene, micas (muscovite and biotite), fragments of felsic volcanic rock, fragments of basalt, clayey aggregates (pelites?). The fabrics of group A are similar to the fabrics of Nishapur studied by Mason. One difference, however, appears. Among the five samples from Nishapur studied by Mason, only one contains fragments of metamorphic rock in very low proportion (<1%) (Mason, 2004, table 6.6, 137). For all the other fabrics, the fact that the kiln clays and those destined for ceramics, glazed or unglazed, are similar suggests a local origin for the raw materials.

Three main types of rock can be recognized among the inclusions present in the clayey matrix of the aluminous fabrics of Nishapur:

- volcanic rocks, as proved by the presence of fragments of andesite, plagioclase feldspars, amphibole and pyroxene
- metamorphic rocks, for the most part schistous: meta-arenite, metasiltite/metapelite
- detritic sedimentary rocks comprising sandstone, siltite and pelite (~argilite)

All these rocks come through the soil a few kilometres to the north of Nishapur, at the level of the southern part of the mountainous belt of the Binalud (Figs 77–78). The volcanic rocks, of the andesite type and the Eocene age, come through the soil to the north-west of Nishapur, on the first slopes of the reliefs of the Binalud (see caption 14 of the extract of the geological map, Fig. 77). Some Miocene conglomerates with sandstone elements and andesite also come through the soil on a wide band several kilometres long at the base of the slopes of the south escarpment of the reliefs of the Binalud. The metamorphic rocks come through the soil just behind this conglomeratic formation with which are associated sandstones and marls. They date from the Jurassic Period and correspond to schists in the form of metapelites and meta-arenites. No town in Khorasan or even in Semnan has these three types of rocks outcropping in the same basin escarpment. The ceramics demonstrating the presence of these three types of rocks or even the first two types were therefore produced in Nishapur. The composition of the fabrics being quite close for the great majority of the samples studied, it is thus very probable that all these ceramics, with the exception of shards nos 38–39, and perhaps shards nos 12, 7, 4 and B, had been produced at Nishapur.

'The clay' (with or without inclusions) could come from the marls or calcareous silts emerging in the environs of Nishapur. A Miocene geological formation principally constituted of red and white marls would have been the clayey source (see caption 21 of the extract of the geological map, Fig. 77 and the red ellipses on the satellite photo, Fig. 78). The geological maps also indicate that these marls run alongside volcanic rocks. Temper and clayey raw material (marl, calcareous clay or calcareous silt) could therefore have come from a very restricted geographical and geological zone situated to the northwest of Nishapur. However, the clayey materials used by the potters could also have been found in the colluvial and alluvial deposits of the areas close to Nishapur (in the form of more or less sandy calcareous silt).

If the potters had used the Miocene marls coming through the soil on the first slopes of the massif of the Binalud (formation no. 21, Fig. 77), the inclusions were added, as this type of clayey rock very rarely contains rock fragments or inclusions coming from rocks of different natures. On the other hand, if the clayey material is a calcareous silt, this could naturally contain a sandy fraction with grains of varying size and nature. The use of a sandy calcareous silt (with a granulometric fraction >62.5 µm) is very probable, given the presence of this type of sediment in the archaeological zone and around it (Fouache and Cosandey 2006; digital geological

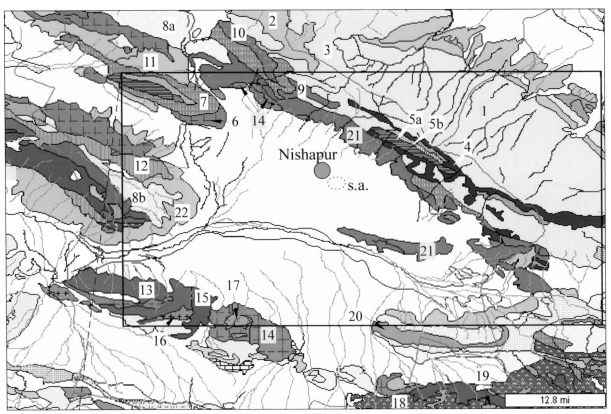

According to the geological map of Iran at 1/1000000 online: http://www.ngdir.ir/ThematicGeology/Geology.asp?#Nod

Captions

  0 (Qft2): colluvions, sediments of dejection cone, alluvial terraces (Quatenary)

  1 (Jph): metamorphic rocks comprising metapeltites, schists and meta-arenites (Jurassic inf.)

  2 (Jd): greenish or greyish clayey limestone, with clay intercalation (mid J. to Cretacious inf.)

  3 (Jl): light grey limestone in thin or thick banks (mid J. to Cretaceous inf.)

  4 (Db): grey to black nodulous limestone with marl intercalation (Devonian)

5a (Pzl): non-differentiated rocks (Cambro-Ordovician)

5b (Cl): dark red arkosic and sub-arkosic sandstone and mica siltites (Cambrian)

  6 (Ea.bvt): non-differentiated volcanic rocks?

  7 (E2sht): metapeltite, tuff and sandstone

8a (PlQc): fluviatile conglomerate (Pliocene)

8b (Plc): sandstone and little consolidated conglomerates

  9 (E2c): conglomerates (Eocene)

10 (E3c): sandstone and conglomerate (Eocene)

11 (E2m): marls, gypsum and limestone marls with nummulites (Eocene)

12 (E2f): sandstone, calcitic sandstone and limestone (mid Eocene)

13 (di-gb): diabase and gabbros (?)

14 (Eav): andesite (intermediary volcanic rock) (mid to sup. Eocene)

15 (sr): serpentine (Cretaceous inf.)

16 (K2avb): non-differentiated volcanic rocks

17 (LE.Ogr) granite (Eocene sup. to Oligocene inf.)

18 (tm): chaotic tectonic mixture comprising pelagic limestones in association with basic and ultrabasic rocks with ophiolite
    complexes

19 (Kurl): chert, radiolarine and with red lutite (Cretaceous sup.)

20 (Mum): red marls, locally gypsous

21 (Mur): red marls, sandstone and conglomerates with elements of sandstone, limestone and andesite (Miocene)

22 (Qftl): colluvial slopes, sediments of the dejection cone, deposits of the fluviatile terrace (Quatenary)

23 (Qftl): colluvial slopes, sediments of the dejection cone, alluvions (silts, sands, conglomerates) + agricultural soils (Quatenary)

x Numbers in yellow: geological formations from which the temper could have come

s.a.: archaeological sector

Figure 77: extract of the digital geological map of Iran made by the 'Geological Survey of Iran' on the basis of maps made by the team of geologists of the oil company of Iran (after geological map of Iran: http://www.ngdir.ir/ThematicGeology/Geology. asp?#Nod).

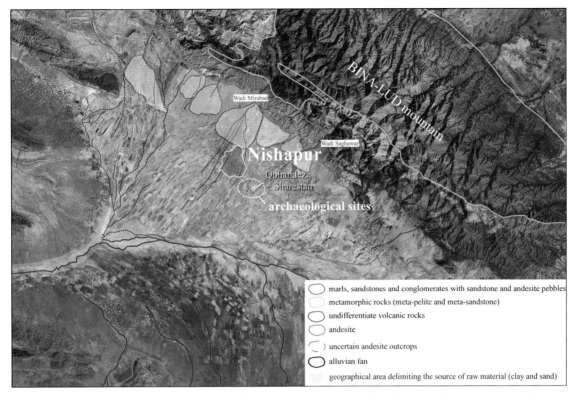

Figure 78: Nishapur: location of the possible principal sources of raw materials for the temper (© Coquinot 2010, from Google Earth).

map of Iran formation no. 23, Fig. 77). This sediment can even contain inclusions like those identified in the ceramic fabrics as it constitutes the soil, and a large part of the superficial formations at the level of Nishapur (yellow zone on Fig. 78) come from the erosion of formations nos 1, 4, 5 and 21 coming through the soil on the southern part of the Binalud massif.

The clayey glazed wares: local productions and imports

As with the ceramics with monochrome green glazes and polychrome decoration, the kiln sticks (nos 34–35, Fig. 50) bear traces of glazes presenting the same petrography and the same chemical composition as the other ceramics analyzed: the production of the glazed ceramics on the site is thus proved. Moreover, the fragments of kiln walls collected on the surface of the Shahrestan bear the clearly visible remains of vitrified materials (nos 36–37, Fig. 50). The PIXE analysis of sample 36 shows a very alkaline glass which does not contain lead or individual oxide colorants (copper, for example) and does not appear to correspond to the vitrification of the subjacent clay. This glass is very certainly proof of materials fired in the kiln, glazes, glass or glass frit.

The imports clearly determined by the analysis are the ceramics with an opaque white glaze (Nos 38 and 39). The chemical composition of the fabrics of the two shards indicates an Iraqi product. The differences in the content of certain elements of the two fabrics could be explained, at least in part, by the different production sites. Concerning shard no. 39, the presence of vitreous inclusions places it in the petrographic group 'Samarra 2' defined by Mason and Tite.[11] The glazes confirm their Iraqi provenance: one of them, at 30% PbO and 7% SnO_2, is close to the glazes of 'Samarra 2' defined by R. B. Mason. The other, more alkaline and much less

[11]   Mason 2004, 211; Mason and Tite 1994, 80. The named 'Baghdad' petrofabric characterized by relict glass fragment inclusions has been found in samples from Samarra, Siraf, Hira, Nippur and from Yemen but ascribed by the authors to Baghdad, on documentary evidence.

plumbiferous, presents characteristics close to those of the ceramics of Basra.

PRODUCTION SITES OF THE SILICEOUS CERAMICS AND THE PROVENANCE OF THE RAW MATERIAL

The production of siliceous ceramic in Nishapur during the medieval period is known from the work of Wilkinson. It nonetheless appears difficult to demonstrate that the seven siliceous ceramics studied were actually produced there. The petrographic characteristics of a large number of siliceous ceramics coming from different archaeological sites in Iran were published by Mason, and Mason and Golombek (Mason 1995; 1996; Mason and Golombek 2003). On the basis of these characteristics Mason defined a certain number of 'petrofabrics', certain of which correspond to an identified production centre. Nonetheless, given the great homogeneity in the nature of the mineral grains present in the fritware (% quartz >80% for most of the samples), it seems very difficult to distinguish the production centres by the facies. The aspect of the quartz (from limpid to very cloudy) was not taken into account in our study as a distinguishing criterion as it can vary significantly from one natural sample to another.[12] The other types of inclusion (amphibole, fragments of volcanic rocks, etc.) can only reduce the possibilities of provenance.

Among the seven fritwares studied, two shards showed particularities allowing the identification of the production site or, at least, restricting the possibilities of provenance. Sample ps7 in fact constituted two ceramics joined together by the same glaze (Fig. 76). They present identical exterior glazes but one of the two presents a black underglaze decoration realized with magnesiochromite. This sample is very probably a firing mishap. It was certainly produced on site in Nishapur. Sample ps3 contains a fragment of volcanic rock. According to the data published by Mason and Golombek (2003, in part. Table 1, 253) and the digital geological map of Iran, the latter could have come from any one of six identified production centres: Tabriz, Rayy, Sirjan, Kerman, Nishapur or Samarkand.

The quartz sand used in the fritware comes from the milling of mono- or poly- crystalline quartz pebbles with crystals of >10 mm in size. The quartz seems to be of metamorphic origin given its typology and the disposition of the fluid inclusions, but also the presence of a few grains presenting an undulant extinction. The milled quartz could also have come from veins of metamorphic formations.

If the compositions of the fabrics at 80% SiO_2 do not allow an origin to be determined with certitude, the glazes of the three shards analyzed suggest a local production. Samples ps1, ps4 and ps6, with alkalino-plumbiferous glazes, are in fact comparable to those of the shards with monochrome glazes coming from the site. Another (ps5) has a transparent alkaline glaze. These shards correspond to two different groups, which according to Mason characterize Iranian fritware. Nevertheless, it should be noted that shard ps5 bears a lustre decoration.[13] If one compares its transparent alkaline glaze with those of lustre objects of the pre-Mongol and Mongol Periods studied within the framework of research on the evolution of lustre (Bouquillon *et al.* 2008), it can be established that it does not correspond with the characteristics of the Iranian glazes which are systematically plumbiferous (20% PbO) and opacified by tin oxide (7 to 9% SnO_2).[14]

---

[12] For the use of the aspect of the quartz grains as a criteria of petrographic characterization of the fritware, see Mason 1995, table 1, 313.

[13] We were unable to analyse the heavily-altered lustre itself.

[14] Sample ps5 more resembles the contemporary Syrian lustre productions by its high SiO_2 content and its absence of PbO. Nevertheless the Na_2O and Al_2O_3 content clearly differentiate the lustre shard ps5 from the lustres from Syria (Mason 2004, table 5.3, 102).

3. Interpreting the analyses: the ceramic groups and their productions

The clayey fabric groups and their chronology

The very homogeneous petrography and chemical composition of the clayey fabrics studied nevertheless leads to the definition of three Nishapur fabric groups (Aa, Ab, and B, Tables 17–18). The cross-referencing of the fabrics analyzed with the chronology of the shards, known from the TL and Archaeomagnetism cross-referencing system[15] and by their stratigraphic position, allows the suggestion that a pottery production industry existed in the Nishapur area at least from Period I onwards. The most ancient shard analyzed, being of the 1st century BC, and the most recent, of the 11th century AD, suggest that for at least 1000 years the raw materials used (clay and inclusion materials) came from the same regional sources. If the source of supply changed during that time, this change occurred on a local scale.[16]

Fabric of type B may have been produced during the more ancient periods recognized and did not persist after Period II. In fact, the group B shard 203 E1 (T26), belongs to Period I, according to the analysis, and the group B shards 110 E6 and 110 E1 (T26) belong to Period II.

The fabric group Ab is attested to Period II (see sample 116 E1, T26). This type of fabric was probably still produced later, following the stratigraphy of two other shards: 110 E2 (T26) and 420 E1 (T10) that belong to Period IIIa.

The most common type of fabric identified (Aa) is attested to from Period I onwards and seems to be the only fabric type produced during Period IIIb. It was, at the least, produced for more than 1000 years, as suggested by the analyses and the stratigraphic position of some shards. Shard 321-2 E1 (T23), which is a fragmentary kiln stick with splashes of glaze, belongs to Period IIIa according to the stratigraphical study. Finally, samples 110 E3 and 110-4 E5 (T26) also belong to Period IIIa. Shard 200 E1 (T26, wall) is, according to the analyses, from Period IIIb. Finally, samples 106 E1, 106 E2, 106 E3, 102 E1, 102-2 E2, 102 E3, 102 E4, 102 E5, 104 E1, 104 E2, 106 E4 (T26) and 419 E1 (T 10) belong to Period IIIb, according to their stratigraphical position, and are all of fabric group Aa.

All the shards – with one exception – coming from the surface layers of the test-pits or from the surface of the Qohandez and the Shahrestan are also of group Aa.[17]

Fabrics and functions: the earthenware types produced

The 12 textural groups of fabrics defined following the inclusions' size and distribution known by petrography (Table 33, Fig. 54) have been observed on material of Periods II, IIIa, IIIb and on the surface shards. They were defined to refine the grouping of the material considering the homogeneity of the petrography, and are thus insufficient to determine some ceramic groups. The diversity of the groups identified by textural discrimination illustrates the variety of earthenware production in Nishapur, especially during Period III, but also during Period II.

The vessels used for the serving and consumption of food and drink were fine to medium in quality. The finest fabrics observed (A1F, A2F and A4F) are mainly used to make small and

---

[15] For the ages of the shards defined by TL, see Chap. II, Table 2.

[16] Some differences of inclusion types observed in Nishapur petrography samples (such as the presence or not of andesite) may be explained by the clay preparation method rather than by a change of raw material (oral comm., Y. Coquinot, C2RMF, 2010).

[17] Samples 301 E1, 302 E1 and 309 E1 (T23); samples 100 E1, 101 E1, 101 E2, 101 E4, 101 E5 and 101 E6 (T26); sample 338 E1 (T18); sample 149-1 E1 (T15). The samples coming the surface of the Shahrestan (kiln material and stick, monochrome glazes), are C2RMF nos 35–37 and nos 40–46.

Table 33: Textural classification of the fabrics.

Code	Granulometry	Fabric quality
A1F	A1=unimodal regular	F=fine
A2F	A2=unimodal irregular	F=fine
A4F	A4=bimodal irregular	F=fine
A1FM	A1=unimodal regular	FM=fine to medium
A5FM	A5=unimodal irregular	FM=fine to medium
A5GM	A5=tri/polymodal regular	FM=fine to medium
A6FM	A6=tri/polymodal irregular	FM=fine to medium
A6GM	A6=tri/polymodal irregular	GM=coarse to medium
B5FM	B5=bimodal regular	FM=fine to medium
B5GM	B5=bimodal regular	GM=coarse to medium
B6G	B6=bimodal regular	G=coarse
B6GM	B6=bimodal regular	GM=coarse to medium
C6G	C6=tri/polymodal irregular	G=coarse

rather thin jugs and jars, and unglazed or glazed bowls. They are proportionally more numerous from Period IIIa onwards (see Chap. IV). The most common type of fabric (A6FM) for every period studied in fact corresponds to all the typology of shapes observed, but is mostly used for the making of jars and glazed or unglazed bowls. The two other types of fine–medium fabrics defined (A5FM and B5FM) are much rarer and, according to the layers where the shards were found, are associated with Period III.

The ceramics made for storage and cooking are more heterogeneous in quality and are fine-medium to coarse. Among the coarser types of fabrics, one was observed for the making of specific objects: the cooking pots are all of B5GM fabric, except one sample which goes in the A5GM textural group. The B5GM fabric was observed from Period II to Period IIIb. Other coarse to medium fabrics (A6GM, B6GM) were observed for lids, basins, pots and jars. They are more common in Period III but were nevertheless observed in Period II material. Finally, the coarser fabrics (B6G, C6G) were used to make the large jars, some lids, basins and pots. C6G fabric was observed from Period I to Period IIIb, and the B6G textural group seems more linked with Period III.

The glazed earthenware: technologies and chronology

The monochrome blue/green glazed wares studied were not visually differentiable. The analysis of samples enabled the definition of two main groups: one calco-alkaline, the other plumbiferous. This very different technology is in fact known from different previous studies (Pace *et al.* 2008, table 3, 599. See also Hill *et al.* 2004, table 3, 600; and Simpson 1997, table on p. 75) to differentiate pre-Islamic and Islamic Period glazed earthenware. The first group, probably linked with the Sasanian Period, corroborates the stratigraphic study concerning the presence in Nishapur of a glazed material pre-dating the Islamic era. The calco-alkaline group, which concerns two of the six samples analyzed (nos 44 and 45, Fig. 66) presents a type of composition that appears to well-characterize the Mesopotamian glazes of the Sasanian Period, datable by stratigraphy to the 3rd–beginning of the 7th centuries AD. In addition, the presence of inclusions in the glaze, such as of bubbles and weathering products (as observed in sample no. 45, Fig. 66), has been observed in pre-Islamic shards. These elements, which give the glazes an opaque appearance, are characteristic of pre-Islamic production and precede the use of tin oxide, in particular in Mesopotamia (Pace *et al.* 2008, 597). The plumbiferous monochrome blue/green glazes present the same composition as the polychrome ones (Tables 25; 29). They are, therefore, very probably contemporary with the Islamic Period.

The polychrome glazed wares analyzed have shown that several technologies were known and used over a rather short chronology, on samples that represent types that all coexisted during Period IIIa (Fig. 85). For instance, the yellow colorations obtained with three different methods appear on shards of buff ware, underglaze painted, monochrome ware types and yellow staining black (samples A, F, M and C/H, Fig. 48). The same technology was observed on the buff ware and underglaze painted samples. Nevertheless, they may be contemporary with the monochrome sample analyzed, which shows a very different technology and belongs to Period IIIa. The same phenomenon of technological diversity was observed for the black colorations. On the shards analyzed (samples C/H and G, Fig. 48) of yellow staining black and slip painted types, the black colour is obtained by two different methods. The use of magnesiochromite observed on the yellow staining black shard was also detected on two fritwares (ps3 and ps7). This could suggest that this technology is later (and thus contemporary with Period IIIb) than the manganese and iron composition used in shard G to obtain the black colouring of the glaze. This last combination was also observed on one shard of the buff ware type (sample B, fig. 48).

The fritwares: technologies and sequence hypothesis

The chemical analyses realized on fritware samples allowed one to distinguish them in terms of composition and technologies. Cross-referencing these data with the sequence observed in the stratigraphy makes it possible to suggest a sequence for these types.

First, two groups of fabrics could be defined by some differences in their chemical composition (Table 19). The samples (Fig. 49) forming Group 1 (ps 1, ps 2, ps 4 and ps 6) are all monochrome shards and those which constitute Group 2 (ps 3, ps 5 and ps 7) are monochrome turquoise, moulded and painted on glaze, and one fragment of lustreware.

Considering the technologies of their decoration, the last two indicate that they may be later than some of the monochrome samples (Rugiadi 2010, 178; Porter 2004–5, 25–27). The glazes of samples corresponding to fabric Group 1 are very different compared to the glazes of fabric Group 2, and are much more heterogeneous. Shard ps6 presents a plumbiferous and tin opacified glaze; ps 1 and ps 4 an alkalino-plumbiferous glaze. The glaze of ps2 presents some diopside crystals: it could also belong to another category of glaze (A. Bouquillon, oral comm., 2010.).

Glazes of samples from fabric Group 2 are, on the contrary, very siliceous: this completely different composition of glazes could corroborate the hypothesis of a change, or more accurately of an enrichment, in technologies during the 12th century AD. From the second half of that century onward, the fritwares would thus also present siliceous surface glazes which partially replaced older ones that were much more plumbiferous. The plumbiferous and opacified glazes (as defined by the C2RMF analyses) were nevertheless still in use at the same time as the siliceous ones, following Mason's results on lustre and *haft rang* types glazes (Mason 2004, table 6.5, 135).

Chapter IV

Chronology of the Qohandez pottery

This chapter introduces the Qohandez pottery in a chronological sequence resulting from our stratigraphical and analytical study. It presents the ceramic material found in all tests excavated (A, B, 10, 11, 12, 13, 15, 17, 18, 23, 26, 27).[1] The pottery discussed comes from the stratigraphical sequence only from Test-pits B, 10, 12, 26 and 27, which are later compared with the other test-pits. All the data have been introduced into a database, permitting the cross-referencing of the different elements concerning the characteristics of the pottery and the analyses carried out in the laboratory. This study allowed us not only to situate our different typologies within their own periods, but also to better define changes in all the different periods.

1. Introduction to the Test-pits

Concerning Test-pit B, the study indicates that the majority of the ceramics recovered were coarse and common wares. The type of this *corpus* was utilitarian (jars, cooking pots). The proportion of fine pottery is much lower: only three glazed wares were found. Quantitative analysis shows that the coarse to medium types are more than 60% more prevalent than the fine types. These pottery data testify to the modesty of the place, with the few architectural structures found during the excavation corroborating this hypothesis (Fig. 25).

Test-pit A proceeds from Test-pit B in the chronological sequence and exclusively concerns Period IIIb. It is situated close to Test-pit B, above it in the upper part of the slope in the central area of the Qohandez. No architectural remains have been found here. The study of the material shows that within the glazed *corpus* the fabric proportion testifies that the clayey wares are equal to the fritwares.

Therefore, regarding both Test-pits A and B, one notices that the period before the 9th century is characterized by a modest status of occupation. In contrast, from the 9th century onwards the quality of the material becomes much richer, suggesting an important change in occupation type which, in fact, becomes richer. This part of the Qohandez may have been converted into a residential area.

Test-pit 10 demonstrates a more complete chronological sequence from the first to the last occupations, just before the Mongol invasion. The ceramic material is well balanced throughout the entire stratigraphy. The coarse to very fine unglazed and the glazed wares are more or less

---

[1] The test-pits here mentioned concern the French team's excavations. In fact, Test-pits C, D, E and the trenches opened in the southern part of the Qohandez, below the possible south gate, excavated by the Iranian team, are not included in our study. The ceramic material of these last test-pits has been exclusively studied by our Iranian colleagues and will be published separately.

equally represented. The main change to have occurred concerns the proportion of the glazed wares. This was visible in stratigraphy from the first level of the section, which here corresponds to the first level of the doorway, transformed into a rich neighbourhood. It seems that the well-represented glazed wares are less luxurious than the material found in Test-pit A.

Test-pit 11 is a group of a few small tests at the foot of T10 which were opened with the aim of understanding the area surrounding the doorway. The material comes only from the upper and surface layers and belongs to Period III. It is of the same type as the T10 material.

Test-pit 12 is situated in the middle of the military building in the northeastern part of the Qohandez. As previously shown, this building lost its military function in the beginning of Period IIIa. This is well corroborated by the ceramic material which is coarse and only utilitarian in the stratigraphical sequence (Period II).

Test-pit 13 was excavated on the north side of the Qohandez, in an area which corresponds with the military fortification of the citadel. The test-pit covered a large irregular area from the interior to the exterior of the northern rampart. There is no material directly linked with the rampart; therefore, there is no possibility of precisely dating this defensive system. Nevertheless, since its observed lower part belongs to the first occupation,[2] one could suggest that this structure belongs to the first architectural phase of the Qohandez. After analysis, this phase can be considered as belonging to Period II (late 4th–early 5th centuries).

The material is essentially composed of coarse to medium quality wares of utilitarian use (jars, basins and cooking pots). The fine unglazed pottery is much less numerous and the glazed pottery is not greatly represented, but shows the main glazed types of Period IIIa.

Test-pit 23 is situated close to Test-pit 13, in the rampart area. The material belongs to the upper and surface layers. The predominant pottery group is composed of jars, of coarse to medium quality, and cooking pots, as in Test-pit 13. Fine unglazed wares are much less represented.

As previously noted, the material from the last two test-pits corresponds well with the military and thus utilitarian character of this area.

In this area two other test-pits, T17 and T18, were opened. Both pertain to the upper and surface layers, as well as to the previously analyzed T23. According to the material studied the ceramic types are more heterogeneous. In fact, coarse to fine unglazed pottery, clayey glazed bowls, and very few monochrome fritwares have been found.

Test-pit 15 is situated in the centre of the military building linked to the northern rampart and the doorway. The material studied is mainly fine and glazed, and is much later than the architecture itself. It should nevertheless be noted that this excavation only concerned the upper and surface layers. This well-identified pottery belongs essentially to Period III.

Test-pit 27 is the only one to be situated in the western part of the Qohandez. The pottery recovered is mainly of coarse and medium quality, with jars and cooking pots being the better represented wares. A few fine unglazed wares (jars and jugs) were also found, as were a few monochrome glazed wares.

Test-pit 26 is situated in the southern part of the Qohandez. The type study indicates a high proportion of fine unglazed jugs and small jars; the proportion of glazed ceramic is relatively low. The presence of fritwares can also be noted, whose types are the latest found in the Qohandez. Accordingly, one can observe that this part of the citadel corresponds to a patrician quarter, a suggestion borne out by comparison with the other excavated areas of the Qohandez.

---

[2] In 2007, we reached the foot of the rampart, 7.50 m lower than the destroyed interface.

2. Chronological sequence of the Qohandez pottery

Period I

Period I (Fig. 79) covers an extended chronology which, when cross-referenced with the Archaeomagnetism results, gives the following interval: ~450 BC–~150 BC.

Period I was identified by three fragments,[3] none of which correspond stratigraphically to this period; in fact, TL and Archaeomagnetism date them to this period, but they have been found in layers of Period II (T26 203 E1; T12 158) and IIIa (T26 110 E4). Only one fragment (TB 260) was found in a stratigraphical context corresponding with this period, but it has not been analyzed by TL. This interpretation was made firstly due to the fact that the TB stratigraphy is the same as that of T12.[4] In this last test-pit, the first dated soil corresponds to layer 158. Two fragments have been found in this layer, the T12 158 and the T12 158 box. The former is dated to Group 1, and the second to Group 2 (Table 2; Fig. 20). The soil layer was therefore dated to Period II. Moreover, layer 164 is situated between the 158 soil and the virgin soil. The TL and Archaeomagnetism dating of fragment T12 158 to Group 1 could mean that layer 164 belongs to Period I. The same stratigraphical sequence appears in the deepest layers of TB (Fig. 25): layer 260 is situated between the virgin soil and the first soil layer of Period II (249). This could mean that the TB 260 fragment could belong to Period I.

The poor quantity of the studied fragments (four shards) of this period is obviously not representative of this cultural context, which means that it is impossible to perform a real study of this period. This is also the reason for the very large time interval of Group 1. Our intention, here, is consequently only to show three fabric types and a pottery form. It is important to note that this occupation period and the associated material are very hard to define with the classical method; the only way to define this chronological period was through the analytical study, as shown by our results. In conclusion, certainly a part of the ceramic material excavated in the Qohandez may belong to this period.

The only shape recorded in TB is a storage jar. The object was almost complete, although only the rim was drawn (Fig. 79/1). Its fabric is coarse (C6G), of buff colour, slightly pink clay, with large gravel grits, small bubbles and fingerprints on the edge. The surface is clear.

The analyzed remains of fragments show two different petrographic categories: A, the most frequent; and B, one of the three B categories represented here. The third shard has not been identified by petrography, but only categorized by its fabric texture. The three fragments are not representative of typology forms. Although belonging to different SU, they belong all to Period I. The coarser fragment is 203 E1 (C6G), which is completely burnt. The medium–coarse is represented by fragment 158 (B5GM), which is certainly a shard of a closed shape; its surface is covered with a beige slip and combed wave. The finest is fragment 110 E4 (A1F), whose surface is engraved.

---

[3] The discovery of a stone pendant in T27, not in a stratigraphic context but found during the cleaning of the slope, bears an inscription, probably Parthian Pahlavi. Unfortunately, this kind of object cannot deliver information about the nature of the area. It is, nevertheless, very important to mention that the site may have had a Parthian occupation (Period I).

[4] Three shards belonging to this test have been analyzed.

Cat.	n°SU	Test	Square	Description
1	158	12	J XV	Shard. See: Table 2.
2	110 (E4)	26	O XII	Shard. See: Table 2; Table 17, no. 18.
3	203 (E1)	26	O XII	Shard. See: Table 2; Table 17, no. 32.
4	260-1	B	LXIV	Top of large jar (LJ5). Buff pinkish coarse fabric (C6G). Finger prints on the rim.

Figure and Legend 79: Nishapur, Qohandez, Period I.

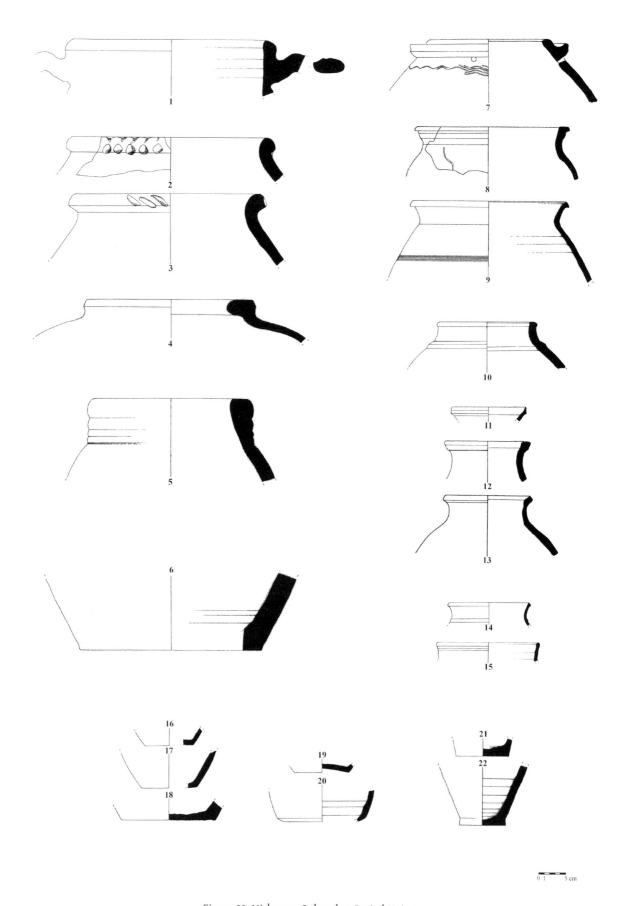

Figure 80: Nishapur, Qohandez, Period II: jars.

CAT.	N°SU	TEST	SQUARE	DESCRIPTION
1	249-4	B	LXIV	Rim of jar with handles (LJ4). Coarse reddish fabric (C6G)
2	517/1	27	JX	Rim of large jar (LJ5). Coarse to medium red fabric (A6GM), finger prints on the rim. Cream slip.
3	116-1	26	O XII	Top of large jar (LJ5). Coarse red orange to buff fabric (C6G), finger prints on the rim. Cream slip.
4	239-11	B	LXIV	Top of jar (LJ9). Very coarse buff fabric (C6G).
5	239-8	B	LXIV	Top of jar (LJ8). Coarse red fabric (C6G)
6	239-6	B	LXIV	Base of jar (Jb3). Coarse red fabric (C6G).
7	424-1	10	L XVII	Top of jar (J10). Medium orange fabric (A6GM). Pinkish buff slip, combed design.
8	424-2	10	L XVII	Top of jar (J4). Very fine red fabric (A4F). Red orange slip.
9	240-2	B	LXIV	Top of jar (J4). Fine pinkish buff fabric (A4F).
10	517/2	27	JX	Top of jar (J1). Rather fine pink orange fabric (A6FM). Cream slip.
11	243-3	B	LXIV	Rim of fine jar (J14). Fine buff fabric (A1F).
12	424-4	10	L XVII	Neck of jar (J14). Fine to medium red orange fabric (A6FM). Pinkish slip.
13	423-5	10	L XVII	Top of jar (J8). Medium buff orange fabric. Clear buff slip. Rim burned.
14	118-2	26	O XII	Rim of jar (J8). Rather fine buff fabric (A6FM).
15	248-4	B	LXIV	Rim of fine jar (J1). Rather fine reddish fabric (A6FM).
16	516/1	27	JX	Base of jar (Jb1). Rather coarse orange buff fabric (A6GM).
17	517/3	27	JX	Base of jar (Jb1).
18	118-1	26	O XII	Base of large jar (Jb3). Coarse red to buff fabric (C6G). Cream yellowish slip.
19	517-518/2	27	JX	Base of jar (Jb5). Rather fine buff orange fabric (A6FM).
20	517-518/3	27	JX	Base of jar (Jb6). Rather fine buff pinkish fabric (A6FM). Cream slip.
21	249-2	B	LXIV	Base of little jar (JsJb5). Fine yellowish fabric (A4F).
22	239-9	B	LXIV	Base of pitcher or jar (JsJb4). Medium orange fabric (A6GM).

Legend 80: Nishapur, Qohandez, Period II: jars.

Period II

Period II is much more represented than the previous one and corresponds to the foundation of the Qohandez. Nine fragments were analyzed and the interval is comprised between the end of the 4th century AD and 785 AD. Among these shards, seven were found in their proper stratigraphical context, and two belonged to higher layers (Period IIIa) (Table 2).

The ceramic material of Period II was found in TB, T10, T12, T26 and T27, showing a homogeneous occupation of the mound (Fig. 8).

The first architectural occupation of the site, and therefore the foundation of the Nishapur citadel, corresponds to this period. The material found during the excavation of T23 and the architectural recognition of the northern rampart showed the same characteristics as the material and structures found in the other parts of the Qohandez. In fact, the massive doorway (T10), the TB structures, the T12 structures of the military establishment and the structures found in T26 – although there are not enough elements to interpret them – correspond to Period II. In terms of interpreting the architecture, a main point of interest could be the study of the different construction materials employed.[5] The walls, all dressed with mud brick, presented the same types of bricks in terms of their dimensions and method of manufacture. The main module of mud brick employed is 40/42 × 40/42 × 10/12 cm, sometimes accompanied by 45 × 45 × 15 cm, and more rarely 48/50 × 48/50 × 15 cm and 38 × 38 × 9/10 cm modules. The composition of the mud bricks is always quite pure and fine.

---

[5] The study of the brick modules is not used here as a dating element.

These homogeneous characteristics are also noticeable in the ceramic material. There are 810 recorded pottery fragments from Period II,[6] of which 48 were studied and drawn. Amongst the ceramic material, the most frequently represented are closed shapes, especially large storage jars. The fabrics identified are of four main categories, from fine to coarse, divided into seven different types: A1F, A2F, A4F, A6FM, A6GM, B5GM, B6GM, C6G. The most common in this period is the coarser fabric C6G.

TB

The ceramic material of this period is characterized by 53% coarse to medium and 14% fine to medium ceramic wares. An increase of large jars, used for storage and transport, can be observed: they represent 22% of the ceramic material in the lowest layers and 72% in the upper ones. These latter also show the appearance of cooking pots. Regarding fine material, the jug is the most represented shape. One glazed shard was found in the upper layers of Period II. The supremacy of storage and transport wares and the topographical situation of the test suggest a possible utilitarian function for this area, which could be interpreted as a storage and/or dump zone.

T10

The ceramic material of the doorway during Period II post-dates its foundation and should correspond to its final blocking,[7] while being anterior to its reconstruction. Of the recorded material, 37.5% comprises coarse to medium fabrics and 50% fine to medium fabrics. The most representative shapes are cooking pots, large jars and basins. Jugs and small jars can be found among the fine shapes. A further 5% constitutes glazed wares, of which one is monochrome green and the other monochrome turquoise. Their fabrics are rather fine and medium-fine. In contrast to the previous test-pit, storage material is much less well represented (12.5%). The most common ware types, small jars, jugs, basins, cooking pots and bowls, were used mainly for cooking and the consumption of food and liquid.

T12

The test-pit was positioned inside the military building and, despite its very limited dimensions, the ceramic material has helped to identify the nature of this area. It is only coarse (98%) and mainly comprises cooking pot (176, forming 67%) and storage jar shards (31%). This zone could, therefore, be identified as the part of the building used for food preparation.

T26

Very few ceramic shards were diagnostic; 91 fragments were recorded, of which only seven fragments were drawn. The main ceramic type is that of the coarse storage jar, corresponding to 36% of the material. The other well-represented coarse wares are cooking pots (13%). The finer wares, jugs and small jars, amount to 21%. No glazed shards were found, but the presence of a single moulded fragmentary flask was noticed.

The proportions of the different categories seem to be more homogeneous than in the other test-pits. This trend diverges from the other assemblages studied and probably suggests a different type of occupation. This was corroborated by the discovery of a massive mud brick structure, constructed of very large bricks (45 × 45 × 15 cm), which was excavated to a depth of more than 7 m (Fig. 36). No other elements exist to better define this architecture. In any case the discovery of a seal, datable to the 6th century AD, and an *ostracon* with a Sasanian Pahlavi inscription could suggest the official function of this monumental structure as well as its quarter.

---

[6] The shards of T26 are not included in this count as they were not precisely counted.
[7] As previously mentioned, this practice was often employed during enemy attacks.

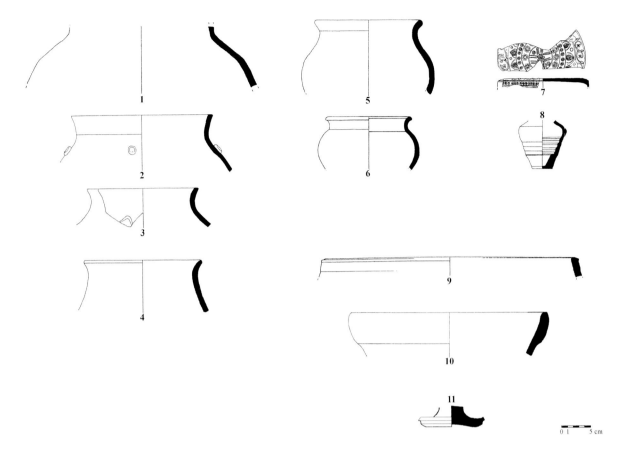

Cat.	n°SU	Test	Square	Description
1	236-3	B	LXIV	Fragment of cooking pot. Coarse, burned fabric (C6G).
2	155-1	12	J XV	Top of burned cooking pot (CP4, B5GM). Applied dots.
3	151-2	12	J XV	Top of burned cooking pot (CP4, B5GM). Combed design.
4	157-1	12	J XV	Top of cooking pot (CP4). Rather coarse buff orange fabric (B5GM). Cream slip.
5	423-5	10	L XVII	Rim of jar (J8).
6	113-1	26	O XII	Cooking pot (CP2). Coarse buff fabric, burned, with sand (C6G).
7	114-1	26	O XII	Part of moulded flask. Fine buff to orange fabric (A6FM).
8	423-3	10	L XVII	Jug (rim missing) (JsJb5). Fine buff fabric (A4F). Cream buff slip.
9	242-7	B	LXIV	Top of basin (Bas5). Fine buff fabric (A2F).
10	423-4	10	L XVII	Rim of basin (Bas9). Fine orange to buff fabric (A6FM).
11	239-10	B	LXIV	Base of lamp (L2). Fine yellow buff fabric (A2F), turquoise glaze.

Figure and Legend 81: Nishapur, Qohandez, Period II: cooking pots and varia.

T27

The material presents very few diagnostic shards: of the 275 shards recorded, only 11 fragments were drawn. As in TB, the percentage of coarse ware here is very significant (76%). The fine shards are, instead, 14% and probably correspond to jugs and small jars. Very few cooking pots were discovered (1%), and in the upper layers of the Period II stratigraphy one glazed shard was found, which is turquoise monochrome on fine yellowish-buff fabric. The absence of elements that could provide better information about the different occupation horizons makes any interpretation of the nature of the northwestern part of the Qohandez difficult.

General interpretation

Period II is characterized by a preponderance of closed shapes corresponding to utilitarian ceramics, mainly employed for storage and cooking. The material discovered is all very fragmentary. Only rims and bases were drawn (Fig. 80). The coarser ceramics also are the larger ones: the storage jars present fabrics corresponding to C6G to A6GM. The most frequent rims are those with vertical necks (Fig. 80/1) and handles (LJ4), or without a neck and a round open rim, LJ5 (Fig. 80/2–3 and Fig. 93/1–4 and 6). This kind of rim is often adorned with fingerprints and twisted decoration. The body seems to have been globular. Another kind of storage jar presents a vertical neck and a flatter body than the former, LJ8 (Fig. 80/5 and Fig. 93/7–8). A large proportion of the storage jars are covered with a cream to yellowish slip, while some jars are covered with a red slip (Fig. 93/9).

The other types of utilitarian wares are cooking pots (Fig. 81/1–6 and Fig. 94/22–24). All fragments were identified by fired traces as well as by the complete burning of the shards. The fabrics are coarse: mostly B5GM, but also C6G and A6GM. The typology was essentially established by the rims. Four types were defined (CP1–CP4): the first is the most represented and characterized by slightly open rims, CP4 (Fig. 80/2–4). The types with hemmed rims, smaller than the former, are also present, CP1–CP2 (Fig. 80/5–6).

This coarse material, of large jars and cooking pots, is much better represented than finer vessels. This could be explained by the nature of the areas dug and also by the culture of food practice. This period is therefore characterized by a restricted variety of pottery types that is traceable in all test-pits, except in T10 (the citadel monumental door), in which the material is more diverse. Concerning the military area of the Qohandez, the material seems to correspond with its function. In the other areas, the absence of relevant elements does not allow the better definition of the functions of structures. However, the material is similar to that found in the military building.

The finer material is mostly jars, small jars and jugs (Fig. 80/7–22 and Fig. 94/1–21), with the majority being jars. They present vertical or oblique rims or short necks (J1, J4 and J10). Other shapes are jugs, probably with handles, J8 and J14 (Fig. 80/11, 14). The preeminent fabric is A6FM. Nevertheless, some small jars are coarser (A6GM, B6GM, C6G; Fig. 80/7, 16, 18, 22) and others are the finest fabrics found at that period (A1F, A4F; Fig. 80/8–9, 11, 21). Some wares are decorated with combed and engraved motifs on the shoulder (Fig. 94/1, 11–13). The finest jugs, with a pale cream yellowish or greenish fabric, JsJb5 (Fig. 94/19–21) were found in the lowest layers of Period II (Fig. 80/21; US soil 249, Fig. 25) and in higher layers (Fig. 94/19–21), which means that this kind of fabric and shape can be dated from the origin of the Qohandez. Finally, the main function of these finer wares was for liquid consumption.

The only open shapes found are basins, of which very few were recorded (Fig. 81/9–10 and Fig. 94/25–26). Among these, two have fine to medium fabrics (A2F, A6FM): one presents a closed rim (Fig. 81/9) and the other an oblique one (Fig. 81/10). Two others are coarser and present a different shape, with a clubbed rim (Fig. 94/25–26).

Very rare fragments of moulded ceramics were discovered in the Qohandez. Only one was stratified (Fig. 81/7 and Fig. 94/27); it belongs to the same flask as another shard, which was found in the surface layers of the test-pit.

Period II is also characterized by the appearance of glazed wares (5 stratified fragments). In all excavated areas where they have been found, the glazed shards belonged to the upper layers. According to the stratigraphy, their appearance could be dated to the last part of Period II. Nevertheless, one glazed shard belongs to a layer in which TL has dated another shard to between 250 and 550 AD. The shapes recognised are probably small jars and one lamp. The glazed fragments (Fig. 94/28–31) recorded can be divided into two groups. The fabrics, on one hand, range from orange-red to red, and on the other hand are yellowish-buff in colour. Their quality is fine medium (FM). The glazes are green to turquoise in colour. It is important to note that the analyzed shard no. 44 (Tables 18 and 24, Fig. 46) is similar to shard no. 31 (Fig. 94) and to the base of lamp found in TB (no. 11, Fig. 81). They present a close fabric type, even if no. 44 is slightly coarser (MG). Moreover, the glazes look exactly the same: they are turquoise in colour and of very good quality. The surface is translucent and cracked. The chemical composition of no. 44 is chalco-alkaline.

Period IIIa

Period IIIa is the most represented and therefore the best known. Six fragments were analyzed by TL and Archaeomagnetism and dated to this period: all of them belonged to this stratigraphical context. The interval corresponding to Period III is 745 to 1165 AD. The chronology corresponding to Period IIIa was determined by a stratigraphical and an architectural study as well as an interpretation of the material. This interval could correspond to 745 AD until the early 11th century.

The material of Period IIIa belongs to TB, T10, T12, T13, T23, T26, T27 (Fig. 8). A large part of the structures visible on the citadel today should correspond to this period. The construction materials are the same as those of the older periods, mud brick and *pakhsa*, even if some changes were observed in the size of the bricks, with the largest mud bricks having disappeared. The early part of this period is still characterized by the use of square mud bricks of 38/40 cm per side. The last part, from the 10th century, is characterized by the use of smaller mud bricks, 27/29 cm per side and 9 cm thick (T10, Fig. 31). It is only later, in Period IIIb, that the appearance of baked bricks is largely observable.

There are 1942 recorded fragments, of which 184 were studied and drawn. The main characteristic of this period is the variety of shapes: the most represented types are storage jars and basins for the coarse wares, and jugs and glazed bowls for the fine ones. In contrast to Period II storage material seems to be less represented, whereas the finer material, used for consumption, has increased. Among this material, the fabrics analyzed are of 11 types (A1F, A2F, A4F, A6FM, A5FM, B5FM, A6GM, B5GM, B6G, B6GM, C6G).

TB

The ceramic material of this period is characterized by 52% coarse to medium and 45% fine to medium wares. The coarse to medium material comprises jars, cooking pots, basins and lids. The finer wares are mainly jugs and bowls and 2% of the recorded material is glazed ware. The proportion of fine material is different to that recognised in Period II at the same test-pit, with the fine material being in more or less equal proportion to the coarser. An increase in bowls and basins is observable, marking a diversity of shapes compared to the former period. A change in the urban context can be perceived.

T10

Four hundred and one shards were found, of which 146 were recorded and 36 drawn. The most important characteristic of this material is the amount of glazed wares, which constitutes 18%. Equilibrium between polychrome and monochrome glazed wares was observed. The ceramics are mainly fine to medium wares (A1F, A2F, A4F, A6FM): jugs and bowls. Among the coarse wares storage and culinary objects are, in contrast, much less well represented: jars (with and without handles), cooking pots, basins and lids (A6GM and C6G). The first two fritware fragments discovered in the Qohandez come from this test-pit. The destruction of the monumental door of the citadel, as well as its redevelopment as rich dwellings, would correspond to this period (most probably during the first part). A first stone levelling of the depression left by the

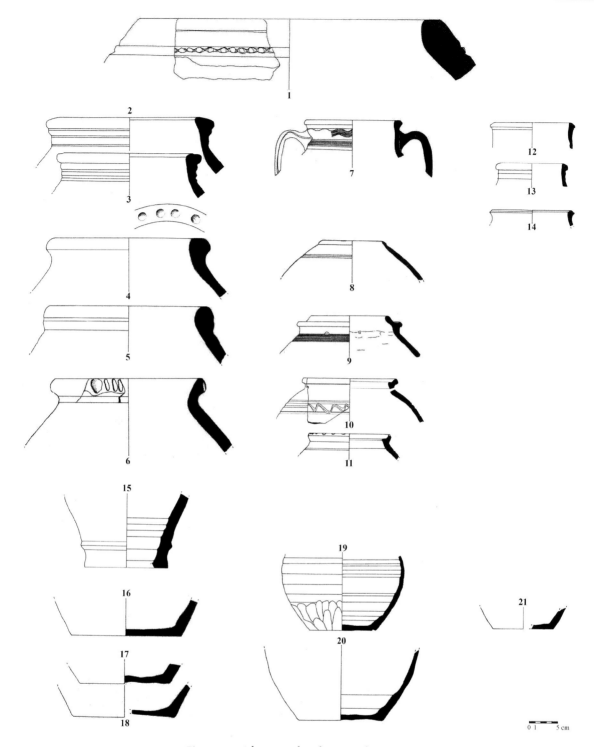

Figure 82: Nishapur, Qohandez, Period IIIa: jars.

destruction, over which a new quarter was created, was clearly observed. The material discovered well corroborates this new urban phase.

T12

The badly preserved upper layers corresponding to this period make the study and the interpretation of the material difficult. The very few shards (41 recovered, of which only six were recorded) do not permit detailed analysis.

Cat.	n°SU	Test	Square	Description
1	418-2	10	L XVII	Rim of storage jar (LJ1). Pinkish buff fabric (C6G). Red orange slip, applied decoration.
2	315-17	13	J XVI	Top of large jar (LJ8). Rather coarse orange fabric (A6GM). Cream yellowish slip.
3	315-18	13	J XVI	Top of large jar (LJ8). Coarse reddish fabric (A6GM). Cream yellowish slip.
4	204-20	B	LXIV	Rim of jar (LJ5). Coarse buff fabric (C6G).
5	509 to 512/6	27	JX	Rim of large jar (LJ6). Coarse pinkish buff fabric (C6G). Cream slip.
6	509 to 512/7	27	JX	Top of large jar (LJ5). Rather coarse red orange fabric (A6GM). Cream slip.
7	418-11	10	L XVII	Top of jar (J11). Buff orange fabric (A6FM). Slip, combed design.
8	330-6	23	G-H-I XV/XVI	Top of jar (J13). Medium orange buff fabric (A6FM). Combed design, cream slip.
9	417-1	10	L XVII	Top of jar (J10). Buff orange fabric (A6GM). Slip, engraved design.
10	110-6	26	O XII	Top of jar (J7). Rather fine pinkish orange fabric (A6FM). Combed design.
11	330-8	23	G-H-I XV/XVI	Rim of jar (J7). Medium orange buff fabric (A6FM). Cream slip.
12	418-4	10	L XVII	Neck of jar (J2). Rather fine orange buff fabric (A6FM). Buff slip.
13	418-5	10	L XVII	Neck of jar (J2). Fine pinkish buff fabric (A2F). Pale slip.
14	330-7	23	G-H-I XV/XVI	Rim of small jar (J12). Medium orange buff fabric (A6GM).
15	311-12	13	J XVI	Base of jar (Jb4). Rather coarse pinkish fabric (B6GM). Cream yellowish slip.
16	227-8	B	L XIV	Base of jar (Jb3). Rather coarse buff fabric with white and sand inclusions (A6GM).
17	506 to 508/2	27	JX	Base of large jar (Jb3). Coarse red orange fabric, overcooked (C6G). Cream yellowish slip.
18	508-509/2	27	JX	Base of large jar (Jb3). Rather coarse buff fabric (A6GM). Cream yellowish slip.
19	421-1	10	L XVII	Part of jar (Jb1). Red orange fabric (A6FM).
20	115-2	26	O XII	Bottom of large jar (Jb3). Rather coarse pinkish buff fabric (A6GM).
21	117-1	26	O XII	Base of jar (Jb3). Medium orange fabric (A6FM). Cream yellowish slip.

Legend 82: Nishapur, Qohandez, Period IIIa: jars.

T13

The total number of ceramic fragments found in this test-pit is 563, of which 250 were recorded and 53 drawn. Among the recorded fragments, coarse to medium wares amount to 57%, fine unglazed material 23% and glazed material 12%. It is clearly observable that the proportion of fine material has notably increased compared to the previous periods. Most of the coarse to medium wares are storage jars (68%), 19.5% are basins, 6% cooking pots and 5% flat lids. The fine material is entirely jugs. The glazed material, mainly polychrome, is essentially composed of bowls and a single closed shape. This period is characterized by the progressive abandonment of the military fortress of the Qohandez, even if the excavation of the northern rampart also shows a possible use during this period. Some other parts were totally abandoned, mostly during the 10th century as shown by the material found in the layers filling the walkway curtain passage. The material culture found in T13, at the centre of this military building, reflects this urban change.

T23

One hundred and forty-three shards were found, of which 25 were studied and drawn. The coarse to medium wares amount to 49% of the material. Most are storage jars, but there are also basins, lids and cooking pots. The fine material essentially comprises glazed wares (21%), mainly bowls. The fine unglazed wares are less well represented (10%) and the best identified shapes are jugs. One turquoise glazed fritware seems to belong to this assemblage.

T26

The total number of shards found is 100, of which 71 were recorded and 34 drawn and studied. The best represented material corresponds to fine wares (47%), mostly jugs. Among this fine

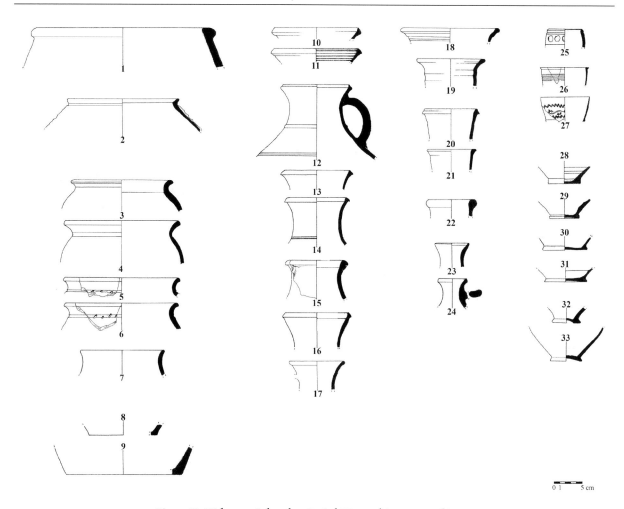

Figure 83: Nishapur, Qohandez, Period IIIa: cooking pots and jugs.

material, 11% are polychrome glazed, mainly bowls. Only 27% of the material is coarse wares: jars, cooking pots and one lid. As with the previous test-pits, the high proportion of fine and glazed material is also clearly observed here. The architecture observed during the excavation does not indicate true changes; the structures found were certainly reused and probably rebuilt.

T27

The total number of shards found and recorded is 396, of which 25 were studied and drawn. Only 12 monochrome glazed wares (3%), of which two are fritwares, were found. The main characteristic observed is a majority of coarse to medium wares (56%) compared to a much less frequent finer material (28%). The coarse wares are essentially storage jars and cooking pots. It seems that the jug is the best represented shape among the fine wares. The absence of structures does not permit the socio-economical status of this part of the citadel to be identified; however, the material suggests a possible modest status.

General Interpretation

UNGLAZED WARES

Period IIIa, like the previous period, is characterized by a preponderance of closed shapes, storage jars and jugs. In addition, an increase in the variety of types was observed. The most frequent shapes among the coarse to medium wares are jars (Fig. 82), which range from large

Cat.	n°SU	Test	Square	Description
1	235-3	B	LXIV	Top of cooking pot (CP9). Coarse greenish fabric (B5GM).
2	311-13	13	J XVI	Top of cooking pot (CP6). Rather fine fabric, burned (B5GM). Applied decoration.
3	504-602/1	27	J X	Top of cooking pot (CP2). Rather coarse buff fabric (B5GM).
4	504-602/2	27	JX	Top of cooking pot (CP2). Rather coarse buff fabric (B5GM). Surface burned.
5	504-505/2	27	J X	Rim of cooking pot (CP2). Coarse pinkish buff fabric (C6G).
6	504-505/1	27	JX	Top of cooking pot (CP2). Coarse buff fabric (C6G).
7	509 to 512/1	27	J X	Rim of cooking pot (CP4). Coarse buff fabric, burned (B5GM).
8	509 to 512/2	27	J X	Base of cooking pot (CP3). Rather coarse greyish fabric, burned (B5GM).
9	213-3	B	LXIV	Base of cooking pot (CP3). Very coarse fabric, burned (C6G).
10	227-6	B	LXIV	Rim of jug or small jar (J5). Medium reddish buff fabric (A6GM).
11	227-1	B	LXIV	Rim of jug or small jar (J5). Medium reddish fabric (B6GM).
12	115-1	26	O XII	Top of jug (J6). Medium pinkish buff fabric (A6FM). Cream yellowish slip.
13	508-509/4	27	J X	Top of neck of jug (J6). Medium red orange fabric (A6FM). Cream slip.
14	420-2	10	L XVII	Neck of jug (J14). Red orange fabric (A6FM).
15	504-602	27	J X	Neck of jug (JsJ3). Medium orange fabric (A6FM).
16	509 to 512/4	27	J X	Neck of jug (J14). Medium orange fabric (A6FM). Cream slip.
17	235-4	B	LXIV	Neck of jug (JsJ1). Fine red fabric (A4F). Trace of handle.
18	205-1	B	LXIV	Rim of jug or small jar (J5). Fine buff fabric (A2F).
19	204-24	B	LXIV	Neck of jug (JsJ6). Fine buff fabric (A1F).
20	202-2	B	LXIV	Neck of jug (JsJ3). Medium red fabric (A6FM).
21	205-4	B	LXIV	Neck of jug (JsJ2). Rather coarse reddish fabric (A6GM).
22	214-9	B	LXIV	Neck of jug (JsJ2). Fine reddish fabric (A4F).
23	504-602/3	27	J X	Neck of jug. Rather fine orange pinkish fabric (A6FM). Cream slip.
24	509 to 512/5	27	J X	Neck of jug (JsJ1). Medium pinkish buff fabric (A6FM). Cream yellowish slip.
25	413-1	10	L XVII	Neck of jug (JsJ5). Very fine grey greenish fabric (A2F). Engraved, finger prints designs.
26	110-5	26	O XII	Neck of jug (JsJ5). Very fine clear buff fabric.
27	110-4	26	O XII	Neck of jug. Very fine clear buff grey fabric (A1F). Combed design.
28	418-7	10	L XVII	Base of jug (JsJb1). Fine buff fabric (A2F).
29	420-3	10	L XVII	Base of jug (JsJb2). Fine pinkish buff fabric (A4F).
30	509 to 512/3	27	J X	Base of jug (JsJb1). Fine pinkish buff fabric (A1F). Cream slip.
31	315-5	13	J XVI	Base of jug (JsJb2). Fine grey greenish fabric.
32	110-3	26	O XII	Base of jug (JsJb2). Fine buff orange fabric (A4F).
33	110-2	26	O XII	Body and base of jug (JsJb2). Fine clear buff fabric (A1F).

Legend 83: Nishapur, Qohandez, Period IIIa: cooking pots and jugs.

storage items (Fig. 82/1–6 and 16, 18; Fig. 95) to much smaller ones (Fig. 82/7–15,[8] 17, 19, 21; Fig. 96/1–12). The fabrics are essentially coarse to medium and a few medium-fine to fine (C6G, B6GM, A6GM, A6FM and A2F).

The LJ5 and LJ8 types, already observed in Period II, were also produced in Period IIIa (Fig. 82/2, 4, 6). Some other types seem to appear in this period, LJ1 (Fig. 82/1) and LJ6 (Fig. 82/5 and Fig. 95/2). The largest (LJ1) is defined by its inverted rim and oblique shoulder, while type LJ6 has a vertical rim and oblique shoulder. As in Period II, some jars bear fingerprint decorations

---

[8]   For a complete handled jar similar to Fig. 82/7, see Wilkinson 1973, 311, n. 63.

on the rim (Fig. 82/4, 6 and Fig. 95/7) and/or on the body (Fig. 95/10). Stamped decoration[9] appears at this period (Fig. 95/8–9). A large proportion of the storage jars is covered in a beige-yellow slip.

The medium to fine jars (Fig. 82/7–15, 17, 19–21) are of several types: with handles and a vertical neck, J11 (Fig. 82/7) or J2 and J12 without handles (Fig. 82/12–14), with a thin inverted rim, J13 (Fig. 82/8), or an open rim, J7 (Fig. 82/10–11). The type J10 was already known in Period II (Fig. 82/9). The fabrics are mainly fine to medium (A6FM), although some are coarser (A6GM). The decorated jars bear combed and engraved motifs (Fig. 95/1, 6–8). The jars are often covered with a beige to yellow slip.

The cooking pots are of five types (CP2, CP3, CP4, CP6 and CP9; Fig. 83/1–9; Fig. 97/1–5). Two fabrics have been identified (C6G and B5GM). Three new types appear in this period (CP3, CP6 and CP9); CP2 and CP4 continued to be produced from Period II onwards. The fabrics, on the other hand, remain the same during both periods.

Concerning jugs, the fabrics observed range from medium-coarse to very fine (Fig. 83/10–33; Fig. 96/13–27). The medium-coarse jugs are of A6GM and B6GM fabrics. Two shapes have been recognised (J5 and JsJ2; Fig. 83/10–11, 21): J5 is defined by a short oblique neck, while JsJ2 is defined by a high vertical neck.[10]

Fine to medium jugs (Fig. 83/12–14, 16, 20, 24; Fig. 96/10, 13, 15) correspond to a unique kind of fabric (A6FM). 4 forms have been identified (J6, J14, JsJ1 and JsJ3), of which the most represented are those with a high flared neck. These jugs are undecorated and some present a coating of beige slip.

Some of the finest closed forms found are small jugs, characterized by a very fine fabric and the width of the profile (A1F, A2F and A4F; Fig. 83/17–19, 22, 25–33; Fig. 96/17–27). The shapes of necks are flared and rounded (JsJ1, JsJ2, J5, JsJ5 and JsJ6). This material, essentially buff to beige in colour, presents combed, engraved, guilloche and fingerprint decorations (Fig. 83/25–27; Fig. 96/17–19).

Among the coarse to medium open shapes, basins are the most represented (Fig. 84/1–6;[11] Fig. 97/6–11). 5 shapes were observed (Bas1–Bas5), of which Bas5 continued to be produced since Period II. The fabrics identified are mainly coarse to medium (C6G and A6GM), with a few finer examples (A6FM). Some objects present tool impressed (Fig. 97/6) and combed (Fig. 97/11) decorations.

The lids are coarse to fine (C6G, A6GM and A2F) and their shape (Lid1, Lid3 and Lid6) and size may depend on their associated vessels. The largest, which may have closed large jars and basins, are flat and usually have a raised knob (Fig. 84/16; Fig. 97/16–17). The finest may have been used for small jars and jugs (Fig. 84/19).

The bowls are medium coarse to very fine (A6GM, A1F, A4F), with most of them being of medium quality fabric (A6FM). Six shapes were identified (Bw1, Bw2, Bw5, Bw6, Bw7, Bw11). The most common profiles are oblique, hemispherical and rounded (Fig. 84/7, 15; Fig. 97/12, 15). Some bowls are covered with beige or beige-yellow slip and occasionally bear combed ornaments (Fig. 97/13).

GLAZED WARES

Glazed wares comprise 8.7% of the material recorded for this period. Most of it is monochrome (53.5%), while polychrome wares form 44.1% of the material. The probably imported ceramics, which are only opaque white wares, comprise 2.3% of the recorded material. Compared to the preceding one, Period IIIa is therefore firstly characterized by the strong increase of glazed

---

[9]   For an example of stamped decorations on a storage jar, see Wilkinson 1973, 309, n. 62.
[10] For the complete shape see Wilkinson 1973, 297, nos 9–10.
[11] For a complete basin shape similar to Fig. 84/3, see Wilkinson 1973, 312, no. 67.

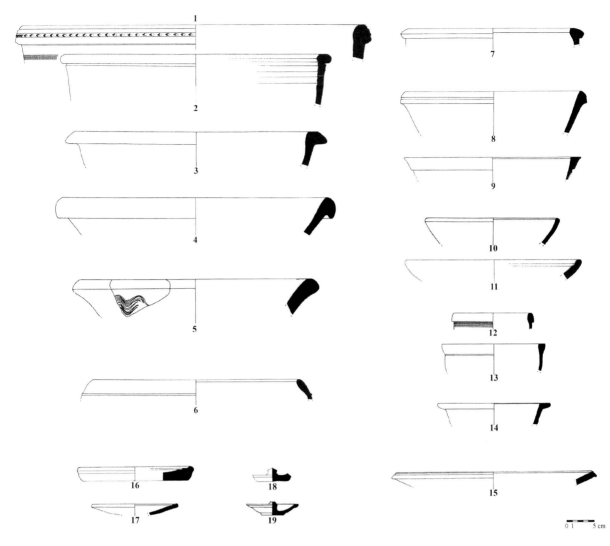

Cat.	n°SU	Test	Square	Description
1	202-36	B	LXIV	Rim of basin (Bas2). Coarse buff fabric (A6GM).
2	202-33	B	LXIV	Top of basin (Bas1). Medium red fabric (A6FM).
3	311-10	13	J XVI	Top of basin (Bas1). Medium orange fabric (A6GM). Buff pinkish slip.
4	418-8	10	L XVII	Top of basin (Bas3). Coarse buff fabric (C6G). Slip.
5	506 to 508/3	27	JX	Top of basin. Coarse pink orange fabric (C6G). Cream yellowish slip.
6	311-14	13	J XVI	Top of basin (Bas5). Medium pinkish orange fabric (A6GM). Cream greenish slip.
7	323-3	23	G-H-I XV/XVI	Rim of bowl (Bw7). Medium pinkish fabric (A6FM). Cream slip.
8	311-9	13	J XVI	Top of bowl (Bw11). Rather coarse pinkish buff fabric (A6GM).
9	315-6	13	J XVI	Rim of bowl (Bw2). Medium orange fabric (A6FM). Cream yellowish slip.
10	509 to 512/8	27	JX	Top of bowl (Bw1). Medium orange fabric (A6FM).
11	204-22	B	LXIV	Rim of bowl (Bw5). Fine buff fabric (A1F).
12	418-12	10	L XVII	Top of bowl (Bw7). Fine red orange fabric (A6FM). Engraved design.
13	311-11	13	J XVI	Top of bowl (Bw7). Medium pinkish fabric (A6FM). Cream yellowish slip.
14	315-7	13	J XVI	Top of bowl (Bw11). Medium buff to pinkish fabric (A6FM).
15	216-12	B	LXIV	Rim of bowl (Bw6). Fine pinkish fabric (A4F).
16	214-2	B	LXIV	Fragment of lid (Lid1). Coarse buff fabric (C6G).
17	330-1	23	G-H-I XV/XVI	Small lid (Lid 6). Fine buff fabric.
18	216-14	B	LXIV	Fragment of lid (Lid3). Coarse greyish buff fabric (A6GM).
19	418-6	10	L XVII	Lid (Lid3). Fine pinkish buff fabric (A2F).

Figure and Legend 84: Nishapur, Qohandez, Period IIIa: basins, bowls and lids.

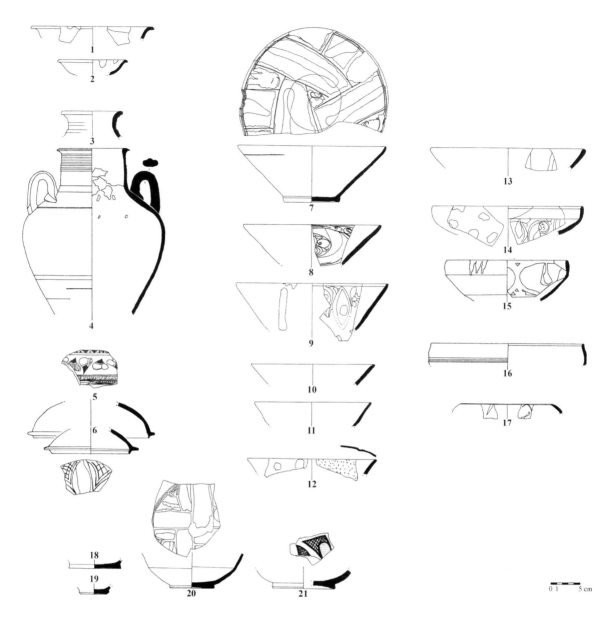

Figure 85: Nishapur, Qohandez, Period IIIa: glazed wares.

wares. It also marks the appearance of the typical Khorasanian polychrome wares known since Wilkinson's publication of the ceramics from Nishapur (Wilkinson 1973). In addition, the uppermost layers corresponding to this period are characterized by the presence of the first fritwares (5 recorded) found in stratigraphic contexts (Fig. 98/30). In addition, a few shards (5 recorded) presented a very hard and very fine clayey fabric, which may be a kind of earthen fritware.[12] As the earliest fritwares discovered, they form 2.2% of the glazed ware fabrics and are all covered with monochrome green or turquoise blue glazes.

The fabrics of the glazed wares are essentially of very good quality, being fine and medium fine (A1F, A2F, A4F, A6FM, B5FM). Some rare examples are coarser (A6GM). Most of the glazed material, when the shapes were well identified, is represented by bowls: *c.* 2.5% are jars and jugs, 1% lids[13] and 1% lamps.

---

[12] This peculiar fabric was observed in the material of T27, T26 and T10.
[13] Concerning this shape see Wilkinson 1973, 65, no. 39; 81, no. 38.

Cat.	n°SU	Test	Square	Description
1	311-7	13	J XVI	Top of bowl (Bw5GL). Very fine cream yellowish fabric (A1F). Cobalt blue painting on opaque white glaze.
2	330-3	23	G-H-I XV/XVI	Small bowl (Bw5GL). Base missing. Fine reddish orange fabric (A4F). Splashware.
3	202-10	B	LXIV	Neck of jar (JsJ6GL). Fine yellow buff fabric (A2F), green glaze.
4	418-3	10	L XVII	Jar (J14GL). Base missing. Fine orange fabric (A2F). Green glaze on white ground.
5	330-4	23	G-H-I XV/XVI	Lid (Lid4GL). Fine buff fabric (A6FM). Buff ware type.
6	330-5	23	G-H-I XV/XVI	Lid (Lid4GL). Fine orange buff fabric (A6FM). Brown and green splash-sgraffiato.
7	425-1	10	L XVII	Bowl (Bw10GL). Red orange fabric (A6FM). Painted sgraffiato on white ground.
8	330-2	23	G-H-I XV/XVI	Bowl (Bw10GL). Base missing. Fine orange buff fabric (A6FM). Brown and green splash-sgraffiato.
9	311-3	13	J XVI	Bowl (Bw10GL). Base missing. Medium pinkish orange fabric (A1F). Splash-sgraffiato.
10	311-5	13	J XVI	Top of bowl (Bw6GL). Medium pinkish fabric (A6FM). White slip under clear glaze.
11	315-1	13	J XVI	Top of bowl (Bw10GL). Fine pinkish buff fabric (A1F), white slip under clear glaze.
12	311-1	13	J XVI	Top of bowl (Bw6GL). Medium pinkish fabric (A6FM). Green painted dots under yellow glaze.
13	311-4	13	J XVI	Top of bowl (Bw10GL). Fine cream to clear buff fabric (A4F). Drips of green and blue glazes.
14	311-2	13	J XVI	Top of bowl (Bw9GL). Pinkish orange fabric (A1F). Splash-sgraffiato.
15	420-5	10	L XVII	Bowl (Bw9GL). Base missing. Fine red orange fabric (A6FM). Slip and glazed painted on white ground.
16	412-7	10	L XVII	Top of bowl (Bw8GL). Very fine orange fabric (A1F). Opacified turquoise glaze.
17	311-6	13	J XVI	Top of bowl (Bw12GL). Medium pinkish fabric (A6FM). Brown painted design on white slip under clear glaze.
18	315-3	13	J XVI	Base of bowl (Bw4GL). Medium orange fabric (A6FM). Turquoise (?) design on white ground, under clear glaze.
19	315-2	13	J XVI	Base of bowl (Bw2GL). Orange fabric (A6FM). Black on white design, under clear glaze.
20	418-19	10	L XVII	Base of bowl (Bw4GL). Fine orange fabric (A4F). Painted on white slip under clear glaze.
21	202-11	B	LXIV	Base of bowl (Bw4GL). Rather coarse reddish fabric (A6GM). Buff ware type.

Legend 85: Nishapur, Qohandez, Period IIIa: glazed wares.

The best represented bowls (Fig. 85) are of two types: the first with oblique walls (Bw6,[14] Bw10[15]) and the second with carinated walls (Bw9[16]). Some bowls belonging to the Bw6 category show Chinese influence in their rim profile (i.e. Fig. 85/12). Other types are less well represented. The shape with curved walls and a rounded flared rim (Bw5[17]) characterises the imported opaque white wares, as their imitations (Fig. 85/1-2). Some types of bowls present an inverted rim (Fig. 85/16–17). The very few lids discovered have a round profile, always with a central knob (Fig. 85/5–6).

[14] Concerning this shape see Wilkinson 1973, 16, no. 52; 25, no. 74; 26, no. 76 ('Buffware'); 68, no. 60 ('color-splashed ware'); 163, no. 13 ('slip painted ware with colored engobe'); 238, no. 43 ('monochrome ware').

[15] *Ibid.*, 20, no. 61 ('Buffware'); 59, no. 8; 60–61, nos 13–14, 20 ('color-splashed ware'); 96, no. 11; 98, no. 19; 100, no. 26 ('black on white ware'); 132, no. 4; 134, no. 9 ('polychrome on white ware'); 160, no. 2; 167, nos 37–38 ('slip painted ware with colored engobe'); 217, no. 8 ('ware with yellow staining black'); 239, nos 45–46 ('monochrome ware').

[16] *Ibid.*, 63, no. 31; 67, no. 58; 70, nos 69–70 ('color-splashed ware'); 105, no. 62 ('black on white ware'); 144, nos 53, 56 ('polychrome on white ware'; 216, no. 3; 217, no. 5 ('ware with yellow staining black'); 236, no. 33 ('monochrome ware').

[17] *Ibid.*, 14, no. 40; 20, no. 62; 22, no. 64 ('buff ware'); 58, no. 2 ('color-splashed ware'); 160–161, no. 3–5 ('slip painted ware with colored engobe'); 183, no. 3; 186, no. 15 ('opaque white ware and its imitations'); 240, no. 50 ('monochrome ware').

MONOCHROME WARES

Amongst the monochrome wares 84.6% are green to turquoise, 13.1% honey to brown and purple, and 2% yellow (Fig. 98/9–12). Very few jar fragments were identified (Fig. 85/3–4; Fig. 98/2–4). The sole jar presenting an almost complete profile, which was found during the excavation, is monochrome green glazed with two symmetrical handles (Fig. 85/4; Fig. 98/2). It has a flat rim, a cylindrical neck, two handles and a bulbous body. The glaze is peculiar, very vivid and clear, covering a white slip ground. This type of glaze on a white slip ground seems to be the same as that covering analyzed shard no. 46 (Fig. 46). The chemical composition of this glaze is plumbo-stanniferous. The type of small jar with an everted neck (Fig. 85/3; Fig. 98/3) visually presents a different glaze; the green is much darker and this glaze may be of a different chemical composition to the former one.

The monochrome bowls are the most common glazed wares. Most of them are green to turquoise (Fig. 85/16; Fig. 98/6–7). These types of glazes of Period IIIa present different visual characteristics: some are characterized by crackles and/or a significant thickness and/or an irregular coating. A large proportion of these glazes are clear, although opaque ones were also recorded. It was therefore observed that these last different aspects cannot define a chronological phase. On the contrary, the chemical analyses of glazes would allow chronological data to be proposed. The monochrome lead glazes, of the same chemical composition as the polychrome ones, are well characterized in the Islamic Period.

OPAQUE WHITE WARES

It seems probable that in Period IIIa this category of wares, as the chemical analyses have shown, was imported from Iraq. Moreover, these ceramics seem to be the only imported material identified in the Qohandez during this period. Four opaque white fragments were found in stratigraphic contexts (T23 and T13), two of them painted with cobalt blue (Fig. 85/1; Fig. 98/1). All have the characteristic shape of a bowl with a curved wall and rounded flared rim. This type of ceramic is here associated with monochrome green to turquoise glazes and also slip wares (splash wares, splash-sgraffiato wares, slip painted wares). In TE (2006), four opaque white fragments were found, also associated with monochrome green and slip painted wares. There also they belong to a stratigraphical context corresponding to Period IIIa.

SPLASH AND SGRAFFIATO WARES

The best represented type within this category is the splash-sgraffiato ware (10% of the glazed material; Fig. 85/6–9, 14; Fig. 98/16–17). The splash wares form 4.7% (Fig. 98/15). Some bowls could be called *painted-sgraffiato wares* because the decoration on the white surface is painted and not splashed. Moreover, the engraved design determines the painted one (Fig. 85/7; Fig. 98/13). The shapes identified among the splash and sgraffiato wares are bowls and one lid. The bowls mainly have oblique walls on a flat base, with the other type presenting a carinated wall. The monochrome sgraffiato wares are less numerous and amount to 1.7% (Fig. 98/15).

SLIP PAINTED WARES

This type of ware forms 17% of the glazed material (Fig. 85/10–11, 19; Fig. 98/20–21, 23–24). The identified shapes are bowls with oblique walls. The shards discovered being very fragmentary, the motifs represented were only partially recognized. Some calligraphic decorations were found (Fig. 98/23), besides abstract and dotted rosettes (Fig. 98/20–21). The colours of the slips are white, black and red. Some wares are in addition polychrome due to the surface glaze, which can be yellow (Fig. 98/24). All these types seem to be contemporary: the assemblages found suggest that there is no evolution between bichrome and polychrome wares.

BUFF WARES

This type of polychrome ware comprises 3.5% of the glazed material during Period IIIa (Fig. 85, 21; Fig. 98/25–29). The shapes identified were round bowls and one lid. It should be noted that the yellow pigment employed, chemically composed of lead and tin (shard A48; Fig. 48), is the same as that found in a yellow and green underglaze painted ware (shard A60; Fig. 48, see Chap. 3). The motifs represented are of vegetal and geometrical inspiration; some of them present a black-hatched background, whose type is contemporary to plain grounds.

OTHER POLYCHROME WARES

The underglaze polychrome decorations (2.9%), as well as the imitations of opaque white wares (1.1%) and, lastly, the yellow staining black type (0.5%) are also found in the same ceramic assemblages (Fig. 85/12; Fig. 98/19, 22).

Period IIIa can be divided into two parts. Most of the material corresponds to the late 9th–early 11th centuries. Concerning the first part of Period IIIa, which would correspond to a period between the late 8th century and the late 9th century, it has been impossible to identify the contemporary material. This lacuna is due to the absence of archaeological and archaeometrical elements. Nevertheless, it is probable that an occupation belonging to this first phase of Period IIIa existed. The layers concerned could have been composed of material produced during this first phase, but mixed with the later, better identified one (see for example the TL realised for T26 US 110). It can be suggested that during the first phase of Period IIIa there was not yet a visible change in material culture. This cultural change is, on the contrary, clearly and forcefully observable during the second phase of Period IIIa.

The ceramic assemblages contemporary to Period IIIa show that all the main types of the Nishapur horizon coexist. Therefore, it is not possible to draw a sequence of the appearance of the different glazed types; for instance, it is not possible to say whether the buff ware type appeared after the slip-painted wares. It is surely assumed that all these types were all produced in the city around the 10th century.

As previously mentioned, the distribution of glazed wares differs from one test-pit to another. They are much more numerous and diversified in T10, T13 and T23. Considering that the distribution of the glazed types on the site is very different, it has been observed that some areas are totally devoid of polychrome wares (i.e. T27). This does not mean that it is more ancient than the other excavated areas, but that this material culture may have been different depending on the areas of the site (Bulliet 1976).

Period IIIb

Period IIIb is not represented in all test-pits, and was identified in TA, T10, T12, T13 and T26. The largest part of this material belongs to TA, which only concerns Period IIIb. As previously specified, the TL analyses performed do not formally show the chronological interval of IIIb; they give the chronological interval for the entire Period III (785–1165). Period IIIb has therefore been identified on the basis of the stratigraphical and ceramic study between the first part of 11th century and 1165 AD.

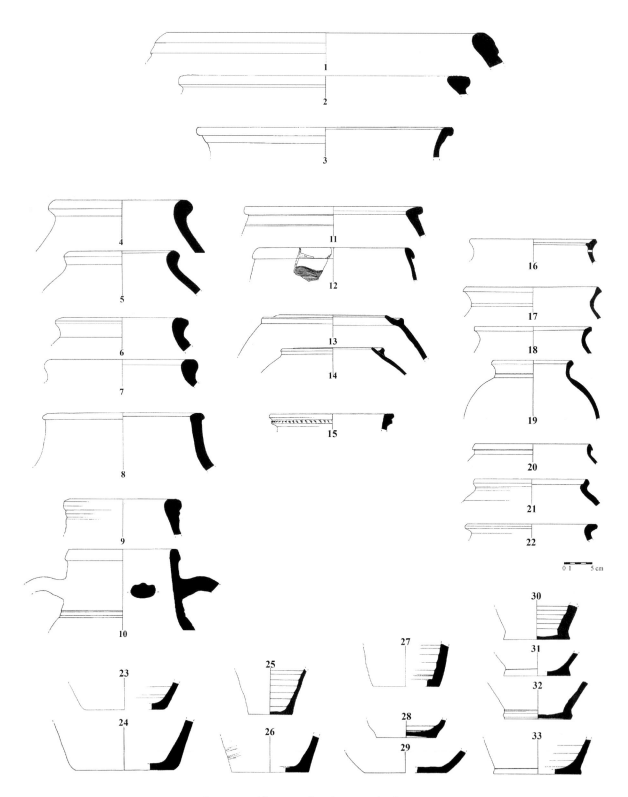

Figure 86: Nishapur, Qohandez, Period IIIb: jars.

Cat.	n°SU	Test	Square	Description
1	106-36	A	L XIV	Rim of storage jar (LJ1). Coarse red orange fabric (B6G). Buff slip.
2	108-1	A	L XIV	Rim of large jar. Coarse pinkish buff fabric (C6G).
3	111-24	A	L XIV	Rim of large jar. Reddish buff fabric with sand (A6FM).
4	108-3	26	O XII	Top of jar (LJ5). Rather coarse red orange fabric (A6GM). Cream slip.
5	108-4	26	O XII	Top of jar (LJ5). Rather coarse red orange fabric (A6GM). Cream slip.
6	106-39	A	L XIV	Rim of jar (LJ5). Red orange fabric (A6GM).
7	105-4	A	L XIV	Rim of jar (LJ6). Buff reddish fabric (A6GM)
8	309-3	13	JXVI	Neck of jar (LJ8). Coarse buff pinkish fabric (C6G). Cream greenish slip.
9	107-79	A	L XIV	Rim of jar (LJ8). Coarse red pinkish fabric (A6GM).
10	111-1	A	L XIV	Neck of jar with handles (J11). Coarse buff fabric (C6G).
11	106-8	26	O XII	Rim of jar (LJ7). Coarse buff orange fabric (C6G). Combed design.
12	106-13	26	O XII	Top of jar (LJ7). Rather fine buff orange fabric (A6FM). Combed design.
13	108-2	26	O XII	Top of jar (J10). Rather coarse red orange fabric (A6FM). Cream slip.
14	106-1	26	O XII	Top of jar (J10). Orange fabric (A6FM). Cream slip.
15	108-9	A	L XIV	Rim of jar (J4). Rather fine pinkish buff fabric (A6FM). Engraved decoration.
16	302-4	13	JXVI	Rim of jar (J7). Medium pinkish buff fabric (A6FM). Cream yellowish slip.
17	327-2	13	JXVI	Rim of jar (J4). Medium buff orange fabric (A6FM). Cream slip.
18	106-2	26	O XII	Top of jar (J4). Fine red orange fabric (A4F).
19	104-6	26	O XII	Top of jar (J8). Rather fine red orange fabric (A6FM). Cream slip.
20	102-5	26	O XII	Top of jar (J9). Buff orange fabric.
21	108-35	A	L XIV	Top of jar. Buff orange fabric.
22	107-80	A	L XIV	Top of jar (LJ5). Fine buff orange fabric (A1F).
23	105-19	A	L XIV	Base of jar (JsJb5). Pinkish buff fabric (A6FM).
24	105-20	A	L XIV	Base of jar (Jb2). Coarse red fabric (A6GM). Pale buff slip.
25	105-17	A	L XIV	Base of jar (Jb2). Rather fine red orange fabric (A6FM).
26	107-81	A	L XIV	Base of jar (Jb3). Coarse buff fabric (C6G).
27	309-1	13	JXVI	Base of jar (Jb5). Medium pinkish buff fabric (A6FM). Greenish cream slip.
28	112-1	A	L XIV	Base of jar (Jb3). Medium reddish buff fabric.
29	308-6	13	JXVI	Base of jar (JsJb5). Pinkish fabric.
30	302-1	13	JXVI	Base of jar (JsJb9). Rather coarse pinkish buff fabric (A6GM).
31	101-16	A	L XIV	Base of jar (JsJb9). Fine pink fabric.
32	327-3	13	JXVI	Base of jar (JsJb9). Medium buff orange fabric (A6FM). Cream slip.
33	101-3	A	L XIV	Base of jar (Jb2). Pinkish pale buff fabric.

Legend 86: Nishapur, Qohandez, Period IIIb: jars.

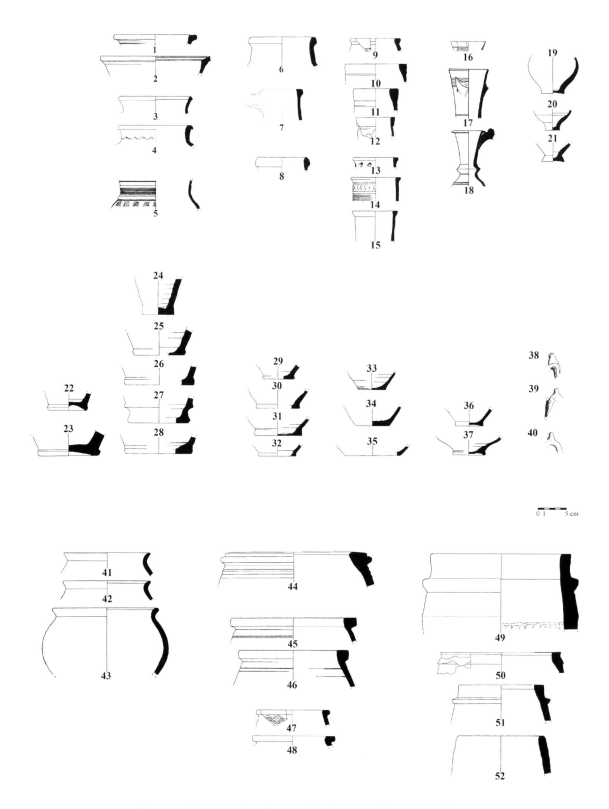

Figure 87: Nishapur, Qohandez, Period IIIb: jugs, cooking pots and pots.

Cat.	n°SU	Test	Square	Description
1	113-36	A	L XIV	Rim of small jar. Rather fine yellowish fabric. Partially burned.
2	114-18	A	L XIV	Rim of small jar (J5). Rather fine reddish fabric (A6FM).
3	111-22	A	L XIV	Neck of small jar (JsJ6). Very fine red fabric (A1F).
4	109-27	A	L XIV	Neck of small jar (JsJ6). Very fine red fabric (A4F). Combed decoration.
5	114-15	A	L XIV	Fragment of jug. Very fine cream fabric (A1F). Engraved decoration.
6	113-11	A	L XIV	Neck of jar or jug (J2). Coarse red fabric.
7	106-56	A	L XIV	Neck of jug (JsJ4). Buff fabric (A6FM). Combed decoration.
8	109-53	A	L XIV	Rim of jug (?). Fine buff fabric.
9	103-13	A	L XIV	Neck of jug (JsJ5). Very fine greyish fabric.
10	109-52	A	L XIV	Rim of jug (JsJ5). Fine pinkish buff fabric (A4F).
11	107-28	A	L XIV	Rim of jug (JsJ5). Fine buff fabric (A4F).
12	107-35	A	L XIV	Neck of jug (JsJ5). Fine buff reddish fabric (A4F).
13	105-6	A	L XIV	Neck of jug (JsJ5). Coarse pinkish buff fabric (A6GM).
14	107-78	A	L XIV	Rim of jug (JsJ5). Fine buff fabric (A4F). Pinched decoration.
15	111-10	A	L XIV	Neck of jug (JsJ5). Very fine grey fabric (A1F). Pinched and engraved decoration.
16	400-22	10	L XVII	Rim of jug. Very fine clear buff fabric (A1F). Engraved decoration.
17	102-7	26	O XII	Neck of jug (JsJ1). Orange fabric (A6FM). Engraved decoration.
18	102-1	26	O XII	Top of jug (JsJ1). Rather fine buff orange fabric (A6FM), cream slip.
19	104-5	26	O XII	Base/body of jug (JsJb7). Fine buff orange fabric (A6FM), cream slip.
20	419-1	10	L XVII	Base of jug (JsJb6). Fine buff orange fabric (A6FM).
21	106-2	26	O XII	Base of jug (J4). Fine buff orange fabric (A4F), cream slip.
22	106-31	A	L XIV	Base of jug or small jar (JsJb7). Red orange fabric (A6FM). Pale buff slip.
23	113-3	A	L XIV	Base of jug or small jar (Jb5). Coarse buff fabric.
24	106-62	A	L XIV	Base of jug or small jar (JsJb4). Coarse red orange fabric (B6GM).
25	113-7	A	L XIV	Base of jug or small jar (JsJb6). Fine buff to pinkish buff fabric (A1F).
26	104-2	A	L XIV	Base of jug or small jar (JsJb6). Reddish fabric.
27	109-33	A	L XIV	Base of jug or small jar (JsJb6). Pale buff fabric (A2F).
28	107-29	A	L XIV	Base of jug or small jar (JsJb6). Pale buff fabric (A2F).
29	105-38	A	L XIV	Base of jug (JsJb4). Fine buff fabric (A4F).
30	105-21	A	L XIV	Base of jug (JsJb6). Fine buff fabric (A2F). Engraved decoration.
31	106-25	A	L XIV	Base of jug (JsJb1). Fine orange buff fabric (A6FM).
32	108-47	A	L XIV	Base of jug (JsJb1). Very fine buff greyish fabric (A1F).
33	113-9	A	L XIV	Base of jug (JsJb4). Rather fine clear buff fabric.
34	107-6	A	L XIV	Base of jug (JsJb5). Pale buff to reddish fabric (A6FM).
35	104-6	A	L XIV	Base of jug (JsJb8). Fine buff fabric.
36	106-61	A	L XIV	Base of jug (JsJb2). Fine buff fabric (A4F).
37	113-1	A	L XIV	Base of jug (JsJb2). Fine yellowish fabric (A4F).
38	105-49	A	L XIV	Handle of jug (H2). Fine buff fabric (A4F).
39	105-32	A	L XIV	Handle of jug (H2). Very fine buff greenish fabric (A1F).
40	107-88	A	L XIV	Handle of jug (H2). Buff fabric (A4F).
41	106-19	26	O XII	Rim of cooking pot (CP1). Coarse buff to grey fabric, burned (B5GM).
42	104-15	26	O XII	Rim of cooking-pot (CP1). Coarse buff to grey fabric, partially burned (B5GM).
43	104-16	26	O XII	Cooking-pot (CP1). Coarse grey fabric, burned (B5GM).
44	108-10	A	L XIV	Top of pot (Pot1). Rather coarse pinkish buff fabric (A6GM).
45	113-13	A	L XIV	Top of pot (Pot1). Buff fabric.
46	113-14	A	L XIV	Top of pot (Pot1). Fine buff fabric.
47	105-42	A	L XIV	Top of small pot (Pot1). Pinkish buff fabric (A6GM). Combed decoration.
48	101-17	A	L XIV	Top of small pot (Pot1). Buff fabric.
49	108-12	A	L XIV	Pot (Pot3). Coarse pinkish buff fabric (C6G).
50	402-6	10	L XVII	Top of pot (Pot3). Buff orange fabric. Cream yellowish slip.
51	109-34	A	L XIV	Top of pot (Pot3). Coarse pinkish buff fabric (C6G).
52	108-4	A	L XIV	Top of pot (Pot5). Coarse buff fabric (C6G).

Legend 87: Nishapur, Qohandez, Period IIIb: jugs, cooking pots and pots.

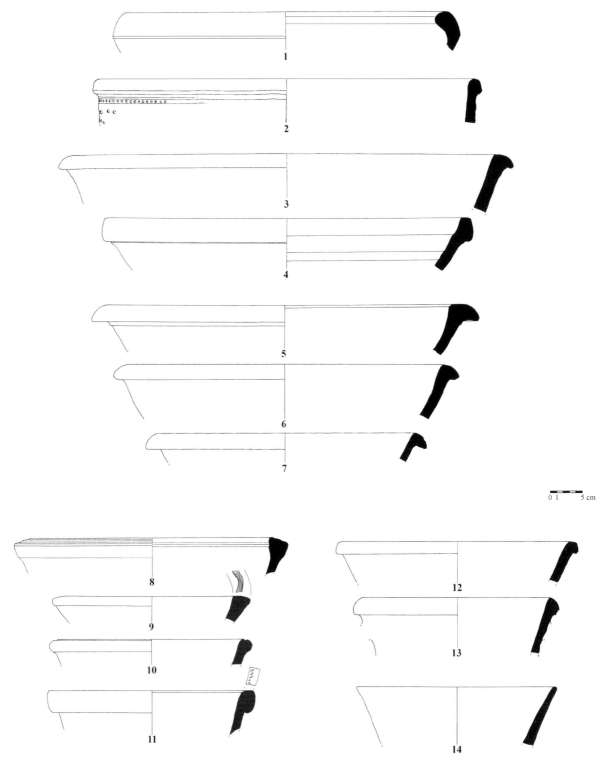

Figure 88: Nishapur, Qohandez, Period IIIb: basins.

Cat.	n°SU	Test	Square	Description
1	105-15	A	L XIV	Rim of basin (Bas5). Coarse red fabric (C6G).
2	108-1	A	L XIV	Rim of basin. Coarse pinkish buff fabric (C6G).
3	106-35	A	L XIV	Top of basin (Bas3). Red fabric (A6GM).
4	318-4	13	J XVI	Rim of large basin (Bas4). Coarse fabric (B6GM). Red slip.
5	318-1	13	J XVI	Rim of large basin (Bas3). Coarse orange fabric (B6GM). Cream slip.
6	105-47	A	L XIV	Top of basin (Bas3). Coarse red orange fabric (C6G).
7	107-53	A	L XIV	Rim of basin (Bas3). Coarse reddish buff fabric (A6GM). Pale buff slip.
8	106-7	26	O XII	Rim of basin (Bas9). Coarse red orange fabric (C6G). Cream slip.
9	308-5	13	J XVI	Rim of basin (Bas4). Medium pinkish fabric (A6FM). Engraved decoration, cream yellowish slip.
10	308-7	13	J XVI	Rim of basin (Bas4). Rather coarse pinkish fabric (A6GM).
11	308-4	13	J XVI	Rim of basin. Rather coarse pinkish fabric (A6GM). Combed decoration, cream yellowish slip.
12	106-7	A	L XIV	Top of basin (Bas4). Red orange fabric (A6GM). Pale buff slip.
13	105-46	A	L XIV	Top of basin. Coarse red fabric (A6GM). Trace of applied handle.
14	302-5	13	J XVI	Top of basin. Medium orange fabric (A6FM).

Legend 88: Nishapur, Qohandez, Period IIIb: basins.

The first appearance of baked brick corresponds to this period, and it was identified in the upper parts of the archaeological remains still visible today. The size of the baked bricks, 23 × 23 × 7/9 cm, is a well-known module attested above all during to the Seljuk Period in Iran.[18]

The total number of fragments recorded is 1941, of which 339 were drawn. It was observed that the general typology is very similar to the previous period (IIIa). The best represented types of coarse wares are storage jars and, in a smaller proportion, basins. The fine ceramic wares are, as in Period IIIa, jugs and glazed bowls. As was already the case during the previous period, the finest and table wares are much better represented than storage ones. Among the material the fabrics identified are of 10 clayey types (A1F, A2F, A4F, A6FM, A5GM, A6GM, B5GM, B6GM, B6G, C6G) plus one fritware type. Compared with the previous period, the absence of the A6FM and B5FM types and the appearance of the B5GM type were observed.

Only two glazed tiles were found in the Qohandez, TB, and are associated with this period (Fig. 106).

TA

The total number of shards recorded is 627, of which 222 were drawn. The material recorded in TA is essentially glazed. In contrast, the unglazed ceramic wares were not systematically recorded. Therefore, their proportion compared to the glazed ones cannot be determined. The largest part of the glazed wares concerning Period IIIb belongs to this test. According to the proportion of shards, 50% of the glazed ceramics are fritwares. Dealing with clayey glazed wares, it appears that the monochrome glazes are much more common than the polychrome ones.

---

[18] In Isfahan, some of the excavated soils of the 11th–12th centuries, composed of the same type of baked bricks, are still today called Nizami (from the Nizam al-Mulk Period) (Scerrato 2001, xxxix and xlii, figs 5, 8–9).

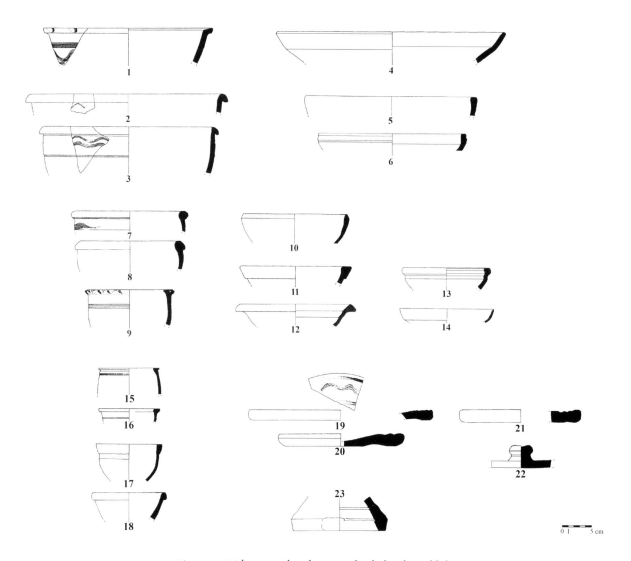

Figure 89: Nishapur, Qohandez, Period IIIb: bowls and lids.

The most represented shapes of coarse wares are mostly handled jars, plus basins and lids, which present combed and engraved designs. The fine unglazed material is mainly constituted of jugs and bowls. The clayey glazed wares are small jars and bowls. The fritware material is mainly constituted of bowls.

T10

The total number of shards is 301, of which 112 were recorded and 25 drawn. The glazed material represents 20%. As observed in Period IIIa, the amount of glazed ceramics is very significant and, in addition, had increased compared to the previous period. On the other hand, Period IIIb shows that monochrome clayey glazed wares (46%) are much more represented than polychrome ones (29.5%). The fritwares represent 24.5% of the glazed material, of which the largest part is monochrome. Concerning the unglazed wares, it has been noticed that the proportion of coarse to medium storage wares (40%) is higher than the fine to medium-fine storage and consumption wares (23.7%). Nevertheless, as in Period IIIa the fine wares, glazed and unglazed, are more represented than the coarser ones. The fabrics identified are mainly fine to medium-fine (A1F, A2F, A4F, A6FM), but one coarser fabric type (A6GM) is also represented. As in Period IIIa, the most represented shapes are large jars, small jugs and glazed bowls.

Cat.	n°SU	Test	Square	Description
1	113-8	A	L XIV	Top of bowl (Bw5). Buff fabric (C6G). Combed and pinched decoration.
2	105-36	A	L XIV	Rim of bowl (Bw7). Fine buff fabric (A4F). Engraved decoration.
3	105-48	A	L XIV	Top of bowl (Bw7). Fine buff reddish fabric (A4F). Combed decoration.
4	111-20	A	L XIV	Top of large bowl (Bw6). Orange to red fabric (A6FM).
5	106-26	A	L XIV	Rim of bowl (Bw1). Fine red orange fabric (A4F).
6	401-11	10	L XVII	Rim of bowl (Bw5). Rather coarse red orange fabric (A6GM). Orange slip.
7	109-35	A	L XIV	Top of bowl (Bw7). Rather fine buff reddish fabric (A6FM). Combed decoration.
8	107-77	A	L XIV	Top of bowl (Bw7). Pinkish buff fabric (A6FM).
9	114-9	A	L XIV	Small bowl (Bw7). Coarse grey greenish fabric (A6GM). Applied decoration.
10	128-1	12	J XV	Top of bowl. Fine buff orange fabric. Cream slip.
11	114-3	A	L XIV	Rim of bowl (Bw2). Medium cream buff fabric.
12	302-1	13	J XVI	Top of bowl (Bw6, A6GM).
13	107-46	A	L XIV	Top of small bowl (Bw1). Fine buff fabric (A4F).
14	107-36	A	L XIV	Top of bowl (Bw5). Very fine buff reddish fabric (A4F).
15	114-14	A	L XIV	Top of small bowl (Bw7). Buff fabric. Engraved decoration.
16	114-32	A	L XIV	Rim of small bowl (Bw7). Yellowish fabric. Cream slip (?).
17	327-1	13	J XVI	Bowl (Bw7). Rather fine orange fabric (A6FM). Cream slip.
18	106-20	A	L XIV	Top of small bowl (Bw4). Buff fabric (A6FM).
19	105-13	A	L XIV	Lid (Lid1). Coarse red fabric (C6G). Combed decoration.
20	106-34	A	L XIV	Lid (Lid1). Coarse pinkish buff fabric (C6G).
21	114-1	A	L XIV	Lid (Lid1). Coarse reddish fabric. The rim is burned.
22	111-4	A	L XIV	Knob of flat lid (Lid2). Coarse reddish buff fabric (C6G).
23	328-1	13	J XVI	Base of lamp-stand (L3). Medium red orange fabric (B6GM). Cream yellowish slip.

Legend 89: Nishapur, Qohandez, Period IIIb: bowls and lids.

To this period corresponds the later and last levelling of the Qohandez, which probably does not concern its entire surface. This levelling, as for Period IIIa, is characterized by a stone layer still visible today. In T10, the strata above it essentially are constituted of destruction layers.

T12

The material corresponding to this period belongs to the surface layers and is the result of the destruction of the upper structures. The total number of shards is 161, of which 46 were recorded and 11 drawn. The material studied presents the same characteristics as the other assemblages of Period IIIb. Nevertheless, as for the previous period, in this test-pit the layers are badly preserved which renders any interpretation difficult.

T13

The recorded shards number 452, of which 115 were studied and 30 drawn. This material comes solely from a large pit excavated from a mud brick soil, which was in use from Period II. As in Period IIIa, the proportion of fine material is much greater than coarse material. Most of the identified fabric types are fine to medium-fine (A1F, A4F, A6FM). The coarser types are A6GM, B5GM, B6GM and C6G. The most common shapes are jars and jugs. As for Period IIIb, this part of the Qohandez remained abandoned and only some parts were reoccupied by houses. The ceramic material found in the large pit excavated in T13, as well as the remains of construction material (baked bricks) also found in it, corroborates this interpretation.

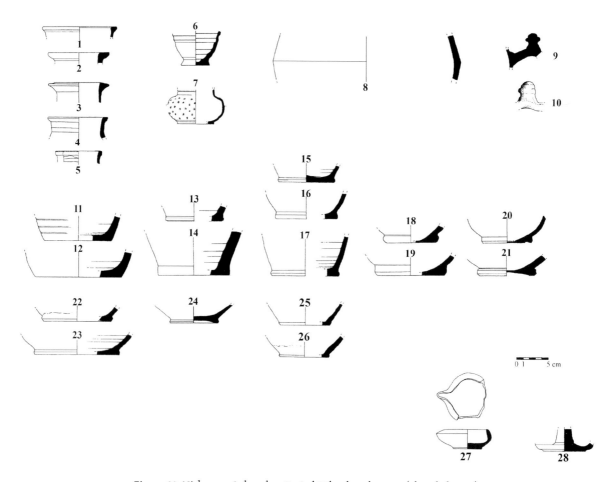

Figure 90: Nishapur, Qohandez, Period IIIb: glazed wares (closed shapes).

T26

More than 400 shards have been recorded, of which 65 were studied and 51 drawn. The material is mainly coarse to medium; fine wares are much less well represented in this area of the site. This contrasts with earlier Period IIIa when the fine material formed the majority. Among the coarse wares, the most frequent shape is the jar, with some basins and lids also observed. The surfaces of these *items* are frequently coated with beige slip. The fine unglazed wares are mainly small jugs, with pale buff to yellow fabric. The glazed wares (clayey and fritwares) form 17% of the recorded material. They are all monochrome, green to turquoise. As far as the urban development of this area is concerned, the structures were definitely abandoned during this period. The numerous pits show and corroborate this historical dynamic.

General interpretation

Unglazed wares

The material of Period IIIb comprises 34.8% coarse to medium fabrics and 24.3% medium fine to very fine fabrics. This period, like the previous ones, is characterized by the preponderance of closed shapes.

Jars are the most represented types at 40.5% (Fig. 86). They range from large storage objects of coarse to medium fabrics (Fig. 86/1–11, 26–27, 29) to smaller *items* of generally finer fabrics (Fig. 86/12–25, 28, 30–36). The largest jars are of coarse fabrics (B6G, C6G and A6GM) and of

Cat.	n°SU	Test	Square	Description
1	114-39	A	L XIV	Rim of jug or small jar (JsJ6GL). Fine yellowish fabric (A1F). Green glaze over white ground.
2	107-60	A	L XIV	Rim of jug or small jar (JsJ2GL). Fine red orange fabric (A1F). Opaque white glaze.
3	327-5	13	J XVI	Neck of jug or small jar (JsJ2GL). Rather fine buff fabric (A6FM). Green glaze.
4	114-40	A	L XIV	Neck of jug or small jar (JsJ6GL). Fine buff orange fabric (A4F). Turquoise green glaze.
5	419-2	10	L XVII	Neck of jug or small jar (JsJ2GL). Very fine pale buff fabric (A2F). Slip painted in black on white, under clear glaze.
6	326-1	13	J XVI	Base of jug or small jar (JsJb6GL). Fine pinkish buff fabric (A4F). Green glaze.
7	113-23	A	L XIV	Small pot or beaker. Rather fine reddish fabric. Green dots under yellow glaze.
8	113-21	A	L XIV	Body of jar. Rather coarse buff pinkish fabric (A6GM). Turquoise glaze.
9	112-15	A	L XIV	Handle with thumber (H2GL). Fine reddish buff fabric. Turquoise glaze.
10	110-43	A	L XIV	Thumber of handle (H2GL). Fine buff fabric (A6FM). Turquoise glaze.
11	106-49bis	A	L XIV	Base of jug or small jar (JsJb5GL). Fine reddish fabric (A1F). Green glaze.
12	109-49	A	L XIV	Base of jug or small jar (Jb3GL). Fine pinkish buff fabric (A4F). Green glaze.
13	106-4	A	L XIV	Base of jug or small jar (JsJb6GL). Pinkish buff fabric (A6FM). Turquoise glaze.
14	111-11	A	L XIV	Base of jug or small jar (JsJb4GL). Rather fine pinkish fabric (A4F). Green glaze.
15	105-41	A	L XIV	Base of jug or small jar (JsJb6GL). Rather fine pinkish buff fabric (A4F). Turquoise glaze.
16	106-9	A	L XIV	Base of jug or small jar (JsJb6GL). Greenish fabric (A4F). Green glaze.
17	105-18	A	L XIV	Base of jug or small jar (JsJb6GL). Buff fabric (A6FM). Turquoise glaze.
18	113-22	A	L XIV	Base of jug or small jar (JsJb6GL). Medium red fabric. Turquoise glaze.
19	110-39	A	L XIV	Base of jug or small jar (JsJb6GL). Fine red fabric (A4F). Turquoise glaze.
20	400-32	10	L XVII	Base of jug or small jar (JsJb3GL). Fine red orange fabric (A6FM). Dark green glaze.
21	402-24	10	L XVII	Base of jug or small jar (JsJb9GL). Fine red orange fabric (A4F). Turquoise glaze.
22	101-9	A	L XIV	Base of jug or small jar (JsJb2GL). Fine red pinkish fabric (A2F). Turquoise glaze.
23	101-1	A	L XIV	Base of jug or small jar (Jb2GL). Rather fine buff fabric (A4F). Green glaze.
24	309-6	13	J XVI	Base of jug or small jar (JsJb2GL). Medium orange to buff fabric (A6FM). Turquoise glaze.
25	103-24	A	L XIV	Base of jug or small jar (JsJb1GL). Fine red orange fabric (A2F). Turquoise glaze.
26	109-13	A	L XIV	Base of jug or small jar (JsJb1GL). Fine red fabric (A1F). Turquoise glaze.
27	327-6	13	J XVI	Lamp (L1GL). Medium red orange fabric (A6FM). Green glaze.
28	110-3	A	L XIV	Base of oil lamp (L2GL). Fine buff fabric (A1F). Turquoise glaze.

Legend 90: Nishapur, Qohandez, Period IIIb: glazed wares (closed shapes).

four main types. One, which occurred in a Period IIIa deposit, is characterized by an inverted rim (LJ1; Fig. 86/1–2). The surface can be coated with buff slip. Another type (LJ5), already present in Period II, is characterized by a round open rim (Fig. 86/4–7; Fig. 99/1–2). The third type of jar (LJ8), known since Period II, presents a vertical and high neck (Fig. 86/8–9). The fourth type of jar (J11) is handled with a narrow high and vertical neck (Fig. 86/10; Fig. 99/4–5). Some other shapes of jars were also recorded, one of which (LJ7) seems to appear during this period and is characterized by a large opening (Fig. 86/11). Some stamped fragments of jars are present in this period, as in the previous one, and emphasise their production during the Islamic period (Fig. 99/7–9). The smaller jars (Fig. 86/13–14, 16, 19–25, 28, 31–36) are usually of fine fabrics (A1F, A4F, A6FM), although some coarser examples were also recorded (B5GM). Two main shapes have been identified, one with an inverted profile and troughed rim (J10; Fig. 86/13–14; Fig. 99/11). The others present an open rim on a round body (J4, J7, J8, J9; Fig. 86/19–24; Fig. 99/12–13). Many of these jars have a coating of beige slip and bear engraved, combed and guilloche motifs (Fig. 99/14–15).

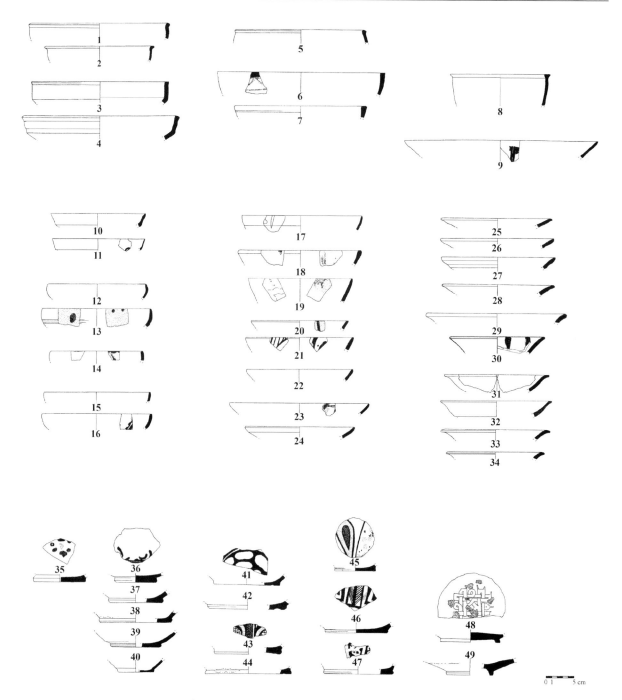

Figure 91: Nishapur, Qohandez, Period IIIb: glazed wares, bowls and dishes.

As in the previous period, the finest unglazed ceramics are jugs (30.2%), of which mainly necks and bases have been found (Fig. 87/1–44; Fig. 99/21–30). Very few jugs are of coarse to medium fabric (A6GM, A5GM and B6GM); most of them are of fine (A4F, A1F and A2F) and of medium to fine fabrics (A6FM).[19] Their colours range from red to cream and grey, although most of them are buff. The largest variety of this category of shape (JsJ1–JsJ6, JsJ9–JsJ10; JsJb1–JsJb9) was observed during this period. It has been observed that the necks can be divided into three categories: large and oblique (Fig. 87/1–5), narrow and rounded (Fig. 87/8–15) and high, narrow flared (Fig. 87/16–18). The largest part of the jug bases is flat (Fig. 87/27–38). Some of the items bear fingerprints, engraved and guilloche motifs on the necks

---

[19] For a complete shape of jug similar to Fig. 87/7, see Wilkinson 1973, 308, no. 59.

Cat.	n°SU	Test	Square	Description
1	110-38	A	L XIV	Rim of bowl (Bw9GL). Yellowish fabric (A4F). Turquoise glaze.
2	113-67	A	L XIV	Rim of bowl (Bw5GL). Fine cream fabric (A4F). Turquoise glaze.
3	114-50	A	L XIV	Rim of bowl (Bw9GL). Fine buff fabric (A1F). Turquoise glaze.
4	110-14	A	L XIV	Rim of bowl (Bw9GL). Buff yellowish fabric(A4F). Turquoise glaze.
5	113-57	A	L XIV	Rim of bowl (Bw8GL). Fine yellowish fabric. Turquoise glaze.
6	110-21	A	L XIV	Top of bowl (Bw1GL). Pinkish buff fabric. Sgraffiato under green glaze.
7	106-41	A	L XIV	Rim of bowl (Bw1GL). Fine buff orange fabric (A6FM). Green glaze.
8	309-5	13	J XVI	Top of bowl (Bw7GL). Fine pinkish fabric (A1F). Dark green glaze.
9	114-45	A	L XIV	Rim of bowl (Bw6GL). Rather fine clear buff fabric (A6FM). Painted in brown/black on white ground.
10	111-63	A	L XIV	Top of bowl (Bw9GL). Fine pinkish buff fabric (A1F). Turquoise glaze.
11	113-83	A	L XIV	Top of bowl (Bw5GL). Very fine white fabric. Brown glaze design on opaque white glaze.
12	106-43	A	L XIV	Rim of bowl (Bw8GL). Fine buff fabric (A4F). Black painted on white slip ground.
13	106-18	A	L XIV	Rim of bowl (Bw1GL). Red fabric (A6FM). Green dots under clear yellow glaze.
14	101-19	A	L XIV	Rim of bowl (Bw8GL). Fine red fabric (A2F). Splash ware.
15	114-75	A	L XIV	Rim of bowl (Bw1GL). Fine red fabric (A1F). Turquoise glaze.
16	106-11	A	L XIV	Rim of bowl (Bw1GL). Rather fine reddish fabric (A6FM). Black slip painted on white ground.
17	402-28	10	L XVII	Rim of bowl (Bw1GL). Very fine orange fabric (A1F). Splash ware.
18	110-35	A	L XIV	Rim of bowl (Bw10GL). Fine pale buff fabric (A2F). Splash ware.
19	109-5	A	L XIV	Top of bowl (Bw10GL). Fine red fabric (A1F). Splash ware.
20	101-21	A	L XIV	Rim of bowl (Bw10GL). Fine pinkish buff fabric (A2F). 'Yellow staining black' type.
21	110-16	A	L XIV	Rim of bowl (Bw10GL). Fine buff yellowish fabric (A2F). Buff ware.
22	111-50	A	L XIV	Rim of bowl (Bw10GL). Fine buff fabric (A1F). Turquoise glaze.
23	110-10	A	L XIV	Rim of bowl (Bw6GL). Fine red fabric (A1F). Splash-sgraffiato.
24	106-45	A	L XIV	Rim of bowl (Bw6GL). Fine red fabric (A1F). Brown glaze.
25	106-23	A	L XIV	Rim of bowl (Bw6GL). Very fine and soft buff yellowish fabric (A4F). Opaque white glaze.
26	107-67	A	L XIV	Rim of bowl (Bw6GL). Buff fabric (A1F). Turquoise glaze.
27	110-7	A	L XIV	Rim of bowl (Bw6GL). Fine red fabric (A1F). Green glaze.
28	114-61	A	L XIV	Rim of bowl (Bw6GL). Rather fine buff fabric (A6FM). Opaque white glaze.
29	105-43	A	L XIV	Rim of bowl (Bw6GL). Fine buff fabric (A4F). Turquoise glaze.
30	106-5	26	O XII	Top of bowl (Bw6GL). Buff orange fabric (A4F). Painted on white slip ground, under clear glaze.
31	100-9	A	L XIV	Top of bowl (Bw5GL). Fine pinkish buff fabric. Opaque white glaze with green design.
32	309-4	13	J XVI	Top of bowl (Bw5GL). Very fine cream white fabric, opaque white glaze.
33	105-28	A	L XIV	Rim of bowl (Bw6GL). Fine pinkish buff fabric (A4F). Opaque yellow glaze.
34	109-22	A	L XIV	Rim of bowl (Bw6GL). Rather fine buff orange fabric (A6FM). Opaque yellow glaze.
35	106-20	A	L XIV	Base of bowl (Bw4GL). Rather fine pinkish buff fabric (A6FM). Splash ware.
36	114-35	A	L XIV	Base of bowl (Bw4GL). Red fabric (A6FM). Painted in brown/black on white slip ground.
37	107-58	A	L XIV	Base of bowl (Bw4GL). Fine red orange fabric (A1F). Splash-graffiato.
38	101-11	A	L XIV	Base of bowl (Bw4GL). Fine pinkish buff fabric (A2F). Turquoise glaze.
39	106-28	A	L XIV	Base of bowl (Bw4GL). Rather fine buff fabric (A6FM). Green splash on white slip ground, under clear glaze.
40	111-51	A	L XIV	Base of bowl (Bw4GL). Red fabric (A6FM). Polychrome painted on white slip, under clear glaze.
41	100-13	A	L XIV	Base of bowl (Bw4GL). Fine red orange fabric. Black slip painted on white slip ground.
42	106-12	A	L XIV	Base of bowl (Bw4GL). Red fabric (A6FM). Turquoise glaze.
43	108-36	A	L XIV	Base of bowl (Bw4GL). Fine buff fabric (A4F). Buff ware.
44	101-13	A	L XIV	Base of dish (D1GL) Fine red to pink fabric. White slip under clear glaze.
45	108-3	A	L XIV	Base of bowl (Bw4GL). Fine buff fabric (A4F). Buff ware.
46	111-53	A	L XIV	Base of bowl (Bw4GL). Fine pinkish buff fabric (A1F). Brown painted on white ground, under clear glaze.
47	108-19	A	L XIV	Base of bowl (Bw4GL). Rather coarse pinkish to buff fabric (A6GM). Buff ware.
48	401-2	10	L XVII	Base of dish (D2GL). Fine red orange fabric (A6FM). Black slip painted on white slip ground, under clear glaze.
49	105-35	A	L XIV	Base of dish (D3GL). Pinkish buff fabric. Green glaze.

Legend 91: Nishapur, Qohandez, Period IIIb: glazed wares, bowls and dishes.

and shoulders (Fig. 87/5, 13–14; Fig. 99/22–24). Only a few wall profiles have been identified and drawn; most of them are rounded and some examples show gadrooned motifs (Fig. 87/21; Fig. 99/25–27).

Cooking pots are very few (*c.* 2%) and much less represented than in previous periods. The material recorded and drawn is homogeneous: only one shape (CP1) and fabric (B5GM) was identified (Fig. 87/42–44; Fig. 100/2–4).

Period IIIb shows the appearance of pots, *c.* 2% (Fig. 87/45–53). They are characterized by three categories (Pot1, Pot3 and Pot5). Pot1 is defined by a thick flat rim on an inverted wall; Pot3 is characterized by a thick wall with lug handles; and Pot5 is characterized by an inverted rim. Their fabrics are medium-coarse to coarse (A6GM, C6G).

As in Period IIIa, the unglazed open shapes are mostly basins, *c.* 10% (Fig. 98). The most represented shapes are Bas3 and Bas4 (Fig. 100/9–17). They are defined by a flared wall and thick (Fig. 98/3, 5–7)[20] or externally thickened rim (Fig. 98/4, 8–10). Bas5 type, already known since Period II, was still being produced (Fig. 98/1). Fabrics are characterized by coarse to medium types (C6G, A6GM, B6GM) and a few finer types (A1F, A4F, A6FM). The largest proportion of the basins is undecorated (Fig. 88), although some of them bear a coating of beige slip (Fig. 100/10–11) or combed designs (Fig. 100/15).

Bowls are well represented in this period at 7.6% (Fig. 89/1–15; Fig. 100/7–8). The shapes are essentially of a round profile (Bw7; Fig. 89/2–3, 7–9, 16–19). This type, already encountered in Period IIIa, is much more represented and diversified here (Bw1,[21] Bw2, Bw4, Bw5, Bw6, Bw8,[22] Bw9). The bowl and basin assemblages are very close in term of fabrics, which range from coarse to fine and are also C6G, A6GM, A6FM, A1F and A4F. Most of them belong to medium to fine quality wares. The decorated bowls are mostly combed.

As in Period IIIa, the lids (Fig. 89/19–22; Fig. 100/18–20), corresponding to 8.3%, are coarse to fine (C6G, B6GM, A6FM, A2F). The most frequent examples are flat and probably associated with large jars and basins or bowls (Lid1, Lid2, Lid3, Lid4).

Some lamp-stand bases also were identified, although they are little represented (Fig. 89/23; Fig. 100/21[23]).

CLAYEY GLAZED WARES

The glazed wares constitute *c.* 19% of the material, of which 9.9% are clayey wares and 9.5% fritwares. Among the clayey wares, monochrome glazes are more numerous (32.4% of the glazed wares) and polychrome types many fewer (18.7%). A *c.* 25% decrease in the polychrome types as compared to Period IIIa has therefore been observed. The other main fritwares are as frequent as the clayey wares. No imports have been identified in this period, with the sole case represented by a shard of Chinese porcelain.[24] Comparison with Period IIIa and the recorded fragments suggest a strong increase in glazed vessels, with the clayey glazed types being the same as in the previous period. The main characteristic of this period is the development of the fritware types.

The fabrics of the clayey glazed material are of good quality. They are essentially fine (A1F, A2F, A4F) to medium-fine (A6FM), and very few examples are medium coarse (A6GM). Therefore, the fabrics employed are of the same kind as in Period IIIa.

---

[20] For a complete shape of basin similar to Fig. 88/3, 5–7, see Wilkinson 1973, 318, no. 87.
[21] *Ibid.*, 17, no. 56; 26, no. 78 ('Buff ware'); 94, no. 5; 97, no. 15 ('black on white ware').
[22] *Ibid.*, 17, no. 59 ('Buff ware'); 58–59, no. 4 ('colored-spalsh ware'); 142, no. 43 ('polychrome on white ware').
[23] *Ibid.*, 349, no. 73.
[24] This shard was found in the surface layers of T26 (nos 100b–9). It was dated by Zhao Bing (CNRS, UMR 8067) to the 12th–13th centuries (oral communication 2008).

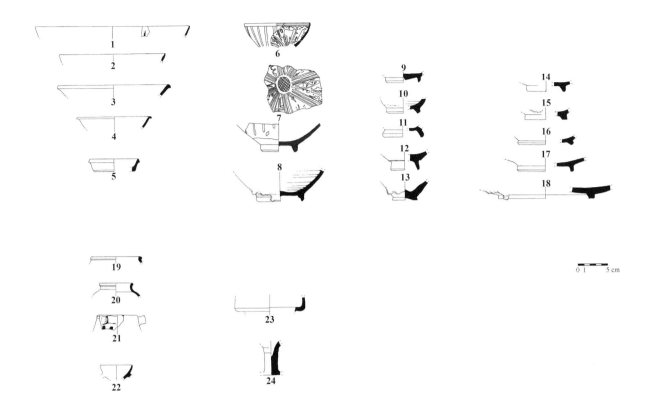

Cat.	n°SU	Test	Square	Description
1	110-48	A	L XIV	Rim of bowl (Bw10GL). White fritware. Cobalt blue painted under clear glaze.
2	114-82	A	L XIV	Rim of bowl (Bw10GL). White fritware, turquoise glaze.
3	101-20	A	L XIV	Rim of bowl (Bw6GL). White fritware. Clear turquoise glaze.
4	100-14	A	L XIV	Rim of bowl (Bw5GL). Pinkish fritware or clayey fritware (?) Turquoise glaze.
5	113-51	A	L XIV	Small bowl (Bw5GL). White fritware, turquoise glaze.
6	419-4	10	L XVII	Rim of bowl (Bw10GL). Fritware, painted in black, turquoise and cobalt blue under clear glaze.
7	419-3	10	L XVII	Base of bowl (Bw4GL). Fritware, painted in black and turquoise under clear glaze.
8	100-2	A	L XIV	Base of jug (JsJb7GL). Hard white fritware. Turquoise (outside) and pale blue (inside) glazes.
9	100-4	A	L XIV	Base of bowl (BW4GL). White fritware. Cobalt blue painted under clear turquoise glaze.
10	104-21	A	L XIV	Base of bowl (Bw4GL). Soft white fritware. Clear turquoise glaze.
11	107-68	A	L XIV	Base of bowl (BW4GL). Soft white fritware. Clear turquoise glaze.
12	111-44	A	L XIV	Base of bowl (Bw4GL). White fritware. Clear cobalt blue glaze.
13	100-7	A	L XIV	Base of bowl (Bw4GL). White fritware. Clear turquoise glaze.
14	113-38	A	L XIV	Base of bowl (Bw4GL). Hard white fritware. Cobalt painted under clear glaze.
15	113-28	A	L XIV	Base of bowl (Bw4GL). Grey fritware, turquoise glaze.
16	112-22	A	L XIV	Base of dish (D2GL). White fritware, turquoise glaze.
17	113-32	A	L XIV	Base of dish (D2GL). White fritware, turquoise glaze.
18	100-5	A	L XIV	Base of dish (D2GL). Hard white fritware. Cobalt blue painted under clear glaze.
19	106-44	A	L XIV	Rim of small pot. Soft white fritware. Clear turquoise glaze.
20	114-44	A	L XIV	Top of small pot (Pot4GL). White fritware, turquoise glaze.
21	114-36	A	L XIV	Top of small pot (Pot9GL). White fritware, turquoise glaze.
22	100-18	A	L XIV	Top of bottle. White fritware. Clear turquoise glaze.
23	106-19	A	L XIV	Fragment of lamp (L1GL). Soft white fritware. Turquoise glaze.
24	100-19	A	L XIV	Fragment of lamp (L2GL). Soft white fritware. Clear turquoise glaze.

Figure and Legend 92: Nishapur, Qohandez, Period IIIb: fritwares.

The best-identified shapes are mainly bowls and jugs or small jars; a few lamps[25] were also recorded (Figs 90–91; Figs 101–102). With a few exceptions, most of the jugs and jars are covered with monochrome glaze. The bowl types are more numerous and diverse than in the previous period. The bowls are carinated (Bw9; Fig. 91/1–12), rounded (Bw1; Fig. 91/7–8, 14–17) or with oblique to very open walls (Bw6, Bw10; Fig. 91/19–31, 34–35).

MONOCHROME WARES

Most of the monochrome wares are green to turquoise (86%), and therefore noticeably more or less the same proportion as in Period IIIa. On the other hand, *c.* 8.7% are honey to brown and purple, showing a decrease in these glazes. Opaque white glazes are well represented (4.3%); the glaze layer directly covers the object, as well a thin slip layer. The jug rims are of two types (JsJ2, JsJ6): they are characterized by a straight neck and a more or less pronounced flat rim (Fig. 90/1–5; Fig. 101/5). The bases could correspond to jugs, small jars, bottles or ewers (Fig. 90/11–26; Fig. 101/1–4). Their profiles are more or less rounded (globular to ovoid; JsJb1, JsJb2, JsJb4, JsJb5, JsJb6, JsJb9).

The monochrome bowls (Fig. 91/1–5, 7–8, 10, 15, 25–29, 32–34, 38, 49; Fig. 101/9–15) are of different types (Bw1, Bw5, Bw6, Bw7,[26] Bw9, Bw10). It has been observed that the recorded carinated bowls seem to be systematically associated with a monochrome glaze. The few lamps recorded are of two types, either footed or with a flat base (Fig. 90/27–28; Fig. 101/16–17).

SPLASH AND SGRAFFIATO WARES

This category is the most numerous of the polychrome types: splash wares form 4% of the glazed material (Fig. 91/14, 17–19, 35; Fig. 102/6–11). In comparison with Period IIIa, and in contrast to the other polychrome categories, the proportion of this type in the glazed assemblage is quite equilibrated. The splash-sgraffiato wares represent 3% of the glazed material (Fig. 91/23, 37; Fig. 102/12–14). The painted sgraffiato found in Period IIIa is here totally absent. The monochrome sgraffiato wares constitute 0.5% (Fig. 91/6; Fig. 102/15). Concerning the shapes, the association between this polychrome category and the Bw1 and Bw10 shapes has been noticed.

SLIP PAINTED WARES

These correspond to 4.5% of the glazed material (Fig. 91/9, 12, 16, 36, 41, 46, 48; Fig. 102/1–5). The shapes drawn are mainly oblique (Bw6) and round (Bw8) bowls. As in Period IIIa, the slips employed are white, black and red. The glazed surface is always clear: no examples of yellow or green clear glaze were found. This type is less polychrome than in the earlier phases of the site. Some calligraphic motifs, as in the previous period, were identified, which are black painted on white ground; some abstract ornaments have also been identified.

BUFF WARES

This category is more poorly represented, at 1.7% of the glazed material (Fig. 91/43, 45, 47; Fig. 102/16–20). No rims have been recorded; therefore, no bowl types can be defined. The fragments discovered have flat bases and the decorations are only geometrical and of vegetal inspiration.

OTHER POLYCHROME WARES

Underglazed polychrome decoration, as observed in Period IIIa, represents 2.8%. The yellow staining black type (0.2%) is even less represented.

---

[25] For this shape see Wilkinson 1973, 56; 245, no. 17; 234, no. 22.
[26] *Ibid.*, 66–67, nos 53–54 ('color-splashed ware').

FRITWARES

Around 50% of the glazed material comprises fritwares (Fig. 92; Fig. 103–104). This *corpus* is essentially composed of bowls[27] and a few dishes[28] (Fig. 92/1–18; Fig. 103/2–7, 9–16; Fig. 104). The identified shapes of bowls correspond to the following types: Bw4, Bw5, Bw8 and Bw10. Some very fragmentary small closed shapes are also represented (Fig. 92/19–22; Fig. 103/5–6). One of the types recorded is a peculiar shape of pot, whose complete profile has been published by Wilkinson (1973, 265 and 278, no. 12). A few fragmentary lamps were also found (Fig. 92/23–24; Fig. 103/17–19). The fabrics cannot be used as provenance or dating indicators due to the strong homogeneity within the analyzed shards. The glazes, however, present some interesting features leading to some suggestions. Analyzed shard ps6 (Fig. 49; Table 12) presents the same chemical characteristics as some analyzed glazes belonging to the monochrome clayey glazed category: they are alkaline-plumbiferous. Shard ps6, turquoise monochrome, was found in the same archaeological context (well 16) as the underglaze painted fritwares (Fig. 92/6–7; Fig. 104/5–6). These last shards, found at the bottom of well 16, provide a chronological *terminus* identifying the beginning of the last occupation of the Qohandez. These ceramics should be the latest of the Qohandez stratigraphy and can be dated to ca. late 12th to early 13th century. Shard ps5 (Fig. 49; Table 12), identified as lustre ware and coming from the upper layers of T26, could belong to the same chronology. It presents, nevertheless, a very different glaze technology characterized by a siliceous chemical composition.

Most of the fritwares (77.9%) are turquoise monochrome, with the other monochrome fritwares being opaque white (7.4%) and cobalt blue (4.4%). The bicolour types are much less well represented, although some turquoise and cobalt (4.4%), turquoise and blue (2.2%), turquoise and white (0.7%) and cobalt and white (0.7%) examples were recorded.

The underglaze painted group represents 2.2% of the fritwares. The silhouette ware type (0.7%) is also present. The overglaze painted group is mainly of the *haft rang* type (3.7%), besides the lustre ware (0.7%).

Period IIIb shows a continuity of the unglazed and clayey glazed types already encountered in Period IIIa. The unglazed types and their proportions are quite similar to the previous period. The appearance of the pot shapes and an increase and development in the bowl typology has been observed. In addition, cooking pots are generally less well represented than before, which could be interpreted as a change in occupation type.

Concerning the glazed material, the main peculiarity of this period is the strong preponderance of the monochrome category. The clayey and the fritware glazed material appears to be mainly monochrome. The polychrome wares, which had defined the Nishapur horizon in the previous period, were still being produced, even if in much lesser quantities. Some types, such as the painted sgraffiato wares and the slip-painted under coloured glaze wares, seem to have disappeared.

The fritwares, which are quite as numerous as the clayey glazed wares, are mostly turquoise monochrome. A chronology of the fritwares can be suggested in relation to the stratigraphy. The first type encountered is the turquoise monochrome; the other monochrome types (mainly cobalt blue and opaque white glazes, but also moulded and engraved monochrome wares), such as the underglaze and overglaze painted ones, appear in the upper layers and on the surface of the Qohandez.

---

[27] Concerning this shape see Wilkinson 1973, 267, no. 22; 269–70, no. 35.
[28] *Ibid.*, p. 264, n. 3; p. 267, n. 22; p. 269, n. 33–34.

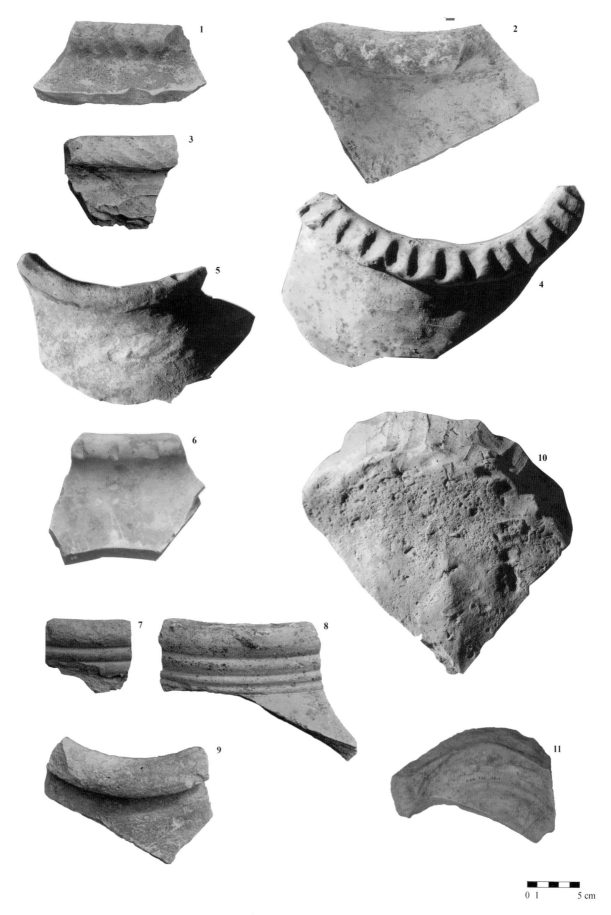

0 1   5 cm

Figure 93: Nishapur, Qohandez, Period II: large jars.

Cat.	n°SU	Test	Square	Description
1	665-678/1	27	JX	see: Fig. 80, n°2.
2	116-1	26	O XII	see: Fig. 80, n°3.
3	237	B	LXIV	Rim of large jar. Coarse to medium red fabric, bow decoration, cream slip.
4	148	12	J XV	Rim of large jar. Coarse red to orange fabric, finger prints on the rim.
5	148	12	J XV	Rim of large jar. Coarse red to orange fabric.
6	424	10	L XVII	Rim of large jar. Medium orange fabric, finger prints on the rim, cream slip.
7	237	B	LXIV	Rim of jar. Coarse red fabric.
8	231	B	LXIV	Top of jar. Coarse red fabric.
9	231	B	LXIV	Top of jar.
10	148	12	J XV	Rim of large jar. Coarse red to orange fabric.
11	118-1	26	O XII	see : Fig. 80, n°18.

Legend 93: Nishapur, Qohandez, Period II: large jars.

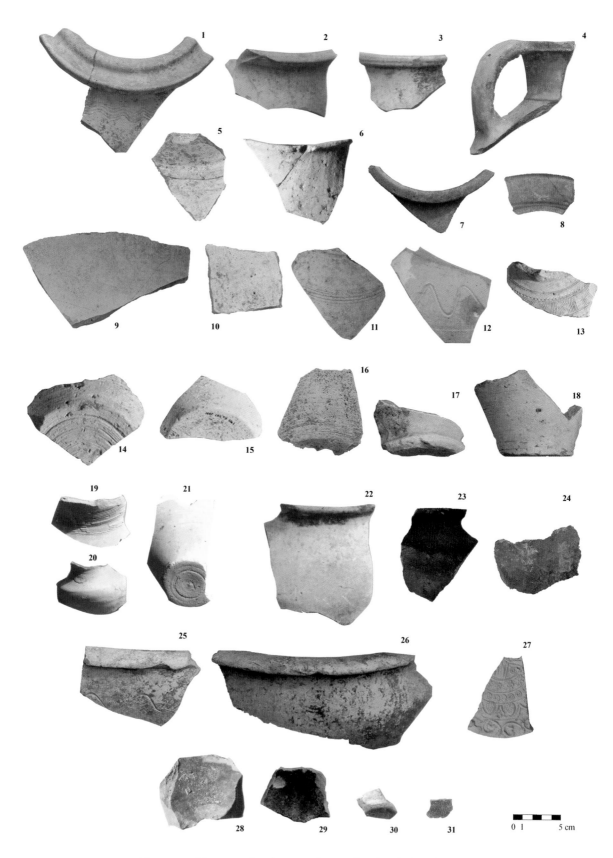

Figure 94: Nishapur, Qohandez, Period II: unglazed and glazed wares.

Cat.	n°SU	Test	Square	Description
1	424-1	10	L XVII	see: Fig. 80, n°7.
2	424-2	10	L XVII	see: Fig. 80, n°8.
3	424-4	10	L XVII	see: fig 80, n°12.
4	424	10	L XVII	Top of jug. Red to orange medium fabric.
5	517/2	27	JX	see: Fig. 80, n°10.
6	157	12	J XV	Top of jar. Red to orange medium fabric.
7	237	B	LXIV	Top of jar. Red fabric.
8	118-2	26	O XII	see: Fig. 80, n°14.
9	114	26	O XII	Fragment of jar (body). Medium buff to red fabric, cream slip.
10	610	27	JX	Fragment of jar (body). Medium buff to red fabric, cream slip.
11	114	26	O XII	Fragment of jar (body). Medium buff pinkish fabric, cream slip.
12	424	10	L XVII	Fragment of jar (body). Fine buff pinkish fabric, cream slip, engraved decoration.
13	246	B	LXIV	Fragment of jar (shoulder). Combed decoration.
14	246	B	LXIV	Base of jar. Medium reddish fabric.
15	236	B	LXIV	Base of jar. Medium reddish fabric.
16	517-518/3	27	JX	see: Fig. 80, n°20
17	237	B	LXIV	Base of jar or jug.
18	231	B	LXIV	Base of jar or jug.
19	423	10	L XVII	Fragment of jug (neck and shoulder). Fine buff pinkish fabric.
20	423	10	L XVII	Fragment of jug (neck and body). Fine buff greenish fabric.
21	423	10	L XVII	Base of jug. Fine deep buff fabric.
22	423-5	10	L XVII	see: Fig. 80, n°5.
23	113-1	26	O XII	see: Fig. 80, n°6.
24	517-518	27	JX	Fragment of cooking pot. Burned coarse fabric.
25	231	B	LXIV	Top of basin. Medium to coarse red fabric. Engraved design.
26	231	B	LXIV	Top of basin. Medium to coarse red fabric.
27	114-1	26	O XII	see: Fig. 80, n° 7.
28	423	10	L XVII	Base of jar. Fine red orange fabric. Green glaze.
29	237	B	LXIV	Base of jar or bowl. Fine red fabric. Green glaze.
30	424	10	L XVII	Base of jar. Fine orange fabric. Turquoise glaze.
31	516	27	JX	Shard. Fine yellowish buff fabric. Turquoise glaze.

Legend 94: Nishapur, Qohandez, Period II: unglazed and glazed wares.

Figure 95: Nishapur, Qohandez, Period IIIa: large jars.

Cat.	n°SU	Test	Square	Description
1	311	13	J XVI	Top of storage jar. Rather coarse buff to red fabric. Cream slip.
2	509 to 512/6	27	JX	see: Fig. 82, n°5.
3	110	26	O XII	Rim of large jar. Medium to coarse red orange fabric. Cream slip.
4	330	23	G-H-I XV-XVI	Rim of large jar. Medium pinkish red fabric. Cream yellowish slip.
5	330	23	G-H-I XV-XVI	Rim of large jar. Medium pinkish red fabric. Cream yellowish slip.
6	257	B	L XIV	Rim of large jar. Coarse red fabric.
7	256	B	L XIV	Rim of large jar. Coarse red fabric.
8	420	10	L XVII	Fragment of large jar (shoulder). Trace of handle. Medium to coarse orange fabric.
				Stamped decoration, cream slip.
9	202	B	L XIV	Fragment of large jar. Coarse buff fabric. Greyish surface. Stamped decoration.
10	323	23	G-H-I XV-XVI	Base of large jar. Coarse buff orange fabric. Finger prints decoration.
11	508-509/2	27	JX	see: Fig. 82, n°18.
12	506 to 508/2	27	JX	see: Fig. 82, n°17.

Legend 95: Nishapur, Qohandez, Period IIIa: large jars.

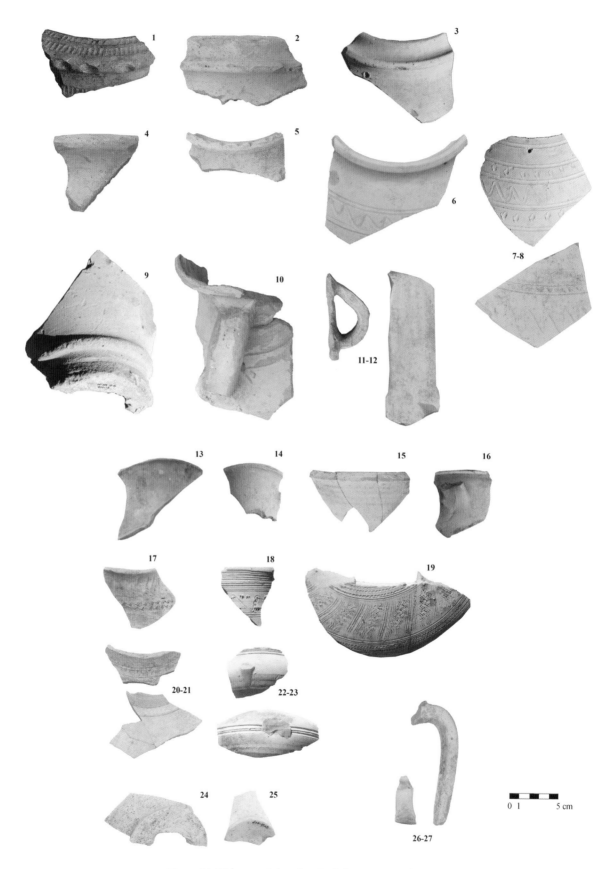

Figure 96: Nishapur, Qohandez, Period IIIa: jars and jugs.

Cat.	n°SU	Test	Square	Description
1	257	B	L XIV	Rim of jar. Red fabric. Stamped or engraved decoration.
2	330	23	G-H-I XV-XVI	Rim of jar. Medium orange pinkish fabric. Cream slip.
3	417-1	10	L XVII	see: Fig. 82, n°9.
4	330	23	G-H-I XV-XVI	Rim of jar. Medium orange pinkish fabric. Cream slip.
5	330-8	23	G-H-I XV/XVI	see: Fig. 82, n°11.
6	110-6	26	O XII	see: Fig. 82, n°10.
7	311	13	J XVI	Fragment of jar (shoulder). Medium buff fabric. Combed/engraved decoration.
8	509 to 512	27	JX	Fragment of jar (shoulder). Medium orange to buff fabric. Combed/engraved decoration.
9	311-12	13	J XVI	see: Fig. 82, n°15.
10	115-1	26	O XII	see: Fig. 83, n°12.
11	506 to 508	27	JX	Handle of jug. Medium orange fabric. Cream slip.
12	110	26	O XII	Handle of jar. Medium pinkish fabric. Cream slip.
13	420-2	10	L XVII	see: Fig. 83, n°14.
14	235-4	B	XIV	see: Fig. 83, n° 17.
15	509 to 512/4	27	JX	see: Fig. 83, n° 16.
16	257	B	L XIV	Neck of jug.
17	420	10	L XVII	Rim of jug. Pinkish buff fabric. Engraved decoration.
18	418	10	L XVII	Neck of jug. Fine buff orange fabric. Combed/engraved decoration.
19	418	10	L XVII	Fragment of jug (shoulder). Fine buff orange fabric. Combed/engraved decoration.
20	110	26	O XII	Neck of jug. Fine buff fabric. Combed/engraved decoration.
21	110	26	O XII	Fragment of jug (shoulder). Fine buff fabric. Combed decoration.
22-23	418	10	L XVII	Fragments of jugs (body). Very fine light buff fabric.
24	330	23	G-H-I XV-XVI	Base of jug.
25	420-3	10	L XVII	see: Fig. 83, n° 29.
26	110	26	O XII	Handle of jug. Fine buff fabric.
27	330	23	G-H-I XV-XVI	Handle of jug.

Legend 96: Nishapur, Qohandez, Period IIIa: jars and jugs.

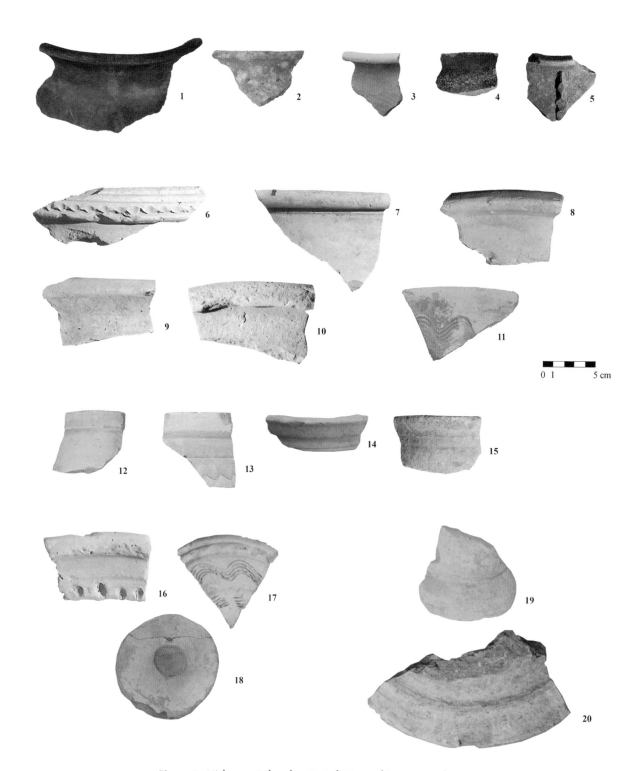

Figure 97: Nishapur, Qohandez, Period IIIa: cooking pots and varia.

Cat.	n°SU	Test	Square	Description
1	504-602/2	27	JX	see: Fig. 83, n°4.
2	504-505/1	27	JX	see: Fig. 83, n°6.
3	504-602/1	27	JX	see: Fig. 83, n°3.
4	509 to 512/1	27	JX	see: Fig. 83, n°7.
5	311-13	13	J XVI	see: Fig. 83, n°2.
6	202-36	B	L XIV	see: Fig. 83, n°1.
7	202-33	B	L XIV	see: Fig. 84, n°2.
8	311-10	13	J XVI	see: Fig. 84, n°3.
9	202	B	L XIV	Top of basin. Coarse buff reddish fabric.
10	418-8	10	L XVII	see: Fig. 84, n°4.
11	506 to 508/3	27	JX	see: Fig. 84, n°5.
12	330	23	G-H-I XV-XVI	Top of bowl. Medium to fine, pinkish orange fabric. Cream slip.
13	330	23	G-H-I XV-XVI	Top of bowl. Medium to fine, pinkish orange fabric. Cream slip, combed decoration.
14	420	10	L XVII	Rim of bowl. Fine red orange fabric.
15	311-11	13	J XVI	see: Fig. 84, n°13.
16	202	B	L XIV	Fragment of lid. Coarse buff red fabric. Engraved decoration.
17	420	10	L XVII	Fragment of lid. Combed decoration.
18	509	27	JX	Lid.
19	330	23	G-H-I XV-XVI	Base of lamp stand. Medium buff orange fabric. Cream slip.
20	229	B	L XIV	Base of lamp stand. Buff orange fabric. Cream slip.

Legend 97: Nishapur, Qohandez, Period IIIa: cooking pots and varia.

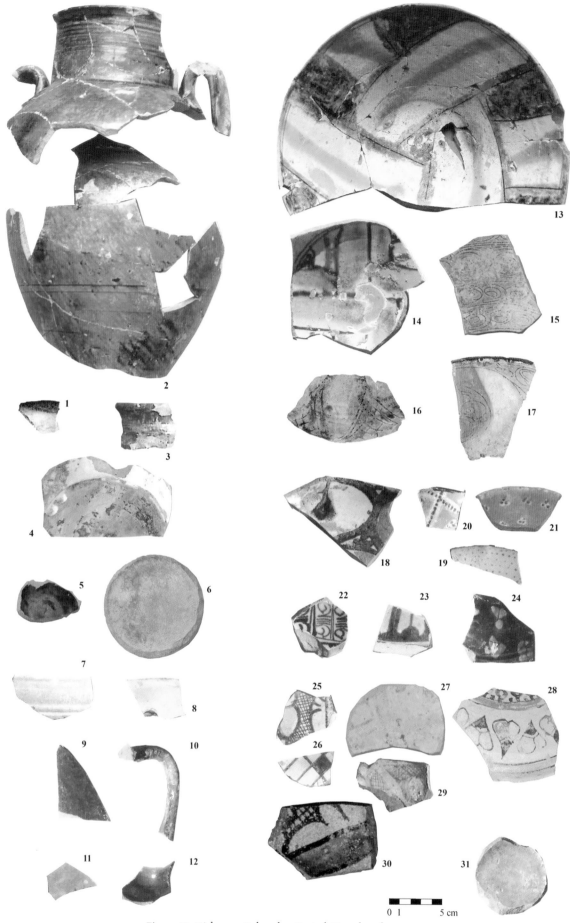

Figure 98: Nishapur, Qohandez, Period IIIa: glazed wares.

Cat.	n°SU	Test	Square	Description
1	311-7	13	J XVI	see: Fig. 85, n°1.
2	418-3	10	L XVII	see: Fig. 85, n°4.
3	202-10	B	L XIV	see: Fig. 85, n°3.
4	420	10	L XVII	Base of jar. Fine to medium red fabric. White slip under clear glaze.
5	323	23	G-H-I XV-XVI	Base of small bowl. Fine red orange fabric. Green glaze on white ground.
6	330	23	G-H-I XV-XVI	Base of bowl. Orange fabric. Green glaze.
7	412-7	10	L XVII	see: Fig. 85, n°16.
8	418	10	L XVII	Fragment of bowl. Fine buff pinkish fabric. White slip under clear glaze.
9	418	10	L XVII	Fragment. Fine to medium red orange fabric. Purple brown glaze.
10	418	10	L XVII	Handle of jug. Fine to medium red orange fabric. Purple brown glaze.
11	418	10	L XVII	Fragment. Bright yellow glaze on white ground.
12	418	10	L XVII	Fragment of jug. Very fine buff orange fabric. Yellow brown glaze.
13	425-1	10	L XVII	see: Fig. 85, n°7.
14	418-9	10	L XVII	see: Fig. 85, n° 20.
15	323	23	G-H-I XV-XVI	Fragment of bowl. Fine to medium buff orange fabric. Sgraffiato under green glaze.
16	330-5	23	G-H-I XV-XVI	see: Fig. 85, n° 6.
17	330-2	23	G-H-I XV-XVI	see: Fig. 85, n°8.
18	420-5	10	L XVII	see: Fig. 85, n° 15.
19	311-1	13	J XVI	see: Fig. 85, n° 12.
20	418	10	L XVII	Fragment of bowl. Fine orange fabric. Black slip painted on white ground, under clear glaze.
21	110	26	O XII	Fragment of bowl. Fine red orange fabric. Black and white slip painted on red ground, under clear glaze.
22	418	10	L XVII	Base of bowl. Black painted on white ground, under yellow glaze.
23	418	10	L XVII	Fragment of inscribed bowl. Fine orange fabric. Black slip painted on white ground, under clear glaze.
24	418	10	L XVII	Fragment of jug? Fine to medium red orange fabric. White slip painted under yellow glaze, on a purple ground.
25	418	10	L XVII	Fragment of bowl. Fine buff ware. Painted in green, brown and yellow under clear glaze.
26	418	10	L XVII	Fragment of bowl. Fine buff ware. Painted in brown and yellow under clear glaze.
27	323	23	G-H-I XV-XVI	Base of bowl. Fine to medium buff orange fabric. Painted in brown and yellow under clear glaze.
28	330-4	23	G-H-I XV/XVI	see: Fig. 85, n° 5.
29	202-11	B	L XIV	see: Fig. 85, n° 21.
30	229	B	L XIV	Fragment of bowl. Painted in green and black on white ground, under clear glaze.
31	417	10	L XVII	Base of bowl. Soft, white pinkish fritware. Turquoise glaze.

Legend 98: Nishapur, Qohandez, Period IIIa: glazed wares.

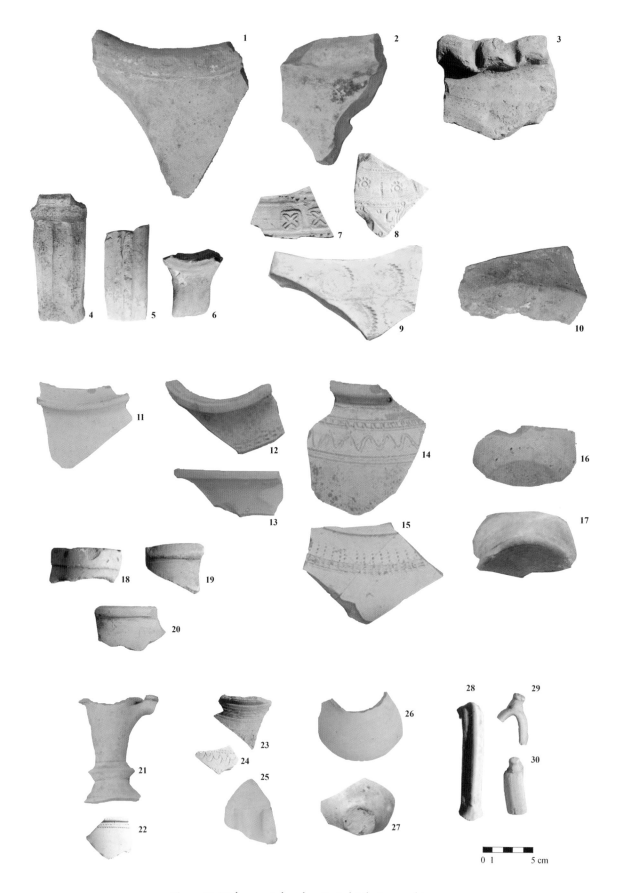

Figure 99: Nishapur, Qohandez, Period IIIb: jars and jugs.

Cat.	n°SU	Test	Square	Description
1	109	26	O XII	Top of jar with round rim. Red orange to buff fabric.
2	108-3	26	O XII	See: Fig. 86, n°4.
3	308	13	J XVI	Rim of large storage jar. Coarse pinkish fabric. Cream yellowish slip.
4	109	26	O XII	Handle of large jar. Fine to medium red orange fabric. Cream slip.
5	411	10	L XVII	Handle of large jar. Fine to medium orange to buff fabric.
6	103-104	A	L XIV	Handle of jar. Medium to fine pinkish buff fabric.
7	411	10	L XVII	Fragment of jar. Medium orange to buff fabric. Stamped decoration.
8	106	A	L XIV	Fragment of jar. Medium pinkish to buff fabric. Cream slip, stamped decoration.
9	132	12	J XV	Fragment of jar. Stamped decoration.
10	109	26	O XII	Base of jar. Coarse red fabric.
11	106-1	26	O XII	See: Fig. 86, n°14.
12	104-3	26	O XII	Top of jar. Fine to medium orange fabric. Engraved decoration.
13	106-2	26	O XII	See: Fig. 86, n° 18.
14	104-2	26	O XII	Top of jar. Fine to medium red orange fabric. Engraved decoration, cream slip.
15	104	26	O XII	Fragment of jar (shoulder). Rather fine cream buff fabric. Engraved decoration.
16	104-14	26	O XII	Base of small jar. Fine to medium red orange fabric. Cream slip. Lowest part of the body cut on the wheel.
17	419	10	L XVII	Base of jug or small jar. Buff fabric.
18	105	A	L XIV	Rim of jug (neck). Fine to medium buff pinkish fabric.
19	104	A	L XIV	Neck of jug. Fine to medium buff pinkish fabric.
20	114	A	L XIV	Neck of jug.
21	102-1	26	O XII	See: Fig. 87, n°18.
22	133-6	12	J XV	Neck of jug. Fine buff fabric. Engraved decoration.
23	114	A	L XIV	Fragment of jug. Fine buff fabric. Engraved decoration.
24	133	12	J XV	Fragment of jug. Very fine buff yellow fabric. Engraved decoration.
25	102	26	O XII	Fragment of jug (body). Very fine cream fabric. Ribbed decoration.
26	106	26	O XII	Fragment of jug (body). Fine buff fabric, polished cream slip.
27	419-1	10	L XVII	See: Fig.87, n°20.
28	327	13	J XVI	Handle of jug. Cream slip.
29	114	A	L XIV	Handle of jug. Fine buff fabric.
30	114	A	L XIV	Handle of jug. Fine cream fabric.

Legend 99: Nishapur, Qohandez, Period IIIb: jars and jugs.

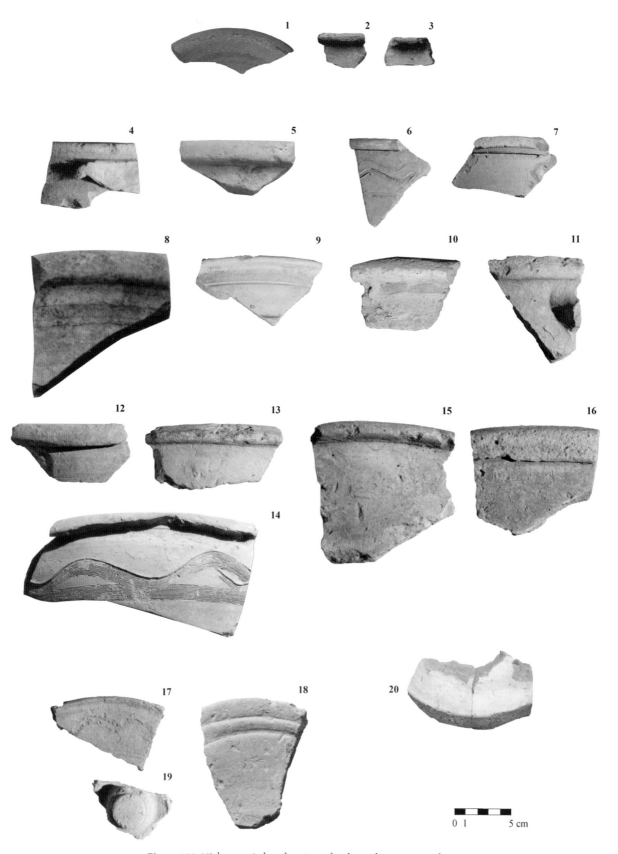

Figure 100: Nishapur, Qohandez, Period IIIb: cooking pots and varia.

Cat.	n°SU	Test	Square	Description
1	302	13	J XVI	Rim of cooking pot. Coarse burned fabric.
2	328	13	J XVI	Rim of cooking pot. Coarse burned fabric.
3	328	13	J XVI	Rim of cooking pot. Coarse burned fabric.
4	402-6	10	L XVII	See: Fig. 87, n°50.
5	419	10	L XVII	Rim of pot. Medium buff orange fabric.
6	105-48	A	L XIV	See: Fig. 89, n°3.
7	308	13	J XVI	Rim of bowl. Medium buff orange fabric, cream yellowish slip.
8	419	10	L XVII	Top of basin. Medium dark buff fabric.
9	323	13	J XVI	Rim of basin. Medium orange pinkish fabric. Cream slip.
10	323	13	J XVI	Rim of basin. Medium red orange fabric. Cream slip.
11	105-46	A	L XIV	See: Fig. 88, n°13.
12	107-53	A	L XIV	See: Fig. 88, n°7.
13	104	A	L XIV	Rim of basin. Medium pinkish fabric. Cream buff slip.
14	400	10	L XVII	Fragment of basin. Medium fabric, cream slip, combed decoration.
15	105-47	A	L XIV	See: Fig. 88, n°6.
16	105	A	L XIV	Top of basin. Coarse fabric.
17	105-13	A	L XIV	See: Fig. 89, n°19.
18	106-34	A	L XIV	See: Fig. 89, n°20.
19	105	A	L XIV	Fragment of flat lid (knob).
20	328-1	13	J XVI	See: Fig. 89, n°23.

Legend 100: Nishapur, Qohandez, Period IIIb: cooking pots and varia.

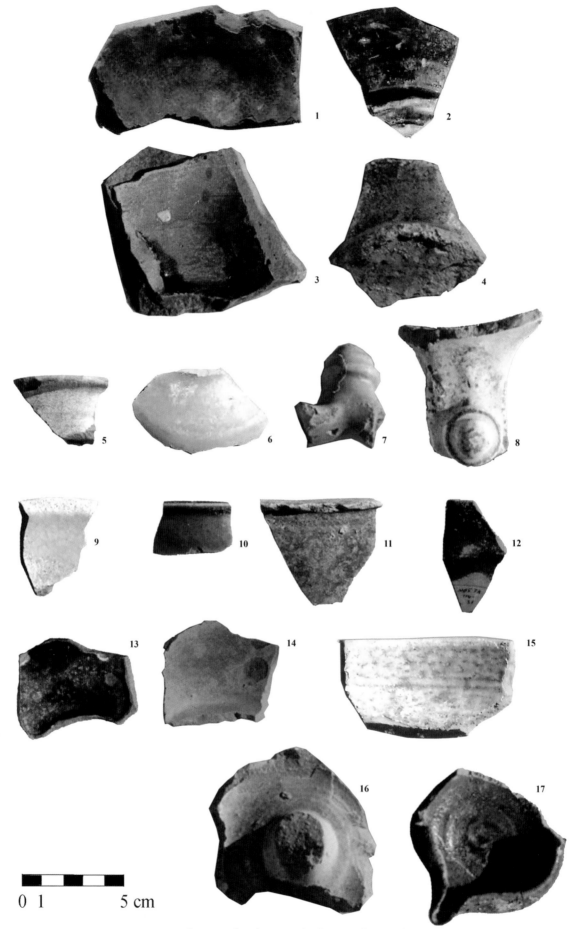

Figure 101: Nishapur, Qohandez, Period IIIb: monochrome glazed wares.

Cat.	n°SU	Test	Square	Description
1	402-24	10	L XVII	See: Fig. 90, n°21.
2	400-32	10	L XVII	See: Fig. 90, n°20.
3	111-11	A	L XIV	See: Fig. 90, n°14.
4	106	A	L XIV	Base of jug or small jar. Fine red orange fabric. Green glaze.
5	114-40	A	L XIV	See: Fig. 90, n°4.
6	400	10	L XVII	Fragment of jug or small jar (shoulder). Very fine buff orange fabric. Turquoise glaze.
7	110-43	A	L XIV	See: Fig. 90, n°10.
8	112-15	A	L XIV	See: Fig. 90, n°9.
9	309-4	13	J XVI	See: Fig. 91, n°33.
10	110-38	A	L XIV	See: Fig. 91, n°1.
11	309-5	13	J XVI	See: Fig. 91, n°9.
12	114	A	L XIV	Rim of bowl. Brown purple glaze.
13	111	A	L XIV	Base of bowl. Brown purple glaze.
14	103-104	A	L XIV	Base of bowl. Turquoise glaze.
15	133-12	12	JXV	Rim of bowl. Fine pinkish orange fabric. Turquoise glaze on white ground.
16	110	A	L XIV	Base of oil lamp. Turquoise glaze.
17	327-6	13	J XVI	See: Fig. 91, n°28.

Legend 101: Nishapur, Qohandez, Period IIIb: monochrome glazed wares.

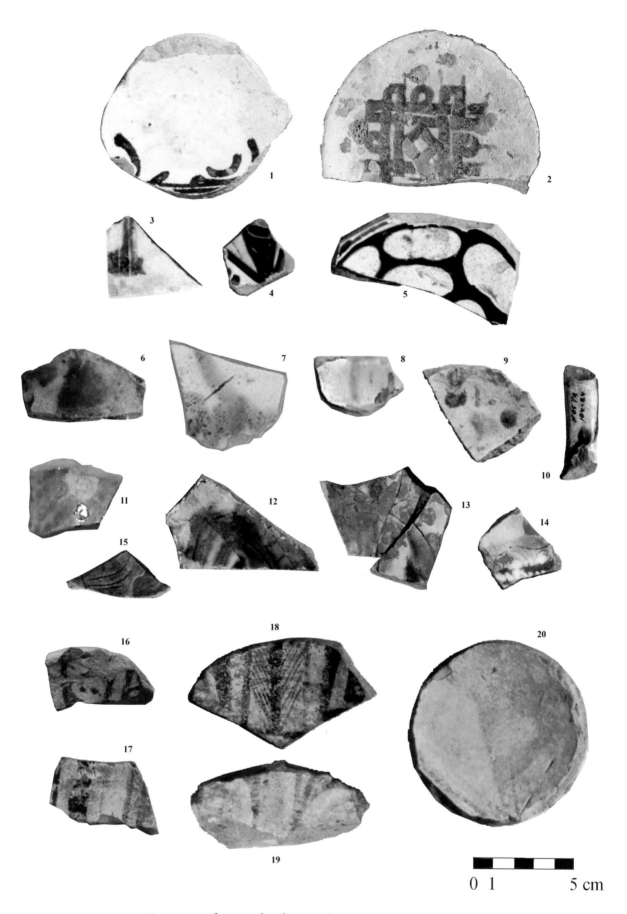

Figure 102: Nishapur, Qohandez, Period IIIb: polychrome glazed wares.

Cat.	n°SU	Test	Square	Description
1	114-35	A	L XIV	See: Fig. 91, n°37.
2	401-2	10	L XVII	See: Fig. 91, n°49.
3	114-45	A	L XIV	See: Fig. 91, n°10.
4	106	A	L XIV	Shard of bowl. Slip painted in black and red on white ground, under clear glaze.
5	100-13	A	L XIV	See: Fig. 91 n°42.
6	109	A	L XIV	Shard of bowl. Green splashware on white ground, under clear glaze.
7	106	26	O XII	Shard of bowl. Fine red orange fabric. Green and brown splashware on white ground, under clear glaze.
8	402-28	10	L XVII	See: Fig. 91, n°18.
9	106-20	A	L XIV	See: Fig. 91, n°36.
10	104-24	A	L XIV	Handle of jug. Fine pinkish fabric. Black and green splashware on white ground, under clear glaze.
11	419	10	L XVII	Shard of bowl? Fine red orange fabric. Painted in green under yellow glaze.
12	111	A	L XIV	Shard of bowl. Green and brown splash-sgraffiato on white ground.
13	107-58	A	L XIV	See: Fig. 91, n°38.
14	106	A	L XIV	Shard of bowl. Green, brown and yellow splash-sgraffiato on white ground.
15	110	A	L XIV	Shard of bowl. Sgraffiato on white ground, under green glaze.
16	108-19	A	L XIV	See: Fig.91, n°48.
17	106	A	L XIV	Shard of bowl. Buff ware, black and green painted under green glaze.
18	111-53	A	L XIV	See: Fig. 91, n°47.
19	108-36	A	L XIV	See: Fig. 91, n°44.
20	108-3	A	L XIV	See: Fig. 91, n°46.

Legend 102: Nishapur, Qohandez, Period IIIb: polychrome glazed wares.

Figure 103: Nishapur, Qohandez, Period IIIb: monochrome fritwares.

Cat.	n°SU	Test	Square	Description
1	418	10	L XVII	Ribbed pearl. White fritware, turquoise glaze.
2	113-57	A	L XIV	Rim of bowl. Fritware, turquoise glaze.
3	113-51	A	L XIV	See: Fig. 92, n° 5.
4	113-67	A	L XIV	Rim of bowl. Fritware, turquoise glaze.
5	114-36	A	L XIV	See: Fig. 92, n° 21.
6	114-44	A	L XIV	See: Fig. 92, n° 20.
7	419	10	L XVII	Rim of bowl. White fritware, engraved decoration under turquoise glaze.
8	419	10	L XVII	Shard of bowl. Pinkish fritware, thick turquoise glaze.
9	104-21	A	L XIV	See: Fig. 92, n° 10.
10	113-32	A	L XIV	See: Fig. 92, n° 17.
11	106	A	L XIV	Base of bowl. Fritware, turquoise glaze.
12	100-2	A	L XIV	See: Fig. 92, n° 8.
13	111	A	L XIV	Base of bowl. Fritware, opaque white glaze.
14	111	A	L XIV	Base of bowl. Fritware, opaque white glaze.
15	111	A	L XIV	Base of bowl. Fritware, cobalt blue glaze.
16	111	A	L XIV	Base of bowl. Fritware, cobalt blue glaze.
17	103	26	O XII	Fragment of lamp. Fritware, turquoise glaze.
18	114	A	L XIV	Fragment of lamp. Fritware, turquoise glaze.
19	100-19	A	L XIV	See: Fig. 92, n° 24.

Legend 103: Nishapur, Qohandez, Period IIIb: monochrome fritwares.

Cat.	n°SU	Test	Square	Description
1	113	A	L XIV	Rim of bowl. Fritware, cobalt blue painted under clear glaze.
2	100-5	A	L XIV	See: Fig. 92, n°18.
3	106	A	L XIV	Shard of bowl. Fritware, black painted under clear glaze.
4	111	A	L XIV	Shard of bowl. Silhouette ware: painted in black under clear glaze.
5	419-4	10	L XVII	See: Fig. 92, n°6.
6	419-3	10	L XVII	See: Fig. 92, n°7.
7	107	A	L XIV	Shard of bowl. Haft rang: black and blue painted on opaque white glaze.

Figure and Legend 104: Nishapur, Qohandez, Period IIIb: polychrome fritwares.

Figure 105: Moulded wares, T 26. Surface (1–2) and Period II (3).

Figure 106: Glazed tiles, TB, Period IIIa.

Figure 107: Moulded and glaze inlaid shards, TB and TC, Period IIIb.

3. Comparative study with the main Khorasanian sites

The aim here is to compare the Nishapur material with the other Khorasanian capitals as well as other sites, whether or not they correspond with the geographical and/or administrative definition of Khorasan, and to attempt to identify a cultural area where it could be possible to demonstrate a similar material culture. The Khorasanian cultural territory seems to change depending on the different periods concerned.

Period II

Tureng Tepe

The Tureng Tepe material, in the present Iranian province of Gurgan, belongs to the phases VIA (3rd–5th centuries) to VIIA/B (7th–8th centuries), and is generally different in comparison to that of Nishapur.

Contrary to Nishapur, no fine wares have been identified at Tureng Tepe during this long period. Instead, as in Nishapur, the most common material is characterized by closed shapes, jars and jugs, whose shapes are different from those of Nishapur. Besides, it can be observed that the typology of bowls is much more important in Tureng Tepe. In addition, the coarse fabrics of Tureng Tepe present very different production technologies: their inclusions are mineral but also organic, shells and bones (Lecomte 1987, 104–119).

The existence of glazed material in Tureng Tepe from this period is unclear. One fragment of a flask with turquoise grey glaze was identified in phase VIA (Lecomte 1987, 106, pl. 60/13 and pl. 137/4).

Some shapes found in Nishapur are, nevertheless, comparable with the Tureng Tepe material. In the Nishapur material, one jar shape (Fig. 80/9) shares very similar characteristics with some jars of phases VIA–VIIA/B in Tureng Tepe (Lecomte 1987, pl. 48/3, 6; pl. 61/9; pl. 66/13). A Nishapur jug type (Fig. 80/11) is also present in Tureng Tepe in phase VIA (*ibid.*, pl. 48/7; pl. 55/11). Moreover, some cooking pot shapes from Nishapur (Fig. 81/5) could also be compared with the material of the same type in phase VIA (*ibid.*, pl. 54).

As in Nishapur, the decoration techniques in Tureng Tepe are engraved and combed (*ibid.*, 116). Additionally, other kinds of decorations were found in Nishapur: beige and red slips, fingerprints and twisted motifs.

Gurgan Plain

In nine[29] of the pre-Islamic and Islamic sites studied by Kiani (1982) some types of jars and cooking pots could essentially be compared with the Nishapur material. According to Kiani, this material would date to the Sasanian Period. The largest part of this pottery is red in colour with a few being grey. The shapes comparable with the Nishapur material are of four types: storage jars (Fig. 80/3–4; Kiani 1982, figs 50, 59), jars (Fig. 80/10, 13; *ibid.*, figs 46, 48), cooking pots (Fig. 81/4–6; *ibid.*, figs 51, 56–58) and one basin (Fig. 81/10; *ibid.*, fig. 44). The decorations observed are incised or stamped (Kiani 1982, 64). Therefore, according to Kiani, for the Gurgan Plain the stamped decorations should be earlier than the same types in Nishapur, according to the results of the Nishapur study.

Following Kiani's investigations in the Gurgan Plain, glazed ceramics have been observed from the early Sasanian Period onwards. The glaze is turquoise to green, defined by Kiani as alkaline. The shapes concerned are storage jars, bowls and flasks (Kiani 1982, 64). It seems, therefore, that the Gurgan Plain glazed material precedes that of Nishapur. Nevertheless, there is no information concerning the production place of this material.

---

[29] Qaleh Paras, Altintokhmaq, Qaleh Qarniareq, Qaleh Kafar, Qaleh Tokhmaq, Qaleh Qabrestan, Qaleh Gabri, Qaleh Polgunbad, Qaleh Kharabeh.

According to Lecomte's study for Tureng Tepe and its province, the ceramic material culture is less regionalist from the 7th–8th centuries onwards. He suggests that the material of Tureng Tepe (phase VIB) could only be compared with the Atrek Valley for the 6th century. The latter material (phase VIIA/B) is, on the contrary, very close to the Khorezm ceramic material (Lecomte 1987, 110, 113–114).

In the Atrek Valley, the survey carried out by the Italian Mission of the Institute of Archaeology of Turin University permitted the publication of ceramic material belonging to the Sasanian and early Islamic Periods. The jugs illustrated, as a type of storage jar, are close to the Nishapur typologies (Fig. 80/3, 11–13; Venco Ricciardi 1980, fig. J, K; 70, fig. L).

Merv

The Sasanian material of Merv has been recently dated through numismatic and statistic study. The chronological sequence has been divided into two main periods (Puschnigg 2006, 116–119): 'early to middle Sasanian' (*c.* late 4th–5th centuries) and 'late Sasanian' (*c.* late 6th century–early Islamic times). Within the published material from Merv, very few shapes can be compared with those of Nishapur; only one type of jar (Fig. 80/8; Filanovich 1974, fig. 26) and one type of fine jug (Fig. 80/11; Puschnigg 2006, 161, fig. 7.10) are comparable in the two sites. The open shapes (bowls and basins) are well represented during the pre-Islamic Period, contrary to what was observed in Nishapur.

In addition to the morphological typology, the other main difference between the ceramic material of Merv and Nishapur is the absence of glazed material in the layers associated with the 'late Sasanian' Period in Merv.

Some comparisons can nevertheless be made concerning the fabric types and the decorations of the vessels. Recent petrographic analyses (Puschnigg 2006, 105–107) indicate that at Merv the fabrics are mainly of fine types (nine types) and the coarse fabric types are much less numerous (three types). Therefore, in Merv the fineware, as in Nishapur, is well represented in addition to coarse types employed for cooking pots and storage jars. Some of the fine fabrics described could be compared with those of Nishapur: fabrics A, B2, G1 and K in Merv seem to be close to fabrics A1F, A2F, A4F and A6FM in Nishapur. Moreover, the decorations observed in Merv are also comparable, as engraved, combed ornaments and coatings with beige and red slips (Puschnigg 2006, 38, 172–173, 176, 178).

Balkh

The 'Sasanian level' in Balkh corresponds to level III, which is divided into two phases: IIIa (3rd–4th centuries) and IIIb (5th–9th centuries). The material of the early Islamic Period is included in this level, for its characteristics remain the same until the 9th century. The layers concerned in the stratigraphic excavation (Tepe Zargaran, sounding E1) are nos 9–8 (3rd–4th centuries), no. 7 (late 4th century) and nos 6–5–4 (5th–8th centuries) (Gardin 1957, 94–95 and 99). The Balkh material, defined by fabrics and surface processing, is characterized by the presence of stamped red wares, smoothed and unsmoothed red wares, and grey wares (*ibid.*, 102–104 and 109–112). There is no mention of any glazed ware for level III. Concerning the closed shapes, the morphological types are not comparable with the Nishapur ones. However the basins, named 'coupes' by Gardin, are close to those discovered in the Qohandez (Fig. 81/9–10; Gardin 1957, no. 11 and R5a pl. III and 110–111, fig. 94/25–26; no. 4 a, b and c, pl. III).

A glimpse from outside Khorasan

The published ceramics of Afrasiab, dated between the 5th and the 8th centuries, are overall very different to the contemporary Nishapur assemblages (Lebedeva 1990, fig. 1; Akhunbabaev and Sokolovskaja 1996, figs 1–13). The vessel types in Afrasiab are common to the other sites in Khorasan as well as in the other Central Asian lands. The shapes shown are, nevertheless, very different.

The ceramic assemblage belonging to the Bukhara Oasis, dated between the 3rd and 7th centuries (Mukhamedjanov 1983, fig. 2; Mukhamedjanov *et al.* 1982, fig. 3; Abdirimov 1979, fig. 3; Suleimanov 1984, 124) is comparable to some extent with the Nishapur material. In particular the presence of fine jars has been observed, which are close to those of Nishapur (Fig. 80/14–15), additionally there are storage jars with rounded rims and/or characterized by fingerprint ornaments (Fig. 80/2–3).

In the same context, the ceramic of Paykend belonging to the 5th–8th centuries also presents the same features as the Nishapur material, such as the storage jars with fingerprint ornaments. Other types, like jugs and small jars, can also be compared (Fig. 80/2–3, 11, 14–15; Semenov 1988, 154–162, figs 8/4–6, 12/6–7, 13/5).

This characteristic jar with fingerprint ornaments on the rim has also been discovered in the Karchi Oasis in Erkurgan and is dated to the 5th–6th centuries (Turebekov 1981, fig. 3/5). The other ceramic types published from this oasis and continuing until the 8th century are nevertheless very far from the Nishapur assemblages (see i.e. for Kultepa, Alimov 1969).

Occasionally some specific types can be compared with the Nishapur material, as in Turktul Tepe, where one type of jar with a moulded rim (3rd–5th centuries) has been found (Fig. 80/8; Raimkulov et *al.* 2008, fig. 2/13).

Concerning the Surkhan Daria region, the site of Dalverzin Tepe shows some assemblages of closed forms from the 6th–7th centuries, in which a peculiar jar type is similar to one in Nishapur (Fig. 80/10; Albaum 1966, fig. 3/10, fig. 4/16).

In the Tashkent Oasis the material (1st–5th centuries) seems to be different to that of Nishapur (Burjakov and Dadabaiev 1973; Abdullaev 1974). Nevertheless, some storage jars, jugs and cooking pots show the same shapes as in Nishapur (Fig. 80/5, Fig. 81/2–4; Abdullaev 1975, fig. 7/39, 83, 103–105).

In the Semnan region (Damghan area) material from the Parthian and Sasanian Periods is known from excavations and extensive surveys (Maurer Trinkaus 1986). Most of the collected material is of fine quality and comprises bowls and jars, and the wares are usually undecorated. According to Maurer Trinkaus there are no contemporary glazed wares. The ornaments observed are slipping of the surface, moulded, applied, incised and punctate (Maurer Trinkaus 1986, 135). Some observed jar shapes in the Damghan area attributed to the Sasanian Period are similar to the Nishapur typology (Fig. 80/4, 8–9, 11, 14; Maurer Trinkaus 1986, fig. 14/8; fig. 18/11; 19/7).

The Central Iranian Plateau shows, contrary to Central Asia, a real difference of pottery types compared with Nishapur. The major sites, Rayy (Rante 2009, figs 265–286), Isfahan[30] and Qasr Abu Nasr (Whitcomb 1985, figs 16–19), also concerning ceramic material of the 5th to the 8th centuries, have been compared with the Nishapur material. Nevertheless, as in Central Asia, two shapes also appear to be shared in the western regions (Figs 92/11–13). The material collected during the extensive survey carried out by Keall in the Central Plateau as well as in Qal'eh Yazdegird mainly concerns the Parthian and Sasanian Periods. This one also shows typological differences compared with the Nishapur contemporary material. Nevertheless, the material testifies to the existence of one peculiar shape of jar with a concave rim (Keall 1981, fig. 10/9–14) also observed in Nishapur.

The appearance of the Glazed Ware

The late part of Period II in Nishapur (7th–8th centuries), as previously seen, is marked by the appearance of monochrome turquoise-green glazed material. Nishapur is, nevertheless, not the

---

[30]   The unpublished material brought to light during the Italian Archaeological Mission in Isfahan (1972–1977) headed by U. Scerrato, dated between the 6th–8th centuries, was referred to (personal archives R. Rante).

only example where this appearance has been noticed prior to the 9th century. In the other Khorasanian main cities in which pre-Islamic material is known, this event seems to be heterogeneous. In Balkh, where it first seems to have appeared, this material (green and white glazes) dates from the 4th century (Gardin 1957, 92). In the Gurgan Plain the turquoise-green glazes probably appeared in the 6th century (Kiani 1982, 73–80). In Tureng Tepe the same glaze type may have appeared during the 7th–8th centuries, even if only one glazed fragment has been recorded (Lecomte 1987, 106). Instead, Merv seems to be the only main city where no glazed wares have been observed before the 9th century (Puschnigg 2006). According to Shishkina and Pavchinskaja (1992, 50), the monochrome green glaze appeared in Transoxiana in the late 8th century.

The presence of glazed material is better attested to in the western side of Khorasan. In Rayy, at the present state of research, the recent excavation in the Shahrestan brought to light some turquoise-green and white glazed fragments from the late 8th century. Many other sites in the Central Iranian Plateau, such as Hamadan, show the presence of glazed material from the Parthian Period.

Period IIIa

Tureng Tepe

In Tureng Tepe Period VIIC corresponds to the 9th–10th centuries (Gardin 1987, 143–154). The ceramic material is mostly composed of red wares and glazed wares; coarse wares (exclusively cooking pots) and so-called 'white wares' (fine yellowish to pinkish wares) are much less well represented in the assemblages (Gardin 1987, 141–142, table 15).

The shapes identified are, for one part, comparable with the Nishapur assemblages; some storage jars with rounded rims (Fig. 82/6; Gardin 1987, pl. 72/36) and some small jars with concave (Fig. 82/11; *ibid.,* pl. 83/n), or everted rims (Fig. 83/3–6; *ibid.,* pl. 73/c–e, pl. 78/h–i), are close. The same types of jug rims have been observed in both sites (Fig. 83/10–12, 15, 20–21, 23–25; Gardin 1987, pl. 77/c–g, pl. 85/h). Besides, some types of bowls are also comparable (Fig. 84/10–11; *ibid.,* pl. 80/d–e).

Unlike Nishapur, the fine fabrics in Tureng Tepe are very few (*ibid.,* 134) and the unglazed ware fabrics seem to be different to the glazed ware ones (*ibid.*). The glazed ceramic assemblage, in Nishapur as well as in Tureng Tepe, is essentially composed of monochrome green wares (Gardin 1987, 142); the polychrome wares are mainly splash wares and buff wares. It seems that some slip-painted types were also found (*ibid.,* 137–142, pls 88–89).

As has been previously mentioned, in Tureng Tepe an absence of certain polychrome ware types was noticed, in particular opaque white, sgraffiato and painted sgraffiato wares. In addition, it seems that slip-painted wares are almost unknown. Therefore, the glazed ware assemblage seems to be less diversified than in the other Khorasanian sites.

Gurgan Plain

The ceramic material of the Gurgan Plain corresponding to Period IIIa is dated to the 9th–10th centuries (Kiani 1984, 46). The published material of this geographical area is few and mainly concerns glazed wares. Some fine unglazed jugs belonging to Gurgan are nevertheless identifiable and comparable with those of Nishapur (Fig. 83/23, 27; Kiani 1984, 42, fig. 14).

The glazed wares assemblage is constituted of monochrome (green, blue, brown and yellow), black and white slip-painted, splash and sgraffiato wares. The absence of buff wares in this assemblage can be stressed. Its dating seems to be confirmed by the presence of Iraqi type lustre wares (*ibid.,* 49, figs 22–23). In the Gurgan Plain has also been observed the so called 'sari' slip-painted type, which seems to be absent in the eastern lands of Khorasan (Kiani 1982, pl. 40.2; 1984, 44/17).

In the Atrek Valley the glazed assemblage recorded for the Islamic Period presents colour splashed, buff and monochrome green glazed wares (Venco Ricciardi 1980, 71, fig. M).

Merv

Few materials have been published for the Medieval Period of the city and the information available for the material belonging to the 9th–10th centuries essentially concerns glazed wares. The proportion coming from Gyuar Kala area 4 is 91% unglazed (bowl and basins of fine white-yellow fabrics) and 9% glazed wares, this last figure is comparable with the amount of glazed wares in Nishapur (8.7%). The glazed wares described, only bowls, are mostly black and yellow slip-painted (77.3%), but also green to turquoise wares (8.5%) and buff wares, splashed decoration on opaque white glazed (14.2%). It has been observed that the sgraffiato types, as well as other types of slip-painted wares, are absent in this assemblage (Herrmann *et al.* 1995, 45–49; 2001, 42–43).

In older publications the unglazed material allows one to carry out morphological comparisons with Nishapur: close types of unglazed jugs, basins, bowls and lids are presented (Fig. 84/2, 14, 16; Lunina 1962, fig. 8; Filanovich 1974, fig. 30, 33). The identifiable glazed wares are only of buff ware type (Filanovich 1974, fig. 30/8, 24, 26, 28).

Balkh

The early 'Muslim' Period (Balkh IV, Gardin 1957, 96) has not been precisely defined (9th–12th centuries). According to the stratigraphical and ceramological study of Balkh material, layer 3^1 corresponds to the 9th–10th centuries (*ibid.*, 99). In this context, the only identified wares pertaining to this period are engraved unglazed wares and, for the glazed material, blue-green splash on opaque white (or imitation) wares (*ibid.*, 72, 96, pl. xvii/4a). Besides, it seems that the stamped unglazed red wares disappear at around the 9th–10th centuries (*ibid.*, 28).

Herat

The absence of stratigraphical data concerning Herat renders this study, and the comparisons with Nishapur, extremely concise. The only information available concerning this period affirms that the 'Islamic sites belong to two major periods, the 10/11th and the 12/13th cent AD' (http://www.dainst.org/en/project/afghanistan-herat-areia-antiqua-i?ft=all). It confirms that the early Islamic Period (9th–10th centuries) has not been found in the excavated areas of the Herat citadel.

A glimpse from outside Khorasan

The very few coarse wares published for Afrasiab and dated to the 10th century can be compared with the contemporary material in Nishapur: some storage jars present the same rims (Fig. 82/1–5; Brusenko 1969, fig. 2/24–26). On the other hand, the cooking wares and the jugs published for the 9th–10th centuries are quite different from the Nishapur assemblage (Rakhimbabaeva 1983, fig. 2; Shishkina and Pavchinskaja 1992, 61–62). The largely published material from Afrasiab is the well-known glazed wares, essentially the slip-painted types. According to Shishkina and Pavchinskaja (1992, 52), the first polychrome glazed type to be produced in Afrasiab is buff ware, whose production would have ended in around 850 AD. In the mid-9th century the second type to appear would correspond to the opaque white splashed wares (Shishkina and Pavchinskaja 1992, 53). The assemblage of all the other polychrome types (slip-painted types, sgraffiato and splash wares on slip ground) would appear at the end of the 9th century and remain unchanged until the end of the 10th century (Shishkina and Pavchinskaja 1992, 53–54; Shishkina 1986, pl. 20/1–2, pl. 22/2, pl. 41).

In this chronological sequence the appearance of buff ware as the first polychrome glazed type seems very odd and completely diverges from the chronological sequence studied elsewhere. Nevertheless, it suggests the production of buff ware in Transoxiana.

Concerning Paykend, the unglazed assemblage of the 9th–10th centuries (Mukhamedjanov *et al.* 1988, 164–171), which was published, is partially comparable to that of Nishapur. Some small jars with concave rims (Fig. 82/10–11; Mukhamedjanov *et al.* 1988, fig. 15/4–5), besides deep basins (Fig. 84/2; *ibid.*, fig. 15/6), drinking jugs (Fig. 83/10–33; *ibid.*, fig. 17) and flat lids (Fig. 84/16; *ibid.*, fig. 16/7) show closed shapes.

The recent discovery of glazed ware workshops in Paykend (Guionova 2011, fig. xv, xxiv) allows one to date the production of the monochrome green glaze and the green painted over opaque white glaze to the 9th century. They lasted until the 10th century, when the production of buff ware and slip painted wares began.

The excavation of the Bukhara Ark (citadel) brought to light some archaeological layers dated by coins to between the late 9th–10th centuries (Nekrasova 1999, 41). An excavated dump from this period contained buff, splashed and monochrome green glazed wares (*ibid.*, 43, fig. 7). Other dumps have been dated to the 10th century and described as filled in a very short time. They contained slip painted, buff, splashed sgraffiato and underglaze painted wares, as well as unglazed jugs and lids (*ibid.*, 44–48, figs 9–12).

Concerning the Tashkent Oasis, the ceramic material of this period is only partially published or imprecisely identified (Iljasova *et al.* 2000). Some unglazed and slip-painted wares from Kavardan have been presented (Burjakov 1977, fig. 5). The material published from Binkata only deals with glazed wares (Filanovich *et al.* 2008, figs 1–6). The slip-painted wares presented for the 10th century are only of two types: black and white, and red, black and white. In Tashkent the slip-painted wares of the 10th century are, in addition, of the green coloured glaze type (Iljasova 2006).

In Hulbuk Tepe the material, which could be dated to around the 9th–10th centuries, is constituted of fine to medium unglazed and glazed wares, comparable to Nishapur ceramics. Medium to fine jugs with rounded necks (Fig. 83/26–27; Simeon 2009, pl. 18/73–76), basins with falling rims (Fig. 84/1–3; Simeon 2009, pl. 50) and large flat lids with combed and engraved decorations (Fig. 84/16; *ibid.*, pl. 57) are quite close to the common and fine vessels of Nishapur. In spite of a too extensive chronology presented (8th–11th centuries), the more or less contemporary glazed wares in Hulbuk Tepe are mainly green and brown splash on opaque white ground (*ibid.*, pls 71–77), slip-painted types (*ibid.*, pls 80–86, 92–108) along with buff ware (*ibid.*, pl. 87) and splash sgraffiato types (*ibid.*, pls 122–143).

Period IIIb

Tureng Tepe

The material recorded as Period VIII in Tureng Tepe corresponds to the 11th–14th centuries (Gardin 1987, 160). This period is not well represented in the site and it has only been identified in two sectors (D–E) of the southern tepe. Only seven glazed shards have been recorded in sector D. The information on this period thus relates to sector E, but very few unglazed wares were recorded (*ibid.*, 154–156). Some of the shapes drawn are close to the Nishapur material: two types of jars are similar in both sites (Fig. 98/12–14; Gardin 1987, pl. 90/a–b). Concerning the glazed material, three types of wares have been observed: monochrome glazes (yellow, brown and green), sgraffiato under yellow-green glazes and under glaze painted fritwares (Gardin 1987, 157–158, pl. 91, 153–154). At this period the splash and buff wares and much of the monochrome green glazes seem to disappear (*ibid.*, 159).

Gurgan

The only clayey fabric glazed ware mentioned for Gurgan is, according to Kiani (1984, 47), the champlevé type and it appears around the 10th century and endures until the Il-Khan Period.

Most of the ceramic material presented again by Kiani (1984, 48–66) seems to be only of fritware types: monochrome, underglaze painted, lustre and *haft rang* wares. According to the author, all these fritwares were produced from the late Seljuk to the Khwarezmshah Periods (11th century–1220 AD), in Gurgan (*ibid.*, 37–38, 55).

Merv

As for the so called 'Seljuk ceramics' in Sultan Kala (Herrmann *et al.* 2000, 16–19, figs 4–6), the most frequently occurring types are plainwares (jars, jugs and pitchers, ewers and flasks). The unglazed wares published by Lunina (1962, fig. 30) are comparable with the Nishapur material, especially the fine jugs and small jars (Fig. 87/1–41). Some moulded jugs or bottles of fine grey to greenish fabric are similar to some found in Nishapur[31] (Fig. 107; Herrmann *et al.* 2000, fig. 4/6). Besides, some deep handled basins also are similar in both sites (Fig. 88/13; Herrmann *et al.* 2000, fig. 5/6), as are other basins and bowls (Fig. 88/3–4, 12; Fig. 89/12; Lunina 1962, fig. 31).

According to the British team in Merv, the contemporary glazes are mainly monochrome green. There is no mention of fritwares other than very rare lustre wares of the Kashan type; therefore, there would not be any fritwares before the second half of the 12th century in Merv (Herrmann *et al.* 2000, 19).

Balkh

According to Gardin (1957, 96–113), the ceramic material corresponding to the pre-Mongol Period is mixed with that of the 9th–10th centuries. It is, therefore, difficult to determine a correct stratigraphical sequence belonging to Period IIIb in order to compare it with Nishapur. Concerning the unglazed wares, no type has been identified in level Balkh IVa (9th–12th centuries) (Gardin 1957, 32, 116–118). In this period the glazed wares are collected in a 'polychrome' group, which is constituted of slip-painted, splash, sgraffiato and underglaze painted wares (*ibid.*, 69–73). It seems that only one fritware was identified and dated to the 12th century (*ibid.*, 73, pl. xviii/4).

Herat

The ceramic material found in the recent excavation of Herat citadel is partially published (Franke 2008). The ceramics corresponding to the *c.* 11th–13th centuries are mostly fine unglazed moulded and painted wares (Müller-Wiener 2008, 55–57, nos 103–107). The clayey glazed wares are slip-painted, splash sgraffiato and buff wares (*ibid.*, 50–52, no. 90–96; Franke 2008, 73, nos 123–124, 117, no. 132). The fritwares are moulded monochrome, underglaze painted (of the Bamyan type) and lustre ware (perhaps from Kashan) (Müller-Wiener 2008, 52–53, nos 97–99).

A glimpse from outside Khorasan

In Afrasiab, the ceramic material corresponding to Period IIIb in Nishapur is less studied than that of other periods. The fine unglazed material described is constituted of moulded grey wares, which developed during the 11th century, according to Shishkina and Pavchinskaja (1992, 65), and it was produced until at least the 12th century (Khakimov 2004, 136–137). Concerning the glazed wares, the main type during the 12th century is turquoise monochrome (Shishkina and Pavchinskaja 1992, 70). It has been observed that the slip-painted type with red

---

[31] Tests C–D of the Qohandez excavation, headed by Dr. Labbaf Khaniki, have not been mentioned here. Only the material was photographed.

and black decorated motifs on white ground lasts until the 13th century[32] (Khakimov 2004, 127–128, no. 205, 207–208). According to Shishkina (1986) the slip-painted wares[33] datable to the 11th–12th centuries present the following motifs: crossed-ribbon (*ibid.*, fig. 20/3-4), of vegetal inspiration (*ibid.*, fig. 22/6; fig. 26/5-6; fig. 27/1; fig. 29/3-4), and calligraphic (*ibid.*, fig. 42/1, 3-4, 6). This period also corresponds to the introduction of the fritwares in Afrasiab: monochrome turquoise (Khakimov 2004, 132–133), painted in black under turquoise glaze (Shishkina 1986, fig. 42/2), *haft-rang* and lustre wares were imported (Shishkina and Pavchinskaja 1992, 70; Khakimov 2004, 130–131).

Most of the material published from the Tashkent oasis is glazed and shows an assemblage constituted of monochrome, sgraffiato and slip-painted wares (Burjakov 1977, fig. 6). The fritwares published are very close to the underglaze painted vessels found in Afrasiab and are of the black under turquoise type (Badanova and Berdimuradov 2006). Some painted unglazed wares, attributed to the 12th–13th centuries and comparable with the Herat material, were nevertheless published (Badanova and Berdimuradov 2006, figs 4-5).

Some fritwares were also found in Kultepa (Ustrushana) as well as in Rabat-e Malik (Bukhara Oasis). Concerning Kultepa, clayey glazed wares and the associated fritwares besides unglazed wares form the assemblage presented for the 12th–13th centuries (Gritsina 1991, figs 2-3). Concerning Rabat-e Malik, one fragment of pre-Mongol Persian lustre ware has been found in a Qaraqanid complex situated at the entry of the Bukhara Oasis (Saparov 2001). In the excavation of the Bukhara Ark, a dump dated to the 11th century contained slip-painted wares. Associated with the later occupation layers were some fritwares with opaque turquoise glaze and also lustre wares (Nekrasova 1999, 52–53, figs 19-20).

As for the western and central parts of Iran, only Rayy and Isfahan can deliver chronological data essentially concerning the fine wares of this period. In Rayy, the material corresponding to Phase 6 (late 11th–early 13th centuries) of the recent excavation (2006-2007) shows some fragments of monochrome turquoise and white fritwares, and lustre ware associated with clayey vessels with turquoise and cobalt glazes inlays (Rante 2009, figs 231, 240). These types are comparable with the contemporary ones in Nishapur: very close inlaid wares were found in the Qohandez (Fig. 107).

The small amount of material presented by Treptow for Rayy from Period IIIb is not in stratigraphical sequence. The same types are, nevertheless, published for the 11th–13th centuries (Treptow 2007, 27, 36–37, 49).

In Isfahan, the rare elements available concerning the material of the excavation (1972-1977) of the Masjid-i Jum'a of Isfahan, studied since 2000 but as yet unpublished, exclusively concern the fritwares of only one part of the religious complex (Rugiadi 2010). In addition, the author only published a small selection of the fritwares found under Nizam al-Mulk's domed hall and thus datable before *c.* 1087 AD, already recognised by Scerrato (1974, 477). Nevertheless, Rugiadi provides some data concerning the assemblages of glazed wares, which comprises 38% fritwares and 46% clayey wares, which are monochrome green and brown wares, splashed wares, four fragments of splash sgraffiato wares and one opaque white glaze considered as being of the Abbasid Period. The fritwares are dishes, bowls and jars, which are mainly monochrome (largely turquoise, but also purple and green). Some bear turquoise or purple splashes under a clear glaze and a few are engraved under a turquoise glaze (Rugiadi 2010, 178, figs 5-9).

---

[32]   In the recent excavation in Paykend, a 10th–11th centuries habitat brought to light a slip-painted ceramic fragment with an inscription mentioning the date 661H/1282 AD.

[33]   In Afrasiab, a kiln also producing slip-painted wares has been excavated. The ceramic material found in it dates to the 10th–11th centuries (Sokolovskaja 1990, 190).

Conclusion

This research permitted us to refine and bring precision to the history of Nishapur. First, a study concerning the site and its chronology, between archaeology and material analyses, has been essential. Consequently, a re-contextualizing of Nishapur into its archaeological environment and cultural region, through the detailed study of the ceramic and its assemblages has been also realized.

Although the archaeologically oldest area (Qohandez and Shahrestan) reveals evidence of ancient settlements (Period I, 450–150 BC), defined on the Qohandez by a non-architectural occupation, Nishapur was founded between the last part of the 4th century and the first years of the 5th century (Period II), and was composed of a citadel (Qohandez) and a lower city (Shahrestan). If the toponomy *Nev-Shapur* really refers to the Sasanian King Shapur, a foundation during the last part of the 4th century would be more probable.[1] At that period, the Sasanian Empire saw its oriental *limes* at the Oxus River, although one century earlier the Sasanian territory probably extended over Soghdian lands (cfr. Honigmann and Maricq 1953). The recent archaeological researches in Paykend, in the Bukhara Oasis, brought to light the foundation of the city in the 4th century, when the Iranian nomadic populations (probably Chionites) came from the northeast (Rante forthcoming). In this period, according to the account of Ammianus Marcellinus (XIV, VIII, 1), the Chionite kings were in accord with the Sasanian kings to support these latter to the other *limes*, in the Roman wars. Both frontiers, Sasanian and Chionite, were bordered by city fortresses, and other city-fortresses were constructed along the Silk Road. It is in this framework that the foundation of Nishapur should be re-contextualized. Its construction was firstly a necessity of defence, although Nishapur was also an important administrative and religious centre; this is easily noticeable from the extremely strong fortifications, as well as the material studied. Thanks to the study of the pottery, it has been observed that the Qohandez was more or less homogeneously occupied in its entire area. The northeastern part is characterized by quite utilitarian coarse wares showing, as does its architecture, a military use of the space. The rest of the Qohandez seems to have been occupied by administrative buildings and traditional houses. The ceramic material belonging to this period (Period II) is characterized by the preponderance of closed shapes, corresponding to utilitarian objects, mainly employed for storage and cooking, presenting coarse fabrics. The fine material, less common, is characterized by small jars and jugs. The comparisons with the closest city of Merv, where at the same epoch fine material has been found in very significant quantity, seem to show the difference of socio-economical *status*. Period II is also characterized by the appearance of glazed calco-alkaline green/turquoise wares.

After the Arabic conquest (651, according to the historical sources[2]), at the time of the formation of the semi-independent states of the East, mostly corresponding to Period IIIa (2nd half of 8th–early 11th centuries), Nishapur clearly shows urban and cultural changes, observable in its second rather than first half of the period. The great extension of the Islamic conquest beyond the lands of Transoxiana assured a more or less political stability for the Khorasanian countries and cities. At this period the Qohandez was characterized by the disappearance of

---

[1] The Archaeomagnetism analyses confirm this chronological tendency towards the end of the 4th century.
[2] Bosworth, 'Nishapur', *EIr* online.

its previous main military function. The northeastern fortress seems to have lost its military function and allowed for restructuring of the urban space, although the old ramparts were still employed and new ones were erected (Fig. 12). At this period, the central eastern part of the Nishapur citadel is characterized by the formation of a large depression, showing several different areas mainly employed for storage and dumps, as indicated by the discovered materials and architectural features. The last part of this period, probably beginning from the 10th century, sees the appearance of a different module of mud bricks, 27 × 27 × 6/7 cm.

Period IIIa is characterized by a preponderance of closed shapes, mostly storage jars, basins and cooking pots, essentially of coarse to medium fabrics, and jugs, essentially of medium-coarse to fine fabrics. The last part of Period IIIa, corresponding to the late 9th–early 11th centuries, shows an important increase in glazed wares. Most of the glazed material is monochrome, even if a large part of it is also polychrome. All the pottery analyzed and studied confirm that it was produced in Nishapur. Only two opaque white glazed wares correspond to importations from Iraq. Amongst the totality of the ceramics are bowls; a few are jars, jugs, lids and lamps. The glazed monochrome wares are of two types, green or turquoise. At this period the appearance of splash, sgraffiato, painted sgraffiato, slip painted and buff clayey wares has been observed, stressing the appearance of cultural handicraft innovations. It is probable that the appearance of fritware was already observable in the late 10th century and at the early 11th century. More than in Period II, in Period IIIa an increase in the variety of earthenware production has been observed. The growth of fine and medium-fine vessels shows a development of the serving and consumption of food and drink production.

During the last years of Period IIIa Nishapur was sacked by different Turkic peoples several times. From Period IIIb, corresponding to the early 11th century to the Mongol invasion, the Seljuks occupied the city and began a vast programme of public works. A further levelling of the Qohandez has been observed, constituted of one or two stone layers. This phenomenon has been also observed during Period IIIa, but only in few places and in a heterogeneous manner, and is therefore hard to confirm. This period sees the appearance of baked bricks (23 × 23 × 7/9 cm), associated with the mud bricks. In this period, no real urban changes in the Qohandez of Nishapur have been observed. As previously, the Qohandez comprised a central eastern depression, probably characterized by the presence of storage buildings and dump sites. The remaining part contained rich houses,[3] once again showing continuity from Period III and a radical change from Period II.

As from Period I, pottery continued to be produced here and the raw materials employed (clay and inclusion materials) came from the same regional sources. This period seems to be characterized by a unique fabric type identified (Aa), which had been present since Period I. As for the previous period, in Period IIIb the finest and table wares are much better represented than the storage ones. Moreover, the general typology is also very similar to the previous period. The most common types of coarse wares are storage vessels and basins, while the fine ceramic is characterized by jugs and glazed bowls. In this period the appearance of pot shapes and an additional increase and development of bowl typologies have been observed. On the contrary, cooking pots are much less well represented, testifying to a probable change in occupation. Concerning the glazed pottery, a preponderance of the monochrome category has been observed in both fabric types, clayey and fritwares. The polychrome glazed ceramic, painted sgraffiato, slip-painted under coloured glaze wares, nevertheless continued to be produced, even if in much lesser quantity. Fritwares, quite numerous, are mostly turquoise monochrome. The early fritware type identified in stratigraphy is the turquoise monochrome. The other monochrome glazed later types (cobalt blue and opaque white, but also moulded and engraved monochrome wares), such as the underglaze and overglaze painted ones, have

---

[3] For more information regarding this, see Bulliet 1972.

been identified in the upper layers and on the surface of the Qohandez. The analyzed shards belonging to this polychrome group of fritwares present a very siliceous glaze, different from the previous one, thus corroborating the hypothesis of an enrichment in technology during the 12th century.

The results acquired with this study on the Qohandez sustain the thesis that Nishapur changed its political *status* and importance into the Khorasanian frontiers, from its foundation to the Mongol destruction. This has been mostly noticed during two large time intervals corresponding to Periods II and III. The defensive reasons of Nishapur's foundation in Period II marked the role of the city in this vast area for the following centuries. Although an important administrative centre in Khorasan, the earliest Nishapur filled its role of capital differently in comparison with the other older and larger capitals of Merv, Bactres and Herat. Period II is characterized by generally local production. Ancient Hyrcania seems to present close material culture characteristics to Nishapur, even if the details are very different. Merv presents a production of good quality and fine vessels, much more than in Nishapur, and for some typologies a greater link between Merv and the more western cities, like Rayy, has been noticed than with the closer Nishapur. The storage and utilitarian pottery in Nishapur at that epoch remains, therefore, much better represented than others. Apart from some few close comparisons with the Semnan region and the Bukhara Oasis (from the 6th century), the other main cities and surrounding Khorasanian territories (Balkh, Herat, Karchi Oasis, Samarkand Oasis, Tashkent Oasis, Iranian Central Plateau) do not present any representative cultural link with Nishapur. This seems to attest that Nishapur's material culture during Period II reflects the influences of the surrounding eastern Caspian area rather than elsewhere.

Late Period II in Nishapur (7th–8th centuries) is marked by the appearance of monochrome green/turquoise glazed material. This phenomenon has been also observed in Balkh from the 4th century, in the Gurgan Plain and Tureng Tepe between the 6th and the 8th centuries, as well as in western Khorasan, such as in Rayy from the late 8th century. Despite the poverty of research in these areas, it seems that the appearance of glazed pottery is observable in Khorasan during the late Sasanian Period.

It is in Period III (essentially from the 9th century) that the city developed its *status* and role in Khorasan, becoming one of the rich and political dynamitic cities. At that epoch, the Tahirid dirham was largely employed in the entire area, also including Transoxiana, as shown by recent discoveries in Merv, Paykend and Balkh. This political situation involved an increase in production and a development of techniques, as well as a growth of trade within and outside Khorasan. The material culture witnesses a growth of fine wares besides coarse ones. This is also thanks to the increase in the production of glazed wares, of which the clayey matrix was mainly of fine fabric. In this wide Period III, a cultural rapprochement between Nishapur and the eastern and northeastern cities and regions, like Balkh, Bukhara, Samarkand, Tashkent and Karchi Oases, is observable, thus determining a cultural homogeneity in the Khorasanian area as well as outside it. The development of fritware in all these regions also corresponds to this cultural expansion and this stresses once more the easy trade links between the far western and far eastern Iranian world, rendering Khorasan the medieval crossroads of cultural and economic exchange.

Bibliography

Abbreviations

AI   *Archéologie Islamique*
AMI   *Archäologische Mitteilungen aus Iran*
BMMA   *Bulletin of the Metropolitan Museum of Art*
GJ   *Geographical Journal*
IJGA   *International Journal of Geomagnetism and Aeronomy*
IMKU   *Istoriia Materialnoj Kultury Uzbekistana*
JACS   *Journal of American Ceramic Society*
JAS   *Journal of Archaeological Science*
JECS   *Journal of European Ceramic Society*
JG   *Journal of Geophysics*
JGG   *Journal of Geomagnetism and Geoelectricity*
JRAS   *Journal of the Royal Asiatic Society*
JS   *Journal of Sciences*
JSP   *Journal of Sedimentary Petrology*
MMAB   *Metropolitan Museum of Art Bulletin*
RM   *Radiation Measurements*
SI   *Studia Iranica*
TOCS   *Transactions of the Oriental Ceramic Society*

Sources

Ammianus Marcellinus, *Rerum Gestarum libri qui supersunt.* Vol. I, Libri XIV–XXV, W. Seyfarth, L. Jacob-Karau and I. Ulmann (eds). Leipzig, Teubner 1978.

Hamzā al-Isfāhānī, *Kītāb tarīkh sinnī mulūk al-ard wa al-anbiyā' 'alahim al-salawāt wa al-salām*, ed. Gottwaldt, Leipzig 1848.

Khalīfa Nīshāpūrī, *Tārīkhī Nīshāpūr*, ed. B. Karīmī, Tehran 1960.

Al-Maqdisī, Muḥammad ibn Aḥmad, *Aḥsan al-taqāsīm fī ma'rifat al-aqālīm*, de Goeje ed., *Descriptio imperii moslemici*, BGA III, Leiden 1877.

Mustawfī Al-Qazwīnī, *Tārīkh-i Guzīdah*, tr. J. Gantin, Maisonneuve et Guilmoto, Paris 1903.

Nāṣir al-Dīn Shāh Qājār, *Safar-nāma-yi Nāṣir al-Dīn Shāh Qājār ba-Khurāsān (safar-I duwwum)*, Tehran 1889.

Studies

Abdirimov, R. (1979). 'K izuceniu pamyatnika aksac tepa'. *IMKU*, 15, p. 79–83.

Abdullaev, K. (1974). 'Kvartal keramistov gorodisha kanka'. *IMKU*, 11, p. 83–92.

Abdullaev, K. (1975). 'Arkheologiceskoe izucenie gorodisha kanka (1969–1972)'. *IMKU*, 12, p. 128–154.

Adamiec, G. and Aitken, M. J. (1998). 'Dose conversion factors: update'. *Ancient TL*, 16(2), p. 37–49.

Aitken, M. J., Allsop, A. L., Bussell, G. D. and Winter, M. B. (1984). 'Geomagnetic intensity in Egypt and western Asia during the second millennium BC'. *Nature*, 310, p. 305–306.

Aitken, M. J. (1985). *Thermoluminescence Dating*. Academic Press, London.

Akhunbabaev, Kh. G. and Sokolovskaja, L. F. (1996). 'Keramiceskie kompleksi afrasiaba konza, VII–VIII'. *IMKU*, 27, p. 100–119.

Albaum, L. I. (1966). 'Gorodishe dalverdzin tepa'. *IMKU*, 7, 1966, p. 47–65.

Alimov, U. (1969). 'Raskopki na kultepa v karshiskom oazise'. *IMKU*, 8, p. 105–114.

Allan, J. W. (1982). *Nishapur: metalwork of the Early Islamic Period*. Metropolitan Museum of Art, New York.

D'Allemagne, H. R. (1911). *Du Khorasan au Pays des Bakhtiaris: trois mois de voyage en Perse*. Vol. III. Hachette, Paris.

Auclair, M., Lamothe, M. and Huot, S. (2003). 'Measurement of anomalous fading for feldspar IRSL using SAR'. *RM*, 37, pp. 487–492.

Azarpay, G., Frierman, J. D. and Asaro, F. (1977). *Sāmānid Ceramics and Neutron Activation Analysis*. Energy and Environment Division, Lawrence Berkeley Laboratory, University of California/Berkeley, August 29, 1977.

Badanova, E. I. and Berdimuradova, A. E. (2006). 'Novie nakhodki keramiki XII–XIII s. iz urgutckogo raiona'. *IMKU*, 35, p. 276–279.

Barbier de Meynard, C. (1861). *Dictionnaire géographique, historique et littéraire de la Perse et des contrées adjacentes, extrait du mo'djem el-bouldan de Yaqout*. Imprimerie impériale, Paris.

Barthold, V. V. (1981). *Turkestan down to the Mongol invasion*. Karachi.

Barthold, V. V. (1984). *An Historical Geography of Iran*. Bosworth, C. E. (ed.). Princeton University Press.

Bouquillon, A., Aucouturier, M. and Chabanne, D. (2008). 'De Terre à Reflets d'Or. La Céramique Lustrée, des Abbassides aux Hispano-Mauresques'. *Techné*, Hors Série, p. 160–167.

Brongniart, A. (1877). *Traité des Arts Céramiques*. Tome 2. 1977 edition. Dessain et Tolra.

Brusenko, L. G. (1969). 'Raskopki kvartala gonchrov X–XI s. na gorodishe afrasiab'. *IMKU*, 8, p. 115–123.

Buck, C. E., Cavanagh, W. G. and Litton, C. D. (1995). *Bayesian Approach to Interpreting Archaeological Data*. Wiley, Chichester.

Bulliet, R. W. (1972). *The Patricians of Nishapur: A Study in Medieval Islamic Social History*. Harvard University Press, Cambridge.

Bulliet, R. W. (1976). 'Medieval Nishapur: a topographic and demographic reconstruction'. *SI*, 5, fasc. 1, p. 67–89.

Burakov, K. S. and Nachasova, I. E., (1978). 'A method and results of studying the geomagnetic field of Khiva from the middle of the sixteenth century'. *Izvestiya, Physics of the Solid Earth*, Engl. Trans., 14, p. 833–838.

Burakov, K. S., Burlatskaya, S. P., Nachasova, I. E. and Chelidze, Z. A. (1982). 'The geomagnetic field in the Caucasus over the past 2000 years'. *International Journal of Geomagnetism and Aeronomy,* Engl. Transl., 22, p. 439–440.

Burjakov, F. and Dadabaev, G. (1973). 'Pamjatniki anticnogo vremeni v tashkentskom oazise'. *IMKU*, 10, p. 39–51.

Burjakov, F. (1977). 'Archeologiceskie materiali gorodisha Kavardan', *IMKU*, 13, p. 70–88.

Burlatskaya, S. P. and Chelidze, Z. A. (1990). Geomagnetic field variations in Georgia during the last 15 centuries B.C. *Izvestiya, Physics of the Solid Earth*, Engl. Transl., 26, p. 602–609.

Burlatskaya, S. P. and Chernykh, I. Y. (1989). Change in geomagnetic field strength in Azerbaijan during last 2200 years determined from archeomagnetic data. *Izvestiya, Physics of the Solid Earth,* Engl. Transl., 25, p. 594–597.

Calligaro, T., Dran, J.-C. and Salomon, J. (2005). 'Ion beam microanalysis, in Non-destructive microanalysis of cultural heritage materials', in Janssens, K. and Van Grieken, R. (eds), *Comprehensive Analytical Chemistry* XLII. Elsevier, Amsterdam, p. 227–276.

Dunlop, D. and Özdemir, O. (1997). *Rock Magnetism, Fundamental and Frontiers*. Cambridge University press, Cambridge.

Filanovich, M. I. (1974), 'Gyaur Kala'. *Trudy YuTAKE,* XV, p. 15–139.

Filanovich, M. I., Iljasova, S. and Baratova, L. S. (2008). 'Nekotorie Dannie o materialnoi culture bintaka'. *IMKU*, 36, p. 227–237.

Fouache, E. and Cosandey, Cl. (2006). *Report for the Irano-French Archaeological Survey of Nishapur*. 1–24 november 2006. Unpublished.

Fouache, E., Cosandey, Cl., Wormser, P., Kervran, M. and Labbaf Khaniki, R. A. (2011). 'The River of Nishapur'. *SI*, 40, 1, p. 99–119.

Franke, U. (2008). 'In search for the historical roots of a region'. In Franke, U. (ed.), *National Museum Herat - Areia Antiqua Trough Time*. Deutsches Archäologisches Institut, Berlin, p. 71–86.

Franke, U. (ed.) (2008). *National Museum Herat - Areia Antiqua Trough Time*. Deutsches Archäologisches Institut, Berlin.

Frye, R. N. (ed.), (1965). *The Histories of Nishapur*. Harvard Oriental Series, Vol. 45.

Gallet, Y., Genevey, A., Le Goff, M., Fluteau, F. and Eshraghi, S. A. (2006). 'Possible impact of the Earth's magnetic field on the history of ancient civilizations'. *Earth and Planetary Science Letters*, 246, p. 17–26.

Gallet, Y. and Le Goff, M. (2006). 'High-temperature archeointensity measurements from Mesopotamia'. *Earth and Planetary Science Letters*, 214, p. 159–173.

Gallet, Y., Le Goff, M., Genevey, A., Margueron, J. C. and Matthiae, P. (2008). 'Geomagnetic field intensity behavior in the Middle East between 3000 BC and 1500 BC'. *Geophysical Research Letters,* 35, L02307, doi:10.1029/2007GL031991.

Gallet, Y., Genevey, A., Le Goff, M., Warmé, N., Gran-Aymerich, J. and Lefèvre, A. (2009). 'On the use of archeology in geomagnetism, and vice-versa: Recent developments in archeomagnetism'. *C. R. Physique* 10, p. 630–648, doi:10.1016/j.crhy.2009.08.005.

Gallet, Y. and Al-Maqdissi, M. (2010). 'Archéomagnétisme à Mishirfeh-Qatna: Nouvelles données sur l'évolution de l'intensité du champ magnétique terrestre au Moyen-Orient durant les derniers millénaires'. *Akkadica*, 131, p. 29–46.

Gardin, J-C. (1957). *Céramiques de Bactres.* Mémoires de la DAFA, XV, Klincksieck, Paris.

Gardin, J-C. (1987). 'La céramique islamique'. In Boucharlat, R. and Lecomte, O., *Fouilles de Tureng Tepe, 1. Les périodes sassanides et islamiques*, Editions Recherche sur les civilisations, Paris, p. 121–170.

Genevey, A., Gallet, Y. and Margueron, J. C. (2003). 'Eight thousand years of geomagnetic field intensity variations in the eastern Mediterranean'. *Journal of Geophysical Research*, 108 (B5), 2228, doi:10.1029/2001JB001612.

Genevey, A., Gallet, Y., Rosen, J. and Le Goff, M. (2009). 'Evidence for rapid geomagnetic field intensity variations in Western Europe over the past 800 years from new French archeomagnetic data'. *Earth and Planetary Science Letters*, 284, p. 132–143. doi:10.1016/ j.epsl.2009.04.024.

Genevey, A., Gallet, Y., Constable, C. G., Korte, M. and Hulot, G. (2008). 'ArcheoInt: An upgraded compilation of geomagnetic field intensity data for the past ten millennia and its application to the recovery of the past dipole moment'. *Geochemistry, Geophysics, Geosystems*, 9, Q04038. doi:10.1029/2007GC001881.

Gritsina, A. A. (1991). 'Materiali XII– nacala XIII s. Gorodisha Kultepa (cevernaja uctrushana)'. *IMKU*, 25, p. 183–199.

Guionova, G. (2011). *Rapport préliminaire des fouilles à Paykend*, Paris.

Gyselen, R. (1989). *La géographie administrative de l'Empire sassanide: les témoignages sigillographiques.* Paris, Leuven.

Gyselen, R. (2002). *Nouveaux matériaux pour la géographie historique de l'Empire sassanide. SI*, Cahier, 24, Paris.

Hansman, J. and Stronach, D. (1970). 'Excavations at Shahr-I Qumis, 1967', *JRAS*, 1, p. 29–62.

Harmatta, J. and Litvinsky, B. A. (1996) 'Tokharistan and Gandhara under Western Türk rule (650–750)'. In Litvinsky, B. A. (ed.), *History of Civilisations of Central Asia*, III, UNESCO, Paris, p. 367–401.

Hartmann, G. A., Genevey, A., Gallet, Y., Trindade, R. I. F., Etchevarne, C., Le Goff, M. and Afonso, M. C. (2010). 'Archeointensity in Northeast Brazil over the past five centuries'. *Earth and Planetary Science Letters*, 296, p. 340–352.

Hauser, W. (1937). 'The Plaster Dado from Sabz Pūshān'. *BMMA* XXXII, 10, p. 23–36.

Hauser, W., Upton, J. M. and Wilkinson, C. K. (1938). 'The Īrānian Expedition, 1937, the Museum's excavations at Nīshāpūr'. *BMMA* XXXIII, 11, p. 3–23.

Hauser, W. and Wilkinson, C. K. (1942). 'The Īrānian Expedition, 1938–1940, the Museum's excavations at Nīshāpūr'. *BMMA* XXXVII, 4, p. 83–119.

Hedges, R. E. M. and Moorey, P. R. S. (1975). 'Pre-Islamic Ceramic Glazes at Kish and Nineveh in Iraq'. *Archaeometry*, 17, p. 25–43.

Hedges, R. E. M. (1976). 'Pre-Islamic Glazes in Mesopotamia – Nippur'. *Archaeometry*, 18, p. 209–213.

Herrmann, G. and Kubansakhatov, K. *et al.* (1995). 'The international Merv project. Preliminary Report on the Third Season (1994). *Iran*, XXXIII, p. 31–60.

Herrmann, G., Kubansakhatov, K. and Simpson, St J. *et al.* (2000). 'The international Merv project. Preliminary report on the eighth season (1999). *Iran*, XXXVIII, p. 1–31.

Herrmann, G., Kubansakhatov, K. and Simpson, St J. *et al.* (2001). 'The international Merv project. Preliminary report on the ninth year (2000). *Iran*, XXXIX, p. 9–52.

Hill, D. V., Speakman, R. J. and Glascock, M. D. (2004). 'Chemical and mineralogical characterization of Sasanian and early Islamic glazed ceramics from the Deh Luran plain, southwestern Iran'. *Archaeometry*, 46, 4, p. 585–605.

Hitti, P. K. (1916). *The Origins of the Islamic State.* New York, Columbia University.

Honigmann, E. and Maricq, A., *Recherches sur les « Res gestae divi Saporis »*, Bruxelles 1953.

Honigmann, E. and Bosworth, C. E. (1993). 'Nīshāpūr', *E.I.²*, vol. VIII, p. 63–65.

Humbach, H. (1978). *The Sassanian Inscription of Paikuli.* Part 1, supplement to Herzfeld's Paikuli. H. Humbach and P. O. Skaervø. The Iranian Culture Foundation, Wiesbaden, Reichert and Tehran.

Hussain, A. G. (1983). 'Archeomagnetic investigations in Egypt: Inclination and field intensity determinations'. *JG*, 53, 131–140.

Hussain, A. G. (1987). 'The secular variation of the geomagnetic field in Egypt in the last 5000 years'. *Pure Applied Geophys*ics, 125, p. 67–90.

Iljasova, S. P. (2006). 'Novie materiali po glazuravannoi keramike tashkenta'. *IMKU*, 35, p. 239–244.

Iljasova, S. P., Makhzaakhmedov, D. K. and Adilov, Sh. T. (2000). 'Srednevekovoe steklo I keramika binkata – Tashkenta IX–XI s'. *IMKU*, 31, p. 228–239.

Jackson, A. V. W. (1911). *From Constantinople to the Home of Omar Khayyam.* New York.

Kaczmarczyk, A. and Hedges, R. E. M. (1983). *Ancient Egyptian Faience.* Aris and Phillips, Warminster.

Kambakhsh Fard, S. and Mahani, A. A. (1965). *The Excavations of Neyshabur and the Persian pottery during the 5th and 6th centuries AH.* Tehran.

Karamanov, A. and Pelino, M. (2006). 'Sinter-crystallization in the diopside–albite system Part II. Kinetics of crystallization and sintering'. *JECS*, 26, p. 2519–2526.

Keall, E. J. and Keall, M. J. (1981). 'The Qal'eh-i Yazdigird pottery: a statistical approach'. *Iran*, XIX, p. 33–80.

Khakimov, A. (2004). *Masterpieces of the Samarkand Museum.* Tashkent, 2004.

Kiani, M. Y. (1982), 'Parthian sites in Hyrcania. The Gurgan plain'. *AMI, Ergänzungsband 9.* Deutsches Archäologisches Institut Abteilung Teheran, Berlin, 1982.

Kiani, M. Y. (1984). *The Islamic City of Gurgan. AMI*, Ergänzungsband 11, Berlin.

Kramers, J. H. and Wiet, G. (1964). *Ibn Hauqal. Configuration de la terre (kitab surat al-ard).* (transl.). Maisonneuve & Larose, Paris.

Kröger, J. (1995). *Nishapur, Glass of the Early Islamic Period.* New York, Metropolitan Museum of Art.

Kühn, H. and Curran, M. (1986). 'Chrome yellow and other chromate pigments'. In Feller, R. L. (ed.), *Artists' Pigments. A handbook of their history and characteristics*, vol. 1, p.187–218

Labbaf, R. Kh. (2006). *Nishapur Excavation.* Unpublished Report.

Lebedeva, T. I. (1990). 'Keramika afrasiaba V–VI'. *IMKU*, 23, p. 160–168.

Lecomte, O. (1987). 'La céramique sassanide', in Boucharlat, R. and Lecomte, O., *Fouilles de Tureng Tepe, 1. Les périodes sassanides et islamiques.* Editions Recherche sur les civilisations, Paris, p. 93–119.

Le Goff, M. and Gallet, Y. (2004). 'A new three-axis vibrating sample magnetometer for continuous high-temperature magnetization measurements: applications to paleo and archeo-intensity determinations'. *Earth and Planetary Science Letters,* 229, p. 31–43.

Le Strange, G. (1340). *The Geographical Part of the Nuzhat-al-qulub, Composed by Hamd-Allāh Mustawfī of Qazwīn in 740,* (transl.), Leyden, London, 1919.

Le Strange, G. (1930). *The Lands of the Eastern Caliphate.* Cambridge University Press.

Lunina, S. B. (1962). 'Goncarnoe proizvodstvo v merve X-nacala XIII s.' *Trudy YuTAKE,* 11, p. 217– 298.

Marquart, J. (1901). *Ērānšahr nach der Geographie des ps. Moses Xorenac'i: mit historisch-kritischen Kommentar und historischen und topographischen Excursen.* Weidmann, Berlin.

Mason, R. B. and Keall, E. J. (1991). 'The 'abbāsid glazed wares of Sīrāf and the Basra connection: petrographic analysis'. *Iran*, 29, p. 51–66.

Mason, R. B. and Tite, M. S. (1994). 'The beginnings of Islamic stonepaste technology'. *Archaeometry*, 36, 1, p. 77–91.

Mason, R. B. (1995). 'Criteria for the petrographic characterization of stonepaste ceramics'. *Archaeometry*, 37, 2, p. 307–321.

Mason, R. B. (1996). 'Petrography and Provenance of Timurid Ceramics'. In Golombek, R. B. and Mason, G. Bailey, *Tamerlane's Tableware: A New Approach to the Chinoiserie Ceramics of Fifteenth and Sixteenth Century Iran.* Toronto and Costa Mesa, California: Royal Ontario Museum and Mazda Press, p. 16–56.

Mason, R. B. and Tite, M. S. (1997). 'The beginnings of tin-opacification of pottery glazes'. *Archaeometry*, 39, 1, p. 44–58.

Mason, R. B., Tite, M. S., Paynter, S. and Salter, C. (2001). 'Advances in polychrome ceramics in the Islamic world of the 12th century AD'. *Archaeometry*, 43, 2, p. 191–209.

Mason, R. B. (2003). 'Petrography of Pottery from Kirman'. *Iran*, 41, p. 271–278.

Mason, R. B. and Golombek, L. (2003). 'The Petrography of Iranian Safavid Ceramics'. *JAS,* 30, p. 251–261.

Mason, R. B. J. (2004). *Shine like the Sun. Lustre-Painted and Associated Pottery from the Medieval Middle East.* Bibliotheca Iranica: Islamic Art and Architecture Series, 12. Costa Mesa, Mazda Publishers & Toronto, Royal Ontario Museum.

Maurer Trinkaus, K. (1986). 'Pottery from the Damghan Plain, Iran: Chronology and Variability from the Parthian to the Early Islamic Periods'. *SI*, 15–1, p. 23–88.

Melville, C. (1980). 'Earthquakes in the history of Nishapur'. *Iran*, XVIII, p. 103–120.

Molera J., Pradell, T., Salvado, N. and Vendrell-Saz, M. (2001). 'Interactions between clay bodies and lead glazes'. *JACS,* 84, 5, p. 1120–1128.

Mukhamedjanov, A. R., Mirzaakhmedov, D. and Adilov, Sh. (1982). 'Keramika nijnikh sloev bukhari'. *IMKU*, 17, p. 81–97.

Mukhamedjanov, A. R. (1983). 'Stratitraficeskii raskop na zitadeli bukhari'. *IMKU*, 18, p. 57–64.

Mukhamedjanov, A. R., Adilov, Sh. I., Mirzaakhmedov, D. K. and Semenov, G. L. (1988). *Gorodishe Paykend.* Tashkent.

Müller-Wiener, M. (2008). 'Islamic Pottery and Ceramics', in Franke, U. (ed). *National Museum Herat – Areia Antiqua Trough Time.* Deutsches Archäologisches Institut, Berlin, p. 49–60.

Nachasova, I. E. and Burakov, K. S. (1994). 'Geomagnetic field intensity from the 3rd century B.C. to the 6th A.D. in Termez (Uzbekistan)'. *IJGA*, Engl. Transl. 34, p. 409–412.

Nachasova, I. E. and Burakov, K. S. (1997). 'Intensity of the geomagnetic field in Central Asia in 2000 BC–1000 BC'. *Physics of the Solid Earth*, Engl. Transl. 33, p. 543–548.

Nachasova, I. E., Burakov, K. S. and Kverikadze, M. V. (1986). 'Intensity of the geomagnetic field in the territory of Georgia to 1000 BC'. *IJGA*, Engl. Transl. 26, p. 301–302.

Nekrasova, E. (1999). 'La citadelle de Bukhārā de la fin du 9e siècle au début du 13e siècle'. *AI*, 8–9, p. 37–54.

Newton, R. and Davison, S. (1989). *Conservation of Glass*. Butterworths, Chichester.

Odah, H., Heider, F., Hoffmann, V., Soffel, H. and El Gamili, M. (1995). 'Paleointensity of the geomagnetic field in Egypt from 4000 BC to 150 AD using the Thellier method'. *JGG*, 47, p. 41–58.

Odah, H. (1999). 'Improvement of the secular variation curve of the geomagnetic field in Egypt during the last 6000 years'. *Earth Planets Space*, 51, p. 1325–1329.

Pace, M., Bianco Prevot, A., Mirti, P. and Venco Ricciardi, R. (2008). 'The technology of production of Sasanian glazed pottery from Veh Ardašīr (Central Iraq)'. *Archaeometry*, 50, 4, p. 591–605.

Porter, Y. (2004–2005). 'Potters, Painters and Patrons: Documentary Inscriptions and Iconography in Pre-Mongol Iranian Ceramics'. *TOCS*, 69, p. 25–35.

Prescott, J. R. and Stephan, L. G. (1982). 'The contribution of cosmic radiation to the environmental dose for thermoluminescence dating. Latitude, altitude and depth dependences'. *PACT*, 6, p. 17–25.

Prescott, J. R. and Hutton, J. T. (1988) 'Cosmic ray and gamma ray dosimetry for TL and ESR'. *Nuclear Tracks and Radiation Measurements*, 14(1/2), p. 223–227.

Puschnigg, G. (2006). *Ceramics of the Merv Oasis: recycling the city*. Left Coast Press, Walnut Creek.

R Development Core Team (2009). *R: A Language and Environment for Statistical Computing*. R Foundation for Statistical Computing, Vienna, Austria. ISBN 3-900051-07-0, URL http://www.R-project.org.

Raimkulov, A. A., Isamiddinov, M. Kh. and Zgamberdiev, F. (2008). 'Rannesrednevekovaja keramika iz turktul tepa'. *IMKU*, 36, 2008, p. 118–127.

Rakhimbabaeva, N. Kh. (1983). 'Raboti 1978–1980. Bliz meceti afrasiaba'. *IMKU*, 18, p. 192–200.

Rante, R. (2008). 'The Iranian city of Rayy: Urban model and Military architecture'. *Iran*, XLVI, p. 189–211.

Rante, R. (2009). Rayy: developpement de l'Urbanisme et culture matérielle. Thèse soutenue le 16 février 2009 à l'Université de Provence.

Rante, R. (forthcoming). 'Fouilles à Paykend: nouveaux éléments', in *20 ans d'archéologie française en Asie Centrale*, Julio Bendezu-Sarmiento (ed.), Paris.

Raverty, H. G. (1881). *Tabakat-i-Nasiri. A general history of the Muhammadan dynasties of Asia including Hindustan from A.H. 194 (810 A.D.) to A.H. 658 (1260 A.D.) and the Irruption of the Infidel Mughals into Islam by Maulānā, Minhāj-ud-Dīn, Abū-'Umar-i-'Usmān,* Translated from Original Persian Manuscripts, reprint, Calcutta, The Asiatic Society, 1995.

Rtveladze, E. (2009). *Civilizations, States and Cultures of Central Asia*. Tashkent.

Rugiadi, M. (2010). 'Processing Iranian glazed pottery of the *masjid-i jum'a* in Isfahan (Adamji project): fritwares from the foundations of Nizam al-Mulk's domed hall'. In Matthiae, P., Pinnock, F., Nogro, L. and Marchetti and N. (eds), *Proceedings of the 6th International Congress of the Archaeology of the Ancient Near East*, 5 May–10 May 2009, 'Sapienza', Università di Roma, vol. 3, Islamic Session, Harrassowitz Verlag, Wiesbaden, p. 173–190.

Saparov, N. J. (2001). 'Fragmenti liustrovoi keramiki c zoomornimi i rastitelnimi siujetami iz Rabat-i Malik'. *IMKU*, 32, p. 199–201.

Scerrato, U. (1974). Ismeo Activities. Reports of Archaeological Researches, in Masğid-i Ğum'a at Isfahān. *East and West*, 24, 1974, p. 475–477.

Scerrato, U. (2001). 'Ricerche archeologiche nella moschea del Venerdi di Isfahan della Missione archeologica Italiana in Iran dell'IsMEO (1972–1978)'. *Antica Persia. I tesori del Museo Nazionale di Tehran e la ricerca italiana in Iran.* Roma, Museo Nazionale d'Arte Orientale. p. XXXVII–XLIII.

Schefer, Ch. (1881). *Sefer Name, relation du voyage de Nassiri Khosrau*, Paris.

Semenov, G. L., Mukhamedjanov, A. R., Mirzaakhmedov, D. K. and Adilov, Sh. T. (1988). *Gorodishe Paykend*. Tashkent.

Shishkina, G. V. (1986). Remeslennaja produkctsija sredne, vekovogo sogda – steklo – keramika (VIII–XIII s.). Tashkent.

Shishkina, G. V. and Pavchinskaja, L. V. (1992). *Terres secrètes de Samarcande. Céramiques du VIIIe au XIIIe siècle*. Exhibition catalogue, Paris, Caen, Toulouse, 1992–1993.

Siméon, P. (2009). *Etude du matériel de Hulbuk (Mā wārā' al-nahr-Khuttal, de la conquête islamique jusqu'au milieu du XIe siècle (90/712-441/1050). Contribution à l'étude de la céramique islamique d'Asie centrale*. Oxford, British Archaeological Reports International Series 1945.

Simpson, St J. (1997). 'Partho-Sasanian Ceramic Industries in Mesopotamia'. In Freestone, I. and Gaimster, D. (eds), *Pottery in the Making. World Ceramic Traditions*. British Museum Press, London, p. 74–79.

Sokolovskaja, L. F. (1990). 'Novie dannie o keramiceskoie macterckoie kvartala keramictov X–XI s. na gorodishe Afrasiab'. *IMKU*, 24, p. 189–198.

Souleymanov, R. Kh. (1984). 'Rezultati predevaritelnojo izucenija gorodisha romitan', IMKU, 19, p. 118–129.

Thellier, E. and Thellier, O. (1959). 'Sur l'intensité du champ magnétique terrestre dans le passé historique et géologique'. *Annales Géophysiques.* 15, p. 285–376.

Treptow, T. (2007). *Daily Life Ornamented. The Medieval Persian City of Rayy.* The Oriental Institute, Chicago.

Turebekov, M. (1981). 'Raskopki bastiona vnutrennei krepostnoi steni erkurgana'. *IMKU*, 16, p. 36–43.

Upton, J. M. (1936). 'The Persian expedition, 1934–1935, Excavations at Nīshāpūr'. *BMMA* XXXI, 9. p. 176–180.

Upton, J. M. (1937). 'The coins from Nīshāpūr'. In Wilkinson, C. K. 'The Īrānian Expedition, 1936, the excavations at Nīshāpūr'. *BMMA* XXXII, 10, p. 37–39.

Venco Ricciardi, R. (1980). 'Archaeological survey in the upper Atrek Valley (Khorassan, Iran): preliminary report'. *Mesopotamia*, XV, p. 51–72.

Vine, A. R. (1937). *The Nestorian Churches*, London.

Whitcomb, D. (1985). *Before the Roses and Nnightingales. Excavations at Qasr-I Abu Nasr, Old Shiraz*, Metropolitan Museum of Art, New York.

Wiet, G. (1937). *Ya'kūbī, les pays* (transl.), le Caire, IFAO.

Wilkinson, C. K. (1937). 'The Īrānian Expedition, 1936, the excavations at Nīshāpūr'. *BMMA* XXXII, 10, p. 3–22.

Wilkinson, C. K. (1943). 'Water, ice and glass'. *MMAB* New Series, 1, 9, p. 175–183.

Wilkinson, C. K. (1950). 'Life in early Nishapur'. *MMAB*, New Series, 9, 2, p. 60–72.

Wilkinson, C. K. (1959). 'The kilns of Nishapur'. *MMAB*, New Series, 17, 9, p. 235–240.

Wilkinson, C. K. (1961). 'The Glazed Pottery of Nishapur and Samarkand'. *MMAB*, New Series, 20, 3, p. 102–115.

Wilkinson, C. K. (1973). *Nishapur: Pottery of the Early Islamic Period*, Metropolitan Museum of Art, New York.

Wilkinson, C. K. (1986). *Nishapur, Some Early Islamic Buildings and Their Decoration*, Metropolitan Museum of Art, New York.

Yaghubpur, A. and Hassannejad, A. A. (2006). 'The spatial distribution of some chromite deposits in Iran, using fry analysis'. *JS*, Islamic republic of Iran 17(2), p. 147–152.

Zink, A. (2008), 'Uncertainties on luminescence ages and anomalous fading'. *Geochronometria*, 32, p. 47–50.

Zink, A. and Porto, E. (2005). Luminescence dating of the Tanagra Terracottas of the Louvre collections, *Geochronometria*, 24, p. 21–26.

Zink, A. and Porto, E. (2009). Compte rendu de mission à Nishapur, Iran, du 6 au 12 Avril 2009, C2RMF, unpublished.

Zink, A. J. C., Querre, G. and Porto, E. (2002). 'Automation of the chemical preparation for luminescence dating'. *Abstracts Book*, LED2002. 24–28 June 2002, Reno (USA).